Pomponius Mela's Description
of the World

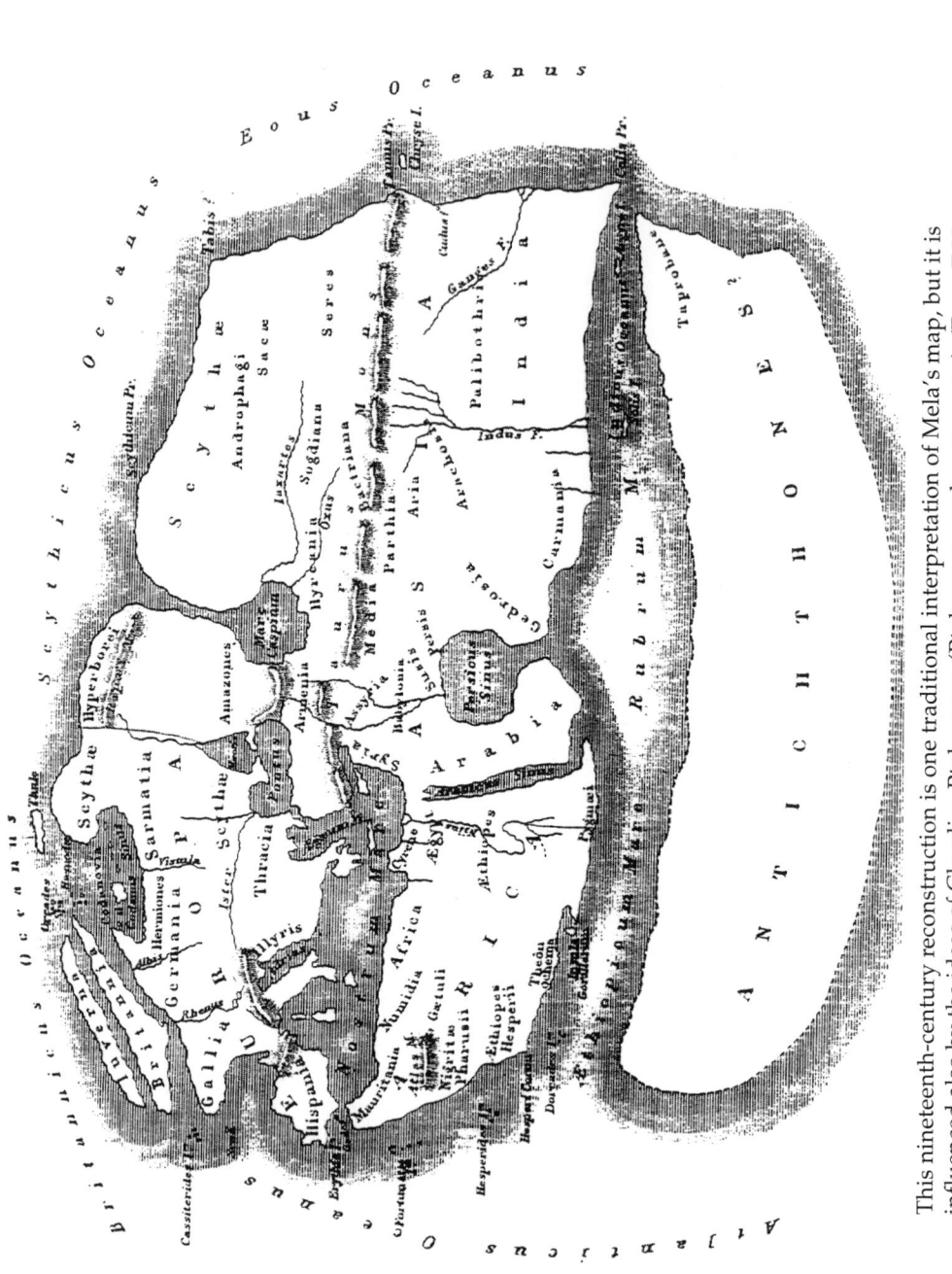

This nineteenth-century reconstruction is one traditional interpretation of Mela's map, but it is influenced also by the ideas of Claudius Ptolemaeus (Ptolemy, second century C.E.). (From E.H. Bunbury, *A History of Ancient Geography*, 2d ed., vol. 2 [London: J. Murray, 1883], opposite p. 368.)

Pomponius Mela's Description of the World

F.E. Romer

Ann Arbor
THE UNIVERSITY OF MICHIGAN PRESS

CANISIUS COLLEGE LIBRARY
BUFFALO, N.Y.

Copyright © by the University of Michigan 1998
All rights reserved
Published in the United States of America by
The University of Michigan Press
Manufactured in the United States of America
♾ Printed on acid-free paper

2001 2000 1999 1998   4 3 2 1

No part of this publication may be reproduced,
stored in a retrieval system, or transmitted in
any form or by any means, electronic,
mechanical, or otherwise, without the written
permission of the publisher.

A CIP catalog record for this book is available from the British Library.

Library of Congress Cataloging-in-Publication Data

Mela, Pomponius.
   [De chorographia. English.]
   Pomponius Mela's description of the world / F.E. Romer.
     p.   cm.
   Includes bibliographical references (p.   ) and index.
   ISBN 0-472-10773-9 (hardcover : alk. paper). — ISBN 0-472-08452-6
(pbk. : alk. paper)
   1. Geography, Ancient.   I. Romer, F. E. (Frank E.)   II. Title.
PA6512.E5   1997
913—dc21   97-40709
                                                               CIP

Acknowledgments

The world is a puzzle, and its sometimes mysterious paths are circuitous and elusive—or so Pomponius Mela has convinced me. Something similar can be said for the path that brought me back to Mela. It will surprise him, but a conversation with David Soren prompted me to pack my bags for this journey. Our conversation focused, innocently enough, on Q. Cicero and the danger of illness even during a winter spent in malarious Sardinia, but it also drove me back to the evidence for Sardinia, then to Mela, and finally to an appreciation of Mela's program in *The Chorography*. It has been fun to discover the pleasures and pitfalls of Mela's coasting voyage, since all projects are journeys, and since all journeys flourish amid the comfort of friends. In traveling these paths and others, I have been fortunate in the friendship and help of many people who go unnamed here, but especially in that of Terry Arendell, Judith-Maria Buechler, Sarah Clay, Diskin Clay, Martin P. Kelly, Barbara Pavlock, John Pollini, Marilyn Skinner, and Tony Tanke. Finally, my personal debt to A.E. Raubitschek, a friend and teacher who has long been both a support and a spur, also needs to be acknowledged here.

In general, my work also has prospered amid the collegiality of the Classics crew at the University of Arizona. The introduction and whole books of the translation were read and criticized by various friends, among whom I thank my colleagues David Christenson, Michael Teske, and Cynthia White, as well as those loyal graduate students Cord Ivanyi, Laura Lane, Kenneth New, and Martha Sowerwine. The students who read Pausanias with me in the fall term of 1995 also endured a large number of generic and cross-cultural explorations between Greek and Roman geographic writing.

Italy and Rome have fostered both my travels and my research in recent years, and one of life's incidental pleasures has been to travel parts of the Italian (and French) coastline with Pomponius Mela in hand. The library at the American Academy in Rome remains a fruitful and congenial place to work away from home, and in Italy Barbara

Pavlock was especially generous in mulling over Mela and his handbook with me.

To examine Mela's world my eye has been on the past, but with an eye to the future I dedicate this book affectionately to my goddaughter, Hilary Clay, and to my niece, Lauren Elizabeth Williams.

F.E. Romer

Reader's Note

Every translator has two goals that conflict with one another. The first is to bring the author's work from one language into another; the second is to introduce the reader as deeply as possible into the culture of the text (in every sense). Translations therefore are a compromise between the claims of the text and the needs of its readers. To bridge this gap and to effect this compromise, a number of principles and devices are used here.

Scholars cite Mela in one of two forms, for example, either as M. 3.87 or as M. 3.9.87. There is effectively no difference between these citations. In the second example, the first number identifies the book, and the third gives the section number. Since these section numbers run continuously from the beginning of each book to the end, the middle number (or chapter) adds nothing and is superfluous. Thus it is omitted here; all citations occur only with the two numbers indicating the book and section. This translation omits these chapter numbers altogether since they appear to be based on an editorial misunderstanding of the proem (1.1–2). Headings and subheadings also have been introduced into the text. Headings are used for the beginnings of the three books, and subheadings within the books generally stand where the chapter numbers were. Angle brackets containing ellipses marks, that is, < ... >, signal places in the text where the true readings cannot even be conjectured.

A map has been provided to show the approximate shape of Mela's world. It originally appeared in Bunbury 1883, vol. 2, opposite p. 368. This map is helpful for conceptualizing the inhabited earth as Mela conceived it, but since Mela's text apparently never contained a map in antiquity, there is room for significant variation in drawing a map to accompany his work, and the reader should be warned that Bunbury's reconstruction is an interpretation that was influenced also by the ideas of the great Claudius Ptolemaeus (Ptolemy, second century C.E.). This reconstruction can be compared with that of H. Philipp, which appears in Brodersen 1994, 24–25. (Brodersen 1994 also includes nineteen regional maps and other illustrations from earlier editions.) The reader is referred to Silberman 1988 for the five newly drawn sectional endmaps included in that edition. Part of the fun of reading *The Chorography,* however, also lies in keeping a modern map at hand, and for that reason the reader is informed, on a regular basis, of the modern names for ancient places. *The Times Atlas of the World,* comprehensive edition (London: Times Books with John Bartholomew and Sons, 1992 or later), is highly recommended for this purpose. This atlas has two immediate advantages: it contains much more information than the reader will need ordinarily, and it adds a significant number of the relevant ancient place-names with their modern counterparts.

Square brackets are used in the translation (a) to translate the original Latin or Greek place-names (marked as Lat. or Grk., respectively) and (b) to give modern place-names. When both a translation and a modern place-name occur in brackets, the translation comes first, followed by a semicolon and the modern equivalent. Square brackets occasionally are used in the translation to enclose letters or roman numerals that help to mark the sequence of ideas in dense passages. In the translated text, regular parentheses and dashes are reserved for remarks that appear to be parenthetical in the original.

Latin or Latinized forms of place-names are retained in the translation as much as possible. Thus a convention, established in some quarters, yields *Aethiopia* and *Aegypt, Aethiopian* and *Aegyptian.* Latin aspiration generally has been kept so that *Bosphorus* (Grk. *Bosporos*) and *Riphaean* (Lat. *Riphaeus;* Grk. *Rhipaios*) are used here. Two exceptions occur, however. The spelling *Adriatic* is universal now, and the alternative Latinate spelling, *Hadriatic,* has disappeared. For this reason the aspiration is omitted from *Adriatic* and related words like *Adria* (Atri). Likewise, the lower Danube, which Greeks called Ister, is more familiar to students of ancient history in its unaspirated Greekish form. The same is true for related terms like *Istropolis* or *Istria,* but even for these exceptions the aspirated forms will be found in the index. The familiar forms *Danube* (wherever Mela uses *Danuvius*) and *Nile* (for *Nilus*) are used in this translation.

Mela uses a number of transliterated Greek names, but his transliterations differ slightly from ours. Besides aspiration, the most conspicuous differences—there are others too—lie in his use of *-oe* for Greek *-oi* in the nominative plural masculine (second declension) and of *-u* for Greek *-ou* in the genitive singular masculine (also second declension), usages I have preserved in the translation. He also varies in using either -*a* or -*e* to represent -*ê* in the nominative singular feminine (first declension), and this variation is preserved too. Wherever they occur in the text, the Latinized forms have been retained in the translation both because they are intelligible and because they have their own interest, but the more familiar endings -*oi* and -*ê* appear in the notes.

The notes to the translation are motivated by items that stand out in Mela's narrative. These notes include cross-references within Mela's text, references to other ancient writers, selected bibliography, and other useful information that suits his miscellany. Abbreviations for ancient authors or works occur in the forms used by the major Latin and Greek dictionaries. Ultimately the notes aim to help readers formulate their own questions about this underappreciated author and to further their own journey.

Contents

Introduction	1
Book 1: Around Our Sea—from the Pillars of Hercules to the End of Asia	33
Book 2: Around Our Sea—from the End of Asia to the Pillars of Hercules	68
Book 3: Around the World—the Circle of Ocean from the Pillars of Hercules	103
Bibliography	133
Index	137

Introduction

Pomponius Mela is a puzzle, and so is his one known work, *The Chorography* (in Latin, *de Chorographia*). Little can be done to unravel the puzzle of Mela the man. Nothing is known about him apart from the two scraps of information he reveals in his monograph. On the positive side, a good deal more can be known about Mela's intellectual project, and the more interesting puzzle of Mela the author is, in proportion, a more rewarding subject. Here his little book can, and does, speak for him.

Pomponius Mela the Man

Mela provides only two items of personal information about himself. First, in a listing of the coastal cities of Hispania Baetica, he blurts out that his hometown, Tingentera, is located in that region. Later Mela gives an indication of his own date when he refers to the current princeps and to the impending celebration of a formal Roman triumph over the British peoples. Neither of these statements, however, is free of difficulty.

The town of Tingentera is otherwise unattested under that name, but Mela's full statement yields a little more information (2.96): "Tingentera, which Phoenicians who crossed from Africa still inhabit—and where we're from too—is located there," that is, near the Strait of Gibraltar on the coast of Hispania Baetica. That Phoenicians, perhaps from Tinge (Tangiers) in North Africa, relocated at Tingentera suggests that the town is probably to be identified with Julia Traducta,[1] which is attested on coins of Augustus, and which is known to have been in this vicinity. Mela's regionalism perhaps shows itself in his proud descrip-

---

1. Strabo's Iulia Ioza (3.1.8). Semitic *Ioza* approximates the Latin *Traducta*, which in turn is paraphrased by M.'s *praetervecti* (crossed). See Silberman 1988, vi–vii, and Parroni 1984, 16, where that author also finds an expression of regional chauvinism at 2.86 (see further, in the present introduction, nn. 2 and 18).

tion of Spain's fecundity (2.86) and in the fact that he devotes more space to Spain (2.85–96, 3.3–15) than to Italy (2.58–72).[2]

The reference to the princeps and to his impending triumph for his British victory indicates that at that time either Caligula (princeps in 37–41 C.E.) or Claudius (princeps in 41–54 C.E.) was in power, with probability pointing to the latter. Caligula's supposed invasion of Britain has left a trail of fact and fiction in the ancient sources, and the modern researcher is hard-pressed to see what really took place. After planning an invasion of the island, however, Caligula probably delayed his own operation until too late. He also had planned an enormous triumph to celebrate his conquests in the north generally, including his victory over Britain, but he never celebrated a full-scale *triumphus*, because he never completed his work in the north.[3] Instead, Caligula made only a preliminary celebration and commemorated his less sweeping accomplishments with the lesser triumph that the Romans called an ovation (*ovatio*).

Claudius, in contrast, did invade Britain in 43 C.E. and marked his success with a formal triumph in the following year. Mela's remarks (3.49) are vivid and convey an air of reality and authority that Caligula's erratic behavior did not deserve:

> Next, as to what kind of place Britain is and what kind of people it produces, information that is more certain and better established will be stated. The reason is that—lo and behold!—the greatest princeps is opening the long-closed island, and as conqueror of previously unsubdued and previously unknown peoples, the princeps brings with him the proof of his own accomplishments, since he will reveal in his triumph as much as he has laid claim to in war.

---

2. On the first point, see Parroni 1984, 341, ad loc.; Silberman 1988, 220 n. 8; Brodersen 1994, 1. Brodersen (ibid.) develops the second point: "Und es ist sicher kein Zufall, daß Mela sein Werk nicht etwa mit der Hauptstadt Rom beginnt, sondern mit der seiner Heimatregion benachbarten Meerenge, zu der er am Ende auch zurückkehrt—und er schließlich III 107 als 'Unsere Meerenge' bezeichnet." See also book 3, n. 70.

3. Barrett (1989, 135–39) argues that Caligula planned an invasion of Britain but postponed it, and that the invasion never materialized. Ferrill (1991, 126–29) argues for a more extreme view of Caligula's personality and refuses to rationalize what he sees as compelling evidence of Caligula's insanity.

"Opening the long-closed island" [aperit iam clausam [insulam]] appears to be a pun on the princeps' name, and it is similar to the pun made on his name a decade later (ca. 54 C.E.) by the younger Seneca in the *Apocolocyntosis* (The pumpkinification [of Claudius]). In that satire, the dead Claudius is knocking on heaven's door, so to speak, and trying to persuade Hercules to let him take his proper place among the gods; Hercules replies (*Apoc.* 8), alluding to earthly matters with heavy irony, "It's no miracle that you burst through the doors of the senate house: nothing is closed to you [*nil clausi tibi est*]." Mela almost certainly alludes to Claudius, whose name sounds like the verb meaning "to close" (*claudere*), but little is at stake in the allusion except that it marks Mela as sharing the spirit of the times and gives a *terminus ante quem*:[4] Mela was writing, in any case, prior to the moment in 44 C.E. when Claudius marked his triumph over the Britons.[5]

The argument can be taken a little further. Claudius was absent from Rome for between five and six months[6] while he took command in the invasion of Britain, and the triumph was held in February 44 C.E. Yet Mela says that the invasion was completed and that the emperor was then on his way to Rome to celebrate the triumph. If time is allotted for conducting the invasion and for the news to reach Rome, the evidence suggests that Mela published his little book very late in 43 C.E. or very early in 44.[7] The air of expectation surrounding Claudius' imminent triumph also suggests that Mela was in Rome when he was writing.

That said, we learn little about Pomponius Mela himself. He was born of an Italic family (as his name indicates) at Tingentera in Hispania Baetica. He was writing, probably at Rome, in the early forties, not long before Claudius' triumph, and his monograph perhaps appeared as late as January or February 44 C.E. These data are enough to identify Mela with one of the leading cultural trends in Rome during the first century C.E. At that time, a large number of Roman writers and

---

4. Romer (1996) suggested that the phrase *tamdiu clausam* (long-closed) as used by M. plays at least in part on the fact that Augustus enjoined his successors from expanding the empire after his death (Dio 56.33.5–6). However important Claudius' British campaign was in the long run, the policy that led to it was certainly anti-Augustan in spirit.
5. Parroni 1984, 16–22, reviews the evidence and arguments for M.'s date.
6. He spent a total of merely sixteen days in Britain (Dio 60.23.1).
7. I have followed here the argument of Wissowa (1916), who urges January or February 44 C.E. as the most likely time of publication.

intellectuals, born of Italic families in Spain, migrated to the capital.[8] These included the two Senecas, M. Porcius Latro (the foremost orator of the day according to the elder Seneca), Lucan, Martial, and Quintilian; perhaps—I go out on a limb here—P. Manilius Vopiscus, a poet and Statius' patron when he was writing the *Silvae*, ought to be added too.[9]

The family of the two Senecas also may be noted in special connection here. This distinguished family included the famous father and son, respectively known for rhetoric and philosophy, and the poet Lucan, who was the grandson of the elder L. Annaeus Seneca. Lucan's father was M. Annaeus Mela, the youngest son of the elder Seneca, and it has been conjectured on the basis of the Mela name that Pomponius Mela may have been connected to the Annaei by a now long-forgotten family tie.

That is all that can be said about Mela's life, and attention now turns logically to his work.

Chorography

Chorography is a perfectly good, but not much used, English word that takes its meaning from its Greek origin, just as its Latin form, *chorographia*, did for the Romans. In Greek technical literature *khôrographia* typically designates a written description (*graphê*) covering a district or region (*khôros*), perhaps a country, but in any case more than one individual place. A *topographia*, in contrast, was a description limited to a single place (*topos*), while in theory a *geôgraphia* would have described the whole earth (*gê*). By genre, then, a work like Mela's *Chorographia* in Latin falls nominally between these two theoretical poles of topography and geography, but it is difficult, if not impossible, to press that distinction very far. In reductive terms, a topography is less inclusive, and a geography more inclusive, than a chorography, but the standard of measurement is subjective and can be elusive. Strabo (2.5.13 and 2.5.34) says that in practice a geographer must restrict the subject matter to the

---

8. It is a familiar rule of thumb that, except possibly for Julius Caesar, the classical Roman writers were born elsewhere than at Rome. Even so, the migration of distinguished writers and intellectuals from Spain in this period stands out.

9. Nothing survives of his poetry. He had a prosperous villa in Tibur (Stat. *Silv.* 1.3), but the family probably originated in Spain and migrated to Tibur at some unknown time: see Fluss (1928), 1143–44.

known world—the *oikoumenê*, in Greek—and it emerges that the ancient difference between chorography and geography lies in scope and detail rather than in the geographic extent of the subject matter per se (cp. Ptol. *Geog.* 1.1).

Chorographia is a rare term in Latin, and few of us run across its English equivalent at all, much less with any regularity.[10] Nevertheless, the poet Varro Atacinus used *chorographia* as a literary title long before Mela, and Vitruvius (8.2.6) also used the plural to include maps. But Mela's treatise is the earliest geographical work of any kind that survives in Latin today, and it is our key to understanding the larger interpretive problem posed by the genre. In actuality, the choice of chorography as a literary genre immediately presents any reader, ancient or modern, with a kind of intellectual puzzle: Where between the poles of topography and geography does any particular chorographic work belong? Where does it strike its own balance?

Mela's *Chorographia*

The manuscript from which all other extant copies of Mela's treatise descend (directly or indirectly) gives the title as *de Chorographia*. Curiously enough, several descendant copies give its title as *de Cosmographia*, and it was under the title of *The Cosmographer* that this work appeared in its first published English translation of 1585. This variation in the title suggests that later scribes (and readers) were confused about the nature of the work they were copying (or reading), and that the title was emended for that reason. Any chorography is enigmatic by nature, but Mela's enigma—as we shall see—is not to be solved by emending the title.

Cosmographia is another Latinized transliteration of a Greek technical term. A *kosmographia* is a written description (*graphê*) of the world as a whole or of the whole universe (*kosmos*). Greek *kosmos*, like Latin *mundus*, emphasizes the orderliness and arrangement either of the universe or of the whole earth,[11] but *kosmographia* is a more appropriate

---

10. In English today the word *geography* often is used generically to designate works that fall into all three ancient genres. A distinction can be made between topography and geography, but chorography has fallen by the wayside.

11. M. uses *mundus* three times. In two instances it means land and sea taken together: *mundus* and the sky (*caelum*) compose a single unity composed of

characterization either for a work dealing with the full implications of the earth's sphericity or for a work like Ptolemy's (second century C.E.) that studies the earth's geography in relation to a system of latitude and longitude based on the positions of the stars. In theoretical terms, Mela's treatise is not a topography, because it does not restrict itself to the description of a single place. It also does not treat the entire universe, but the question remains whether it treats the earth as a whole. It certainly treats in relative detail (cp. "with greater preciseness" at 1.2 and 1.24) the entire inhabited world insofar as it was known, what the Greeks called the *oikoumenê*; but in Mela's own technical analysis this *oikoumenê* is not the earth taken as a whole. Mela picks out and surveys the places and features that he finds to be the best-known, the most important, or the most interesting, while omitting lesser places that would have claims on the completeness of a true geography. In this context, his principle of selection already prevents his work from being a geography in any expected etymological sense, but more can still be said.

Cosmography is simply a misnomer here. That word implies a work whose limits either match or exceed in detail, comprehensiveness, and scale those of a mere geography, but Mela consciously describes his project as something less than a geography. In fact, he limits himself to describing one and only one region or district of the earth—one zone, that is, of the earth's five—and that region is defined as the known world, "our world" [noster orbis] (1.24). His proper subject is announced in the very first words of the monograph: "A description of the known world [*orbis situs*] is what I set out to give, a difficult task and one hardly suited to eloquence, since it consists chiefly in names of peoples and places and in their fairly puzzling arrangement."

Mela's subject does not emerge definitively, therefore, unless the reader reflects on what *orbis* means in his technical vocabulary. The

---

land, sea, and air (1.3); and the breathing of the animate *mundus* accounts for the tides of Ocean (3.2). Here M. considers the *mundus* to be animate and to be made up of land and sea. Elsewhere he distinguishes earth (*terra*) and the heavens (*mundus*) and seems to identify the *mundus* with "the movements of the sky and of the stars, and what the gods intend" (3.19), a view that he attributes to the Druids, but which also conforms in the abstract to the tenets of Stoic thought. Both usages of *mundus* fall within the word's semantic range, and M. thus uses the word in its ordinary senses. See book 3, n. 3.

issue here is how Mela used the word, not simply how lexicographers define it. In the sentence just quoted, I have translated *orbis* as "the known world," whereas its lexicographic range includes (a) a wheel or disk; (b) a sphere or globe (typically, as applied to celestial bodies);[12] (c) a disk-shaped surface, a ring, that is, the cross section of a sphere; (d) the centrally located land mass surrounded by ocean, that is, the three known continents of Africa, Asia, and Europe; and (e) a climatic or other zone or subdivision of the earth conceived as a sphere.

Here Mela must be our guide, and he could not be clearer. He knows that the earth is a sphere (1.4), even if he does not recognize the full consequences of that idea. The earth is divided into northern and southern hemispheres, with five horizontal zones, only two of which are habitable—one in each hemisphere. The southern habitable zone is an *antichthôn* or antiworld—that is, a counterworld—but Mela is fuzzy about its reality. That southern zone, where he says the Antichthones live, is unexplored and unknown in one place (1.4), and yet elsewhere he is uncertain whether this second habitable zone (also called an *orbis*) even exists and whether Antichthones actually inhabit it (1.54).[13] As a result, Mela restricts his narrative to the *known* world, which he will describe not completely but in some detail.[14]

---

12. *Orbis* does not apply to the earth as a whole, even when the earth is conceived as a sphere (*sphaera*); cp. (e) in this list.

13. At 3.70 (see also n. 51 there) M. does not know that part of the evidence for his own theory of the counterworld (*antichthôn*) had been obsolete for almost four centuries. The term *Antipodes* (following Eratosthenes' usage) implies "a strict symmetry across the equatorial plain," a one-to-one correspondence between the northern and southern hemispheres, while the term *Antichthones* assumes the opposite, a general dissimilarity and asymmetry between the two orbs: see Romm 1992, 128–33. The terms sometimes may become loosely interchangeable, but M.'s consistency and the way he speaks of the *antichthôn* at 3.70 appear to assume its asymmetry with the northern hemisphere.

14. By the strictest etymological standard, then, a complete *geôgraphia* was impossible to write, and hence arose the flexible boundary between *khôrographia* and *geôgraphia* as literary genres. Ptolemy distinguishes scientific geography by its comprehensiveness, exactitude (including astronomical precision), proportional representation, and emphasis on the unity and continuity of the known world (*Geog.* 1.1; cp. Strabo 2.5.13). In contrast, M. has no interest in exact measurements or proportionality, and he can omit entirely, for example, the interior of the continents. Strabo (1.1.20, 2.5.1–2) recognizes the importance

The habitable northern zone is the one he intends to describe in this handbook (1.4) and is the one he labels "our world" [noster orbis] (1.24). In this work *orbis* is used for both habitable subdivisions of the earth conceived as a sphere, but only one of these subdivisions forms the proper subject of the book. Based on ancient literary practice, the phrase *orbis situm*, with which the preface begins, defines Mela's subject and should also clarify his title. It turns out, then, that *orbis situs* doubles as the correct Latin translation for the Greek idea of *khôrographia*, and it therefore is translated correctly as "a description of the known world."[15] Mela's work thus falls between a topography and a geography in the strictest sense: it describes more than one place but deliberately describes neither the whole earth nor the inhabited *orbis* in the necessary detail. Mela plays with literary-critical issues that impinge on the reader's interest, and hence *Chorographia* is likely to have been Mela's own title, with the Latinized Greek term apparently identifying for the Roman audience the expected genre and nature of this literary production.

Yet there is something unexpected and exciting about this title. Since neither geography nor chorography was an established genre in Latin letters, no one could have faulted Mela if he had called his book a geography. After all, geography books were restricted by practice and necessity to the known world, and an expansive Augustan example in Greek can be found in the *Geôgraphika* of Strabo.[16] The author's choice of genre here is both important and fully considered. Mela knew that he could

---

of astronomy and has a greater sense of detail than M., but he regards geography as a practical study that underlies political theory (1.1.18), unlike Ptolemy who conceives of geography as a science in its own right. Strabo's point of view affects his literary agenda in the *Geographika*.

15. Some scholars might consider this idiomatic translation of *orbis situs* controversial, but the ordinary logic of language makes it difficult to distinguish in speech between the thing described and the words used to describe it. The equivalence of Latin *orbis situs* and Greek *khôrographia* is born out by the fact that they are interchanged as titles in the later manuscript tradition of M.'s work. Thus Silberman (1988, 1, with explanation at 97 n. 1) translates *orbis situs* at 1.1 as "une description des régions de la Terre." If Silberman is right about the meaning of this phrase, then it is natural to extend his observation, as he does, by implication to *illius* [*orbis*] *situs* and literally to *huius* [*orbis situs*] in the final lines of 1.4 as well.

16. Dilke (1985, 62) notes that Strabo apparently was not read in first-century Rome. In practical terms Dilke means that the elder Pliny did not cite Strabo.

not aim at a full description of the terrestrial sphere, not even at a full description of the inhabited *orbis*, and this recognition also reveals something about his abiding curiosity concerning the theory of the counterworld (*antichthôn*), a theory with which he had not yet come to terms at this point in his (young?) life.

A certain brashness marks this choice of subject and genre, and that brashness is highlighted when Mela begins his account. Greek geographic writers regularly began their descriptions of the Mediterranean littoral at the Strait of Gibraltar, which the ancients called the Pillars of Hercules, but they typically began with the European littoral and moved in a clockwise direction around the Mediterranean. When Mela began his narrative, he broke the Greek pattern.[17] First, in his overview (1.9–23) he treated the continents in the order Asia, Europe, Africa, but then, curiously enough, in his more precise description he proceeded counterclockwise around the Mediterranean, through Africa first (1.25–48), then Asia (1.49–117), and Europe last (2.1–96), before treating the outer coasts in the narrative order of his imaginary voyage—Europe, Asia, Africa (3.1–117).

The Puzzle

Mela the author was described above as a puzzle, and the choice of this term is deliberate. The author's style, the book's genre, its subject matter and purpose, its mode of presentation, and even the reader's expected response are all puzzling to one degree or another. In the first lines of his preface, Mela describes the subject matter as consisting "chiefly in names of peoples and places and in their fairly puzzling arrangement [*eorum perplexo satis ordine*]" (1.1). This sentence underlines the main stylistic problems of the genre (repetitiveness and the necessary inclusion of catalogues) and its primary intellectual difficulty of understanding the order, or *ordo*, of the world. Thus, the subject mat-

---

17. Jacoby (1963, 48–49) identifies the Greek pattern. But it should be noted that in his description of the world (*Astronomica* 4.585–710) Manilius also varies from the Greek order. Manilius gives first an overview of the compass points (4.585–96); then a sketch of the Mediterranean lands in the order Africa, Europe, and Asia, with a review of the major islands at the end (4.597–641); then a sketch of Ocean's other points of entry into the landmass (4.642–57); and finally further details about the continents in the order Africa, Asia, and Europe (4.658–95), with a zodiacal coda connecting this geographical digression to his main subject (4.696–710).

ter is puzzling by its nature, yet the author proceeds in a way that persuades the reader to follow him through the maze. Mela views the geography of the known world as a puzzle, and it is his task to "untangle" (*expediam*, 1.2) its order and to help the reader explore it.

In the proem at 1.1 *ordo* describes the complex arrangement of peoples and places in the known world, but at 1.24 the *ordo* of the world becomes the *ordo* of the narrative when Mela says that "the course [*cursus*] of the work now begun" is "to skirt the shores in the order [*ordo*] they lie in," just as the *cursus* of the work now becomes the circumnavigation of the known world. Once (1.29), *ordo* is used neutrally to describe the file of mountains known as the Seven Brothers (Ceuta) without any explicit notion that their exact order necessarily parallels the progress of the narrative journey, but everywhere else *ordo* retains its mixed sense (1.84, 1.91, 2.58, 2.94, 2.100), often with an indication that the narrative will visit the named places in the order specified. The manual itself is, paradoxically, both an embodiment of the world's puzzle and the solution to it.

At 2.97 the island of Gades (Cádiz) "advises" or "reminds" (*admonet*)[18] Mela to treat the islands that have been omitted or passed by[19] for the convenience of the narrator/narrative: "The island of Gades, which meets travelers as they exit the strait, is a reminder [*admonet*] to mention all the other islands before the narrative [*oratio*] proceeds, as we promised at the beginning, to the shores of Ocean and the earth's periphery." At this moment the narrative enhances its status as a rhetorical, geographic, and navigational *ordo* and becomes, in effect, an oration (*oratio*) as well.[20] While *oratio* can mean narrative order in general, it typically has that meaning in oratorical analysis.

---

18. The vividness of the remark reflects M.'s personal enthusiasm as he enters the territory where he was born (2.96), another mark of his chauvinism.

19. M. follows a similar principle to describe the islands of Ocean. At 3.46 Gades again draws his attention, this time because it is the first island on the Atlantic side of the Strait of Gibraltar. He adds, "Of those islands not happily *passed by*, though, Gades is on the Strait" [sed earum quas *praeterire* non libeat Gades fretum adtingit]. *Praeterire*'s etymological meaning is "to move past" or "to pass by," but it also has the common rhetorical meaning of "to omit" or "to leave out." The use of this verb is one of the subtler ways that M. reinforces the narratological fusion of the narrative and the journey.

20. Parroni (1984, 41) does not note the text's personification here but does draw attention to other aspects of animation in it. M. is playing with the rules of genre again: according to Cicero (*de Leg.* 1.5), historical writing (which includes chorography as a subgenre) is *opus maxime oratorium*.

Ordo is used just once more (2.100), and the reader is left feeling that *oratio* and *ordo* are one thing. The text, in fact, has fused *ordo* and *oratio*. Neither term appears hereafter in *The Chorography*, and whatever they have become in fusion is embodied and exemplified in book 3.

The *ordo* of the narrative, as we have seen, both incorporates and becomes the *ordo* of the world. Narratologically, the text becomes what it describes, and it succeeds through the fiction that the readers are pursuing a journey of their own: the reader is the traveler, and the mixed geographic and narrative *ordo* becomes the reader/traveler's *ordo*, or itinerary. In Mela's day, travel was relatively common for reasons of public and private business as well as for scientific curiosity. Unlike readers of Pausanias' *Guide to Greece* or modern travel books of various kinds, however, Mela cannot have expected his readers to make the journey he described or even a significant part of it. Mela has made explicit what was known intuitively all along, not only that the narrative's order is the order of the journey, but that this journey depends on the power of speech. Speech, then, preserves all the memorable persons, places, and other phenomena of the known world.

The fiction of the narrative as journey and of the reader as tourist is also apparent throughout. With the proviso that special narrative accommodation be made to include islands (2.97), the narrative is a circumnavigation, or *periplus*, of the known world. Mela is explicit about this design (1.24): ". . . until the course of the work now begun sails around both the inside and the outside of the known world and returns to that place whence it began" [. . . donec cursus incepti operis, intra extraque circumvectus orbem, illuc unde coeperit redeat]. "The course of the work now begun" is the voyage. It guides the reader around the continental shores, describes the coastlines, and gives the chief topographical and ethnological features of the immediately adjacent inland regions (remoter inland regions are ignored). The reader's journey is marked in several ways: by vocabulary, by the order in which the coasts are described, by emphasizing the interiority of the adjacent lands from the narratological point of view, by progressing along the coast from *here* to *there* and stressing terms like *next* or *following* in reference to place, and by other devices as well.[21]

---

21. These are the reasons of Silberman 1988, xvi–xvii; cp. Brodersen 1994, 5. Bunbury (1883, 355) notes the defects of the *periplus* as a narrative technique: (a) the narratives of Gaul and Spain "are divided into two separate portions, described in different parts of the work," and (b) the deeper interior of Europe

In book 1, after a general description of the three continents (Asia, Europe, Africa), Mela begins the envisioned journey on the African side of the modern Strait of Gibraltar and proceeds along the coast of North Africa and the Mediterranean (and Black Sea) littoral of Asia. In book 2 he traverses the Mediterranean (and Black Sea) coast of Europe before he interrupts his progress to report on the islands, which, for convenience, he had omitted from the main narrative. In book 3, outside the Strait of Gibraltar, he proceeds up the Spanish coast, Gaul, Britain, Scythia, and the far sides of Asia and Africa, back to the Strait.

Mela is interested generally in anthropological curiosities, natural phenomena, supernatural phenomena, and the lay of the land. He does not spend much time describing man-made structures, and once when he does give sufficient detail, the description rivets our attention. Mela's depiction of Psammetichus' labyrinth in Aegypt (1.56) even becomes emblematic because it represents (a) Mela's own work, (b) the puzzling order of the known world as a whole, and (c) the reader's journey:

> The Labyrinth . . . has one passageway down into it but almost countless paths inside; many confusing paths turn back on themselves this way and that but extend in both directions with a continuous winding and with porticoes that are often circular; with these paths promptly making one circle on top of others, and with the curve of a circle promptly bending back as far as it had advanced, the Labyrinth is puzzling [*perplexus*] with its long, yet solvable [*explicabilis*], wandering path [*error*].

The playful Mela emerges in the concluding sentence here, and his playfulness justifies taking the labyrinth as emblematic of his project.[22] The labyrinth is puzzling (*perplexus*) just like the order of the known

---

and Asia—including inland Germany, the Alpine and Danubian provinces, Dacia, Drangiana, Margiana, and Sogdiana—find no mention, while (c) Medes, Bactrians, and Arians are merely mentioned but not treated. (The mythical creatures assigned to the interior of Africa, it should be added, reflect a larger ignorance of that continent's interior.)

22. This aspect of M.'s image is unknown to Doob (1990, 21–22). Like other scholars, Doob regards M. merely as a technical writer (cp. her p. 20, "in the historical-geographical tradition") and ignores the literary claims he makes on his readers, but it seems inappropriate simply to lump M. with Pliny, as Doob does, as being "interested chiefly in the *facts* of the ancient labyrinths, their status as

world (1.1), which is Mela's proper subject, and in Latin a journey on any puzzling and uncertain course is an *error*. But as Mela knows, this particular *error* can be unraveled (*explicabilis*) and at the same time the reader saved from making a mistake (*error*).

The image of unraveling not only recalls Ariadne's thread that saved Theseus from the horror of the primordial Cretan labyrinth but also returns the reader to the beginning of this work, where the textual voice announced its first task as the untangling (*expediam*, 1.2) of "the things that are most unambiguous" (a phrase that emphasizes that even the starting point of the reader's *error* is not entirely free from difficulty). While the world's *ordo* is *perplexus* and the text holds the solution to the puzzle for the reader, the traveler who embarks on a puzzling and uncertain journey also needs to be provided with a solution and saved from *error*. For the traveler the device that both embodies the puzzle and provides its solution is a map, and the enigmatic word *chorographia* also means "map" (cp. Vitr. 8.2.6 and this introduction, n. 31). The reader's text becomes the metaphorical traveler's map, and as such it is the Ariadne's thread that unravels the puzzle of the world's labyrinthine ways.

Mela's Reader

Mela also has a complex relation to his reader. At certain points in the narrative the reader is addressed personally. In describing Gaul's Rocky Beach (the Crau), the legendary site where Jupiter rained rocks down on two sons of Poseidon who were fighting with Hercules, Mela says directly to the reader, "You would believe [*credas*] that it had rained rocks" (2.78). As Mela's narrative moves from Gaul to Spain, he describes the Mediterranean littoral "if you coast along the shores" [si litora legas] (2.89). In the plains of Armenia the movement of the smooth-flowing Araxes (Araks) cannot be detected "even if you watch it closely" [quamquam intuearis] (3.40). This usage is sometimes called

---

buildings, their design and purpose, the skill of their architects" (18). By contrast, it is Doob who is interested in the facts of M.'s description: "But an intriguing hint of confusion between unicursal and multicursal designs may be found in Pomponius Mela's account of the Egyptian building. . . . Mela seems to want it both ways. . . ." To be fair to Doob, M.'s literary-theoretical concerns are not treated by classicists, and her professed goal is to win access to certain poetic fictions, especially those of the Middle Ages.

the impersonal *you* and often is translated as "one," but to translate it as the impersonal *one* misses the point and does any author a disservice. This device is anything but impersonal. An author uses it as a rhetorical strategy to address the reader personally and individually and to implicate each reader more intimately into the text. However effective this trope might be, its use marks a direct and personal address from the author—or better, from the text—to the reader.[23]

A closely related and truly impersonal construction occurs in a parenthetical remark about the mythical creatures—the Goat-Pans, Blemyes, Gamphasantes, and Satyrs—that are supposed to inhabit an interior part of Africa. Mela invites his readers, in essence, to make up their own minds about the mythical creatures that are said to inhabit the interior of Africa—"if one wants to believe it" [si credere libet] (1.23). Throughout the narrative this author evinces a certain skepticism about mythological or legendary events and persons. At such moments he typically suspends his own specific judgment and lets the reader decide about the factuality of the item in question. Mela engages his readers, then, by inviting them to make up their own minds about certain sights on the journey.

Among other devices that reinforce the idea of the reader's journey are two features of Latin that stand out. One is the dative of reference; the other is the Latin verb *legere*. The dative of reference, as its name implies, gives the reference point from which the content of the clause or sentence is to be understood. An example is found right at the beginning of the journey (1.25): "From here, *for those traveling into Our Sea*, Spain is on the left, Mauretania on the right . . ." [hinc *in Nostrum mare*

---

23. The so-called editorial or royal *we* and the impersonal *you* would be better named the conspiratorial or implicative *we* and *you*. Both devices mark deliberate attempts to focus the reader's attention on a particular item and thereby to implicate the reader in the author's point of view. Not all will agree about the successful effect of such usages on the reader, but the logic of the grammatical structure is transparent. The point I have argued here is, in fact, reinforced also by M.'s use of the editorial *we*: M. (a) uses thirteen different verbs in the first person plural on thirty-eight occasions, (b) implies such verbs four times by using the first person plural *nos* [*we*], and (c) deploys the possessive pronoun *noster, nostra, nostrum* [*our*] twenty-seven times. Perhaps the cleverest example occurs at 2.96, when M. identifies author, reader, and text with his hometown (*atque unde nos sumus*, "and where we're from too"), which is echoed again in the last sentence of book 3 when, for the first time, he calls the Strait of Gibraltar "Our Strait."

pergentibus laeva Hispania, Mauretania dextra est . . .]. The italicized phrase is the dative of reference in its purest form, sometimes called the historical or geographic dative in this usage, and that construction recurs many times throughout the work, so often that it is a distinct feature of Mela's style. In one stroke, this usage gives the necessary bearings in the narrative and effectively identifies the reader and the reader's interest with the traveler and the traveler's interest. This identification is reinforced further both by the narrative's progress and by the way the author makes the acts of writing, reading, and traveling problematic.

The verb *legere* in Latin is common and almost predictable in its meanings of "to pick" (or "to choose") and "to read." Mela uses the verb five times, but never in its usual sense of "to read" and only once in the ordinary sense of "to choose." At 3.86 certain Aethiopians are said to "choose" their chief by his strength and appearance. In the other four instances (1.24, 2.27, 2.44, and 2.89), the verb has the specialized meaning of "to sail along the coast," that is, to pick one's way among the coastal reefs, shoals, and other barriers. Once, at 1.24, where Mela states his methodology, he tells us (a) where he will begin his narrative, (b) that he will "skirt the shores" (*stringere litora*) of the Mediterranean in their natural order, and (c) that, when these shores have been "traversed" (*peragratis*), he will "coast along" (*legere*) Ocean's seaboard. The author's approach and the journey that forms the narrative become fused to one another, with the consequence that the act of reading becomes problematic for the reader who also picks her or his way along these coasts with Mela. In this way, author and reader become bound narratologically to one another and to the journey as well.

The Structure of *The Chorography*

Only now are we prepared to examine the program that Mela outlines in his introduction. The formal proem to the work as a whole (1.1–2) explains the author's purpose and describes generally the overall shape of *The Chorography*, but it does not detail the author's exact plan for the main narrative. The proem justifies the author's overview of the world (as described in 1.3–23), before a second introduction at 1.24 refers back to the proem and lays out the exact plan for the rest of the book.

The proem is divided into two parts. One part (1.1) announces, in its first three words, what Mela's project is, namely, to give a description of the known world (*orbis situm dicere*). In the rest of the paragraph the author expresses reservations about the subject matter and his own literary ability to capture it. To describe the world, he says, is

> a difficult task and one hardly suited to eloquence, since it consists chiefly in names of peoples and places and in their fairly puzzling arrangement. To trace this arrangement completely is a time-consuming, rather than a welcome, subject, but nevertheless a very worthwhile thing to consider and understand. It repays the effort of those who give it attention—at least by the very act of contemplating it, if not by the richness of this supplicant's natural talent.

These are formal reservations, though, with a long rhetorical history of their own, and these gestures are intended to focus the reader's attention more keenly on the content. Chorography is a risky subject for an author because of its catalogues and the world's complexity, but Mela also reminds the reader that careful reading will reap its own reward.

The second paragraph of the proem (1.2), however, has presented a greater challenge to critics, and the key to reading and understanding this manual rests in its first sentence:

> *Dicam autem alias plura et exactius, nunc ut quaeque erunt clarissima et strictim. Ac primo quidem quae sit forma totius, quae maximae partes, quo singulae modo sint atque habitentur expediam, deinde rursus oras omnium et litora ut intra extraque sunt, atque ut ea subit ac circumluit pelagus, additis quae in natura regionum incolarumque memoranda sunt. Id quo facilius sciri possit atque accipi, paulo altius summa repetetur.*

> [*I should, however, say more elsewhere and with greater preciseness. Now let me address the things that are most unambiguous, as they all certainly will be, even in a summary treatment. To start with, in fact, let me untangle what the shape of the whole is, what its greatest parts are, what the condition of its parts taken one at a time is, and how they are inhabited; then, back to the borders and coasts of all lands* [a] *as they exist to the interior and on the seacoast,* [b] *to the extent that the sea enters them and washes up around them, and* [c] *with those additions that, in the nature of the regions and their*

inhabitants, need to be recorded. So that this outline can be known and grasped more easily, its full extent will be revisited in a little more depth.]

What does Mela mean by "elsewhere" [*alias*] and "with greater preciseness" [*exactius*]? Does he mean elsewhere in *The Chorography*? Or does he mean in a separate, more detailed work? Erasure in this sentence in Vat. lat. 4929 shows both that the passage was considered to be a problem not long after our earliest manuscript was copied and that clarification was deemed necessary. Previous scholars have fallen into three camps. One thinks that Mela alluded here to two separate works—a larger and more detailed treatment, which he reserved for another occasion, and the summary account or compendium that has survived as *The Chorography*.[24] The second camp argues that Mela's description in 1.2 corresponds exactly to the plan he executed in the surviving work. A third group argues that Mela's phrase *alias . . . nunc* means that in some parts of the present work he will proceed with broad summary strokes, while in other places in it he will proceed with more detail.[25] This problem cannot be resolved by paleography or by purely stylistic or linguistic arguments.

Content is a more secure guide to what any author is doing in his or her own work, and Mela signals at 1.24 what the phrase "with greater preciseness" applies to in *The Chorography*: "Now for me, as I begin to describe its coastlines and regions with greater preciseness . . ." [nunc exactius oras situsque dicturo . . .]. That description does not end until he finishes the work. In other words, the more precise or more detailed description begins with 1.24 and constitutes, in fact, the remainder of the entire work. The second part of the proem, then, tells the reader both the shape of the whole work and how to understand the overview

---

24. In his edition of 1530 (Paris) Ioachim Vadianus articulated the theory of an *editio minor* (the existing work) and a proposed *editio maior* (never realized). Parroni (1968 and 1984, 23–27) has examined and defended this theory, but his arguments do not satisfactorily explain away the exact symmetry between the proem and M.'s opening chapters. See, in the present introduction, n. 36.

25. The three camps are summarized by Parroni (1968, 188). The argument of Parroni 1968 is reprised more concisely by Parroni 1984, 23–27. The third group takes M.'s phrase *alias . . . nunc* as equivalent to *alias . . . alias* or *nunc . . . nunc*. This third interpretation is, by far, the hardest to defend; such usage is unparalleled in Latin.

of the earth contained in 1.3–23, while the methodological statement at 1.24, with its deliberate verbal echo of the proem (1.2), both terminates the broad sweep of 1.3–23 and leads the reader to focus on the more precise treatment that follows it.

In brief, the proem explains, as it should, the structure of the whole work to follow. First the general characteristics of the terrestrial sphere will be given (1.3–23), then the important features of our habitable *orbis* will be reprised in more detail (1.25–3.107). To comprehend the proem requires the reader, as we have seen, to understand both the meaning of chorography in the author's scheme and the place of the known world (*orbis*) in that scheme. The table illustrates the correspondences between 1.2 and the opening chapters of *The Chorography*. The overall symmetry between the plan laid out in 1.2 and the structure of the rest of the book is so exact that readers can hardly doubt the author's narrative design.

Style and Content

The Chorography is a surprisingly engaging work. Mela wrote it in a pleasing and graceful style that mediates, as he intended, between the repetitiveness of the subject and his audience's curiosity. The book has been described as "clear and simple" and as "written well and in a captivating manner, but really superficial from the viewpoint of its content."[26] Mela's style is smooth, and the reader tends to overlook the catalogues and repetitiousness that the author had warned about at the outset. His style, however, can also be jejune and can suffer from the necessary overuse of the same devices that otherwise would relieve the narrative. It can be judiciously or tediously full of chiasmus, antithesis, parallelism, and asyndeton, and it can also be elliptical and artificial, even without being entirely artless, unnecessarily repetitive, or stiff. In short, he shares the virtues and vices of other Latin writers in the Silver Age.

The subject matter, after all, is both restricted and restrictive. To succeed, Mela needed to describe and locate the same kinds of features in each of the regions he treated—mountains, rivers, seas, peoples, cul-

---

26. Silberman (1988, xv) calls it "claire et simple." Wissowa (1916, 89) writes, "das gut und fesselnd geschriebene, aber inhaltlich recht oberflächliche geographische Handbuch." Parroni 1984, 51–53, also summarizes M.'s language and style.

Table of Correspondences

M. 1.2	Correspondence	Execution
"I should . . . say more **elsewhere** and **with greater preciseness**."		
"Now let me address the things that are most unambiguous . . . even in a summary treatment."	1.3	"Whatever all this is, therefore, on which we have bestowed the name of world and sky, it is a single unity and embraces itself and all things with a single ambit. It differs in its parts."
"Shape of the whole":	1.3–4	—compass directions
1. "its greatest parts"		—land mass of our *orbis* —hemispheres
2. "the condition of its parts"		—zones and climates
3. "how they are inhabited"		—habitability or not
"borders and coasts of all lands":	1.5–8	—land mass and seas (described abstractly)
a. "as they exist to the interior and on the seacoast"		—three continents (main features described)
b. "to the extent that the sea enters them and washes up around them"		—two rivers that divide the land mass into three continents
c. "with those additions that, in the nature of the regions and their inhabitants, need to be recorded."	1.9–23	Continents and seas described in specific outline; ethnography and political geography: 9–10: Asiatic geography 11–14: Asiatic peoples 15–17: European geography 18–19: European peoples 20–21: African geography 22–23: African peoples
"So that this outline can be known and grasped more easily . . ."	1.24	"This is the full extent of our world. These are its largest parts, its shapes, and the nations of its parts."
"its full extent will be revisited in a little more depth."	1.24	"**Now** for me, as I begin to describe its coastlines and regions with greater preciseness, . . ."

tural habits, important cities, coasts, the adjacent interior, and so on. He varied the subject matter by adding a nontopographic, nongeographic criterion, fame or memorability, as well as numerous digressions. Climate, locale, natural resources, or architecture can underlie a city's or region's claim to fame, of course, but more typically fame depends on wealth and power, history, or legend. Mela looks for what is worth remembering, without ever forgetting that his descriptions are limited to a brushstroke or two. There is little or no room for rhetorical or contextual development, which further restricts the work's appeal.

It is as if Mela wrote *The Chorography* as much for himself as for others. He expresses occasional skepticism about the legends, or *fabulae*,[27] that have come down, and he takes particular care to locate various places in the geography of mythology. The intended audience is not easily identifiable except in general and predictable terms—as the educated upper classes. The reader with an historical bent appreciates the geographic sorting out that occurs in the text because Mela was working with one or more detailed geographic sources, but without the reader's interest in ethnography, legends, and fame, *The Chorography* would offer little more than the flat verbal picture of a map.

As far as can be known, and despite its title's pun, *The Chorography* never circulated in antiquity with a map,[28] and an explanation is now available: for this author, as we have seen, the text doubles as its own map. (One nineteenth-century interpretation of the world as described by Mela is embodied in the map at the front of this volume.) Mela's device is charming, and the author has emerged as the popularizer that he was.[29] The genre of the *periplus* was ordinarily practiced either by

---

27. *Fabula* applies to what English calls myth and history. Since we make a distinction in this regard that Romans did not always make, I settled on "legend" as the universal translation of *fabula* in *The Chorography*.

28. Dilke (1985, 66) notes, "... there is no evidence that it contained maps." And no map circulated with *The Chorography* in the Middle Ages: see Gormley et al. 1984, 268. Gormley et al. indicate (300–301) that *The Chorography* had no influence on medieval cartography, and they discuss (314–19) the first known manuscript to contain a map, that of Philastrius in 1417, while Brodersen (1994, 23–26; cp. 17–20) indicates that the first printed edition to do so came from Salamanca in 1498. (In both cases these were later maps based on Ptolemy's ideas.) Silberman (1988) offers reconstructions of M.'s world in five end-maps outside his text. See, in this introduction, n. 31.

29. Bunbury (1883, 2:355) writes, "It is evident that Mela intended his work as a popular compendium of geography, rather than as an introduction for the

explorers who reported their own adventures (the *Periplus* of Hanno) or by practical writers giving directions to traders and navigators (the *Periplus of the Red Sea* or the *Periplus* of Scylax),[30] but *The Chorography* of Pomponius Mela is not like these other treatises. Mela drew virtually everything from the works of others (from books certainly, from a map or maps possibly),[31] not from his own experience. It cannot be proved, then, that Mela used the world map that was begun by Agrippa, completed by Augustus, and on display in the Porticus Vipsania at Rome, but it is hard to imagine that the most scientifically up-to-date and politically important world map of the early imperial era did not play some part in Mela's conception. Whether or not Agrippa's map underlies the actual outline of the world as given by Mela cannot be known with certainty, but *chorographia* was nevertheless the Roman name for public maps. If the Augustan map was known either formally or informally as the *chorographia*, then both Mela's title and his subject matter deliberately ring with echoes of the Augustan project. In a literary-theoretical sense Mela cast his work as a map, as we learned from the image of the labyrinth, and it may not be stretching the point to suggest that the voice of Mela's textual *oratio* was meant at least to respond to the great *chorographia* of Augustus.[32] However that may be, for Mela

---

use of the student; hence he not only dismisses the whole idea of mathematical geography with the very few words to which we have already adverted, but he nowhere enters into questions of measurements and distances...." He continues (367), "It may be said indeed with regard to the treatise of Mela in general, that, with the exception of the countries immediately bordering on the Mediterranean, it was rather calculated to supply to its readers a compendious collection of the stories current with regard to different countries and their inhabitants, than to furnish them with any correct geographical information."

30. For Hanno, see Blomqvist 1979; for Scylax, Peretti 1979; and for the *Periplus of the Red Sea*, Casson 1989. Although it postdates M.'s work, Arrian's *Periplus of the Pontus Euxinus* (ca. 131 C.E.) deserves to be mentioned here as the memoir (written in Greek) of a Roman official.

31. There can be little doubt that M. used maps or at least authors that used maps. His geometric descriptions of Sicily (2.115), Sardinia (2.123), Britain (3.50), and Ireland (3.53) reflect Eratosthenes' systemization of mapping, and elsewhere he appeals to visual images that directly or indirectly reflect the use of a map for the Black Sea (1.102), a peninsula in the Ukraine (2.5), the Peloponnese (2.38), and the Persian Gulf (3.73). See the following note.

32. On this Augustan project and the epigraphic (public) meaning of *chorographia*, see Nicolet 1991, 98–111. Pliny (*HN* 3.17) refers to the project as "orbem terrarum urbi spectandum" (where *urbi* is certainly Pliny's, even if *orbis spectan-*

himself the practice of chorography was a literary genre first and foremost, and his playful little book embodies his thorough reflection on that genre.

Technique and Purpose

Mela does give more than a verbal map. Even when he errs in specific details, his aim is to inculcate in the reader a sense of place and to convey the same kind of excitement that Sidonius Apollinaris expressed four centuries later when he actually made the journey from Gaul to Rome. Sidonius marveled at the historical and mythological sites he passed on his way down (*Ep.* 1.5.3): "At Ticinum [Pavia] I boarded a 'mailboat' (that's the boat's generic name), and I sailed swiftly on it to the Po and laughed at the daughters of Phaëthon, whom we often sing about in festivals, and at their fabled [*commenticias*] tears of arboreal amber."[33] Here the Christian Sidonius revels in the myths and feelings of pre-Christian Rome. Sidonius actually visited the sites in question, but what is important here is the sense of connection between place and legend, or between place and history. Similarly, Mela's reader is separated by time and space from places and events mentioned in his text, but it is the purpose of Mela's narrative journey to give the reader a feeling of immediacy and familiarity.

Mela strongly conveys this sense of place, of being there, when he alludes to *fabulae* that he and his audience had heard all their lives. Some of these *fabulae* were historical, some mythological; and to the Roman way of thinking, all fell within the range of what we call legend. Mela played on his readers' mental images of persons, places, and things, and he offered his audience a kind of armchair travelogue in prose. It is brief and to the point, the Roman written equivalent of the cinematic travelogue made famous by Lowell Thomas earlier in our own century.

---

dus might be the map's heading), but the *Divisio orbis terrarum* (15R) calls it *chorographia*. Romer (1996) urged that M.'s *Chorographia* resonates from Agrippa's world map (*chorographia*).

33. Contrast Pausanias' matter-of-factness (Paus. 1.4.1) when he gives the locale of Phaëthon's daughters only as incidental information about a location that is removed from his narrative. Earlier in this same epistle (*Ep.* 1.5.1), Sidonius expresses the feelings and hopes of the educated Roman traveler of his own day. Like any tourist, Sidonius also thrills at the history of the places he passes through (cp. *Ep.* 1.5.7).

Introduction 23

The Chorography offered its readers the pleasures of *fabulae*, and the readers, in turn, acquired an intellectually multidimensional view of the world that an even more stripped-down description could not have conveyed at all. Mela's description is pared back already, to be sure, but his concise narrative allows the reader to enjoy the chorography of the whole *orbis* in a practical and convenient time span. The danger is that this author will make mistakes and mislead his readers, and Mela does make his share of errors. There is no doubt that this book is a work of compilation. His style and his errors suggest that, as he wrote, Mela was both acquiring—primarily but not necessarily exclusively from literary sources—and organizing the same data that his audience would acquire from reading his account. By matching his "map" to the data of history and mythology, Mela thickened his own knowledge and benefited his audience at the same time. I suggest that *The Chorography* is a young man's project and that its jejune style may reflect its author's naïveté as well as his youthful ambition. In a sense, this book shows Mela as being close to the literary and rhetorical roots of Roman education, and in it he struggles to be creative and inventive under the double burden both of the rhetorical constraints he acknowledged at the outset (1.1) and of the long cultural traditions that inform his narrative throughout.[34]

This searching on his own part brought Mela to his literary pretensions, so that even as he was composing a popularized account of the *orbis terrarum*, he reflected on and made his medium itself problematic. Several times in books 1 and 2 he lets his readers make up their own minds concerning the truth or falsity of certain claims about the world, but his awareness of the research available in his own day is appalling. For example, at 2.104 he alludes to researchers (*consectantes*) whose theories explain the shrinking distance between Pharos and Aegypt, but at 2.83, where he describes the floating island in a marsh on the Gallic coast, Mela observes, ". . . Greek writers, and even our own, thought it right, either from ignorance of the truth or else from the pleasure of lying (even for sensible writers), to pass on to posterity the story that in this region a fish was pulled from deep within the earth because, after the fish had penetrated from the sea to this place, it was killed by a blow

---

34. Other possible signs that M. was young when he authored *The Chorography* include his lack of preparation for technical geographic writing (3.70), avoidance of hard critical judgment (2.83), blind modernism (3.45), and ambivalence about the *antichthôn* (1.4, 1.54).

from its captors and brought up through those holes." It remains the readers' job, then, not Mela's, to separate fact from fiction for themselves.

When Mela qualifies his statements with phrases like "they claim," "according to tradition," and so on,[35] he gives a sense that he has something to come back to, something further to examine and discuss. No one seriously doubts that Mela planned more work, although scholars strongly disagree about what conveys this sense to his readers, and it is hard to decipher exactly what any future project might have been.[36] (I cannot begin to say whether his next work or works would have been more historical than mythological, vice versa, or even mixed—much in the way *The Chorography* is—or something else entirely.) *The Chorography* shows the same groping for a subject that sometimes marks the efforts of first-time writers today.[37]

---

35. For example, for claims, see 1.26, 1.34, 1.64, 1.92, 2.102, 3.19, and 3.87; for traditions, see 1.27, 1.59, 1.93, 1.103, 3.37, 3.66, 3.82. This list is not exhaustive.

36. Scholars have guessed at M.'s future project. Some have taken proem 2 (that is, 1.2) to mean that *The Chorography* was the sketch of the whole earth promised there and that the future project would be his "more precise" treatment of the same subject. Others have taken M.'s remarks about Britain to be the promise of a future work: "Next, as to what kind of place Britain is and what kind of people it produces, information that is more certain and better established *will be stated* [*dicentur*]" (3.49). But M. depends on Claudius' conquest as the source of these statements, echoes the spirit of Claudian triumphalism, and implies that his own statements will be verified by the princeps' triumph: "the princeps brings with him the proof of his own accomplishments, since he will reveal in his triumph [*triumpho declaraturus*] as much as he has laid claim to in war." Apparently M. expects Claudius' victory parade to have the same kinds of floats, placards, and tableaux that marked the triumph of Cornelius Balbus after he reached the Fezzan (see Pliny *HN* 5.36–38; and in this translation, book 1, n. 19). In any case, M.'s news about Claudius' affairs seems to be current: (a) the cessation of human sacrifice by the Druids (3.18) recalls Claudius' suppression of their cult (Suet. *Claud*. 25), and (b) M.'s reference (3.23) to the familiarity of the port of Gesoriacum (Bay of Boulogne) suggests that Claudius probably mounted his expedition from there. On M.'s future project, see the following note.

37. If M. does give a clue to his future project, it may be stated in one passage that is so obvious it has been ignored in this connection: ". . . Rome, long ago founded by shepherds, now a second book in itself if there is to be discussion on the topic" (2.60). Even this remark, however, may be only a topos of the genre (cp. Pliny *HN* 3.40). This statement also resembles claims made about

Mela's own inquisitiveness is real enough but is not very broad or imaginative. As I already indicated, he knew that the earth was a sphere, but he did not appreciate the consequences of that idea. Nor did he evince much independent scientific curiosity of his own about, for example, the tumulus of Aratus, which he described at 1.71: ". . . the funerary monument of the poet Aratus must be mentioned for this reason: because—no one knows why—rocks that are hurled on it burst apart."

It is odd, then, that in book 3 Mela mentions sources by name more often than he does in either of the two preceding books. To prove that Ocean surrounds the known world (3.45), Mela mentions Homer and the natural philosophers but relies on Cornelius Nepos as being more modern and therefore more trustworthy. In addition, he cites the evidence that Nepos used—an account of Q. Metellus Celer, who reported that, as proconsul of Gaul ca. 62 B.C.E., he had confronted some Indian merchants whose itinerary in reaching Gaul proved to Metellus' satisfaction the theory of the circumambient Ocean. As ordinary readers we wonder what is at stake here, but as informed modern readers we also marvel at the falseness of the evidence and recognize the inherent self-referential and self-explanatory power of the ancient theory of the circumambient Ocean.

At 3.90 Mela knows about the attempted circumnavigation of Africa by Hanno the Carthaginian, and he cites Nepos again, this time as a source for the story that a certain Eudoxus also sailed once from the Arabian Gulf (Red Sea) around Africa to Gades (Cádiz). At 3.93 he cites Hanno again but gets the details wrong: Mela speaks of "hairy women" without men, whereas Hanno spoke of gorillas and probably of his own inability to capture a male. In this instance some of the confusion is due to Mela, some to the Greek translation of Hanno's book (see book 3, n. 64).

Most revealing perhaps is Mela's observation (3.70) about Sri Lanka, ancient Taprobane, which

---

Athens (2.41), Italy (2.58), and New Carthage (2.94), although it is more precise than those other claims: Athens, Italy, and New Carthage are too well known to need any description at all, but Rome requires a second book if there is to be discussion. The characterization of the other three cities forestalls further discussion, but the remark about Rome seems to invite it. M. would be neither the first nor the last visitor to fall in love with the city and its people.

is said to be either a very large island or the first part of the second world, but because it is inhabited, and because no one reportedly has circumnavigated it, the latter interpretation is as good as true.

Again Mela's limited sense of the earth as a sphere confronts the reader. The "second world" is the antichthonic one about the existence of which Mela is relatively secure in one place, doubtful in another. Furthermore, an embassy even came from Taprobane to Rome during Claudius' principate, and as a consequence Roman scientific knowledge about the island was put on a sounder footing (see book 3, n. 51). It is one thing to say that Mela's knowledge of the island was not up-to-date (the embassy may well have arrived after he had published *The Chorography*), but Taprobane had been circumnavigated in the time of Alexander the Great, and Mela shows no knowledge of it. His armchair travelogue takes on an obviously theoretical air. As Mela's narrative touches the rim of Ocean, its theoretical aspect increases, since these shores and their peoples were either unknown or less well known to the Greeks and Romans than were their Mediterranean counterparts. His own unfamiliarity and insecurity alert the reader to the dangers of this genre.

For Mela, as for other Greek and Latin writers before and after him, geography and ethnography are essentially interconnected studies[38] that are joined together as a branch of philosophy. Strabo (1.1) described geography as a philosophical study that combined other subjects into a whole with practical and theoretical consequences:

> We accept that the practice of geography, which we now intend to examine, belongs to the philosopher's field, if anything at all does. That our acceptance is not careless emerges from many signs. The first ones who dared to tackle the subject were very much philosophers. . . . And the encyclopedic learning, by which alone this task can be accomplished, characterizes no one other than the observer of divine and human things, because they say

---

38. I follow Rawson 1985, chap. 17, "Geography and Ethnography." Rawson cites the passage from Strabo that concludes my next sentence in text. She documents the decline in the Roman practice of geography, as contrasted with the Greeks'. On this last topic, see also Silberman 1988, xxv–xxix. In general, Rawson has a fuller discussion of geography than ethnography, and recourse to Trüdinger 1918 is still useful for Greek and Roman ethnographic writing.

knowledge of these things is philosophy. And so, in the same way too, its usefulness is something diverse—relating both to political and military action and also to knowledge of the heavens and of the animals, plants, and fruits on land and sea and to knowledge of everything else that can be seen in individual places—and that usefulness describes one and the same person, the individual who contemplates skill-for-living and happiness.

Mela was a minor writer, a popularizer, not a first-class geographer or even—so far as we can tell—an aspiring technical geographer. One important, shocking reason for his choice of genre and his literary pretensions now emerges. His preparation was insufficient for technical writing in geography. *The Chorography* functioned for its author much like an intellectual map of his own interests. He pointed out curiosities and phenomena that might deserve his time and effort in the future. His literary ambitions in the capital were well served by his salute to Claudius, and why no other work survives from the stylus of Pomponius Mela is as mysterious as the other details of his life.

The Text and Translation

The timing of Mela's publication was fortunate, and his book more or less burst on the scene with a flourish ca. 44 C.E. Among the subjects and sources of the *Historia Naturalis (Natural History)*, published posthumously after 79 C.E., the elder Pliny listed Mela as an authority for no less than nine books, including all four geographic ones.[39] Unfortunately, nowhere in the remaining thirty-six books did Pliny cite Mela by name; thus we cannot assess his direct influence on the encyclopedist. After that Mela went underground, and the brief litany of citations is familiar to specialists: the widely read compiler Solinus (third century C.E.), the very influential encyclopedist Martianus Capella (fifth century), and the important historian Jordanes (sixth century) are known for their systematic use of *The Chorography*.[40] Vat. lat. 4929, the ninth-century manuscript that underlies our text of Mela, is itself the copy of

---

39. M. is cited for *HN* books 3–6 (the geographic books), 8, 12, 13, 21, and 22.

40. Silberman (1988, lii–liii) summarizes the details and gives the exact bibliographical references and publishing information. Brodersen (1994, 14–20) expanded the subject into a fuller discussion of M.'s text and its afterlife, followed by a further discussion of printed editions and maps (20–26).

a lost fifth-century exemplar of Fl. Rusticius Helpidius Domnulus (see book 3, nn. 80 and 81), and that exemplar may ultimately be the indirect source of Jordanes' ten citations. Furthermore, ad hoc citations appear in a scholiast to Juvenal (*Sat.* 2.160) and in Servius' *Commentary on Vergil's Aeneid* (on *Aen.* 9.30–31 with Mela named and on *Aen.* 4.46 anonymously), while after late antiquity Einhard and the so-called Anonymus Leidensis, author of two books called *de Situ Orbis*, both knew Mela's work.

In France the copy of *The Chorography* now known as Vat. lat. 4929 was annotated by Heiric of Auxerre (ca. 841–76) between 860 and 862, and it resided at Orléans from the tenth to the twelfth century. *The Chorography* did not circulate widely in France during this time, nor did it circulate outside of France at all until it made its way to Avignon, whence it was reclaimed for posterity and brought to Italy by Petrarch (1304–74) in the form of a twelfth-century copy. In Italy another copy of the work was exploited by Boccaccio (1313–75), who published his own *de Montibus, Lacubus, Fluminibus* (On mountains, lakes, rivers) the year before he died.[41] Vat. lat. 4929 reached Italy in 1451 and the Vatican in 1612, where it acquired its now familiar identifying number.[42]

After Mela's description of the inhabited world (the Northern *orbis*) crossed into Italy, its circulation increased steadily, even as a school text,[43] well into the Age of Discovery. The Portuguese captain Pedro Álvares Cabral (ca. 1467–ca. 1520), often called the discoverer of Brazil, thumbed well his own copy of Mela and annotated its margins extensively with an eye toward the Southern *orbis*.[44] In addition, when

---

41. According to Billanovich (1958, 101–2), it is likely that Boccaccio made his own copy directly from the one Petrarch owned. On the tradition, see Parroni 1984, 55–81, in general; Silberman 1988, xlvi–xlvii, and Brodersen 1994, 16–17.

42. See Parroni 1984, 59.

43. See Brodersen 1994, 22.

44. Cabral's copy of M. is now Huntington Library no. 87547 (Proctor 9569, Hain 11021). When he landed on the coast on 23 April 1500, Cabral may not have been the first European to reach Brazil, but he did claim the territory for Portugal. The Spaniard Vicente Yáñez Pinzón reportedly reached the coast in January 1500, and other Portuguese traders may have been there even earlier. Cabral's arrival in Brazil ignited scholarly controversy, because he had set out for India. See William Brooks Greenlee, ed. and trans., *The Voyage of Pedro Álvares Cabral to Brazil and India From Contemporary Documents and Narratives* (London: Hakluyt Society, 1938; reprint, 1972, xxxix–lxvii) on Cabral's life and voyage.

Cabral set sail on 9 March 1500 from the mouth of the Tagus River, he carried on board a Spanish physician and astronomer named Joan Faras, who in the 1490s had become the first translator of *The Chorography* into Spanish.[45]

We have no fewer than 121 manuscripts, and there have been more than 150 printed editions since the editio princeps of 1471.[46] In a scholarly sense *The Chorography* is now a hot topic again, with the Latin text having been edited three times in three different countries over the last twenty-five years. There have been new editions by Gunnar Ranstrand (Göteborg, 1971) and Piergiorgio Parroni (Rome, 1984), a new edition by A. Silberman with a facing translation into French (Paris, 1988), a bilingual Latin-German version by Kai Brodersen (Darmstadt, 1994), and a concordance by Carmen Guzmán and Miguel Perez (Hildesheim, 1989). Only these recent editions have proceeded on the proper recognition and inspection of Vat. lat. 4929 (ninth century) as the manuscript from which all other surviving copies are direct or indirect descendants.[47] To be fair, Frick (1880) had appreciated this fact.[48] He did not, however, inspect the manuscript personally or in facsimile but worked instead from notes compiled by A. Mau. As a result, his text is unsystematic and wrong in a number of places.

Scholars continue to correct and comment on Mela's text and his ideas. Parroni and Silberman added extensive notes and solid introductions to the main scholarly issues, and Brodersen has written an introduction that is a succinct and scholarly statement of the primary questions that arise for the modern reader who confronts *The Chorogra-*

---

45. See Carvalho 1974, 25–29, on the evidence: virtually nothing is known of Faras, who was both an astronomer and the court physician of King Manuel I of Portugal, who commissioned Cabral's voyage. Carvalho's book is an edition of Faras' translation, but Gormley et al. (1984, 320 n. 191) correct Carvalho 101: the text Faras based his translation on was apparently the edition printed at Rome in 1492/93.

46. Gormley et al. (1984, 319) note, "of the 121 manuscripts that survive, fully 117 date from the fifteenth century or later." Parroni (1984) describes the manuscripts (55–81) and the printed editions (83–93), etc.

47. Vat. lat. 4929 is described in detail by Barlow 1938.

48. The principle was articulated by Bursian (1869) in his review of Parthey 1867. I have not seen the review, but it is widely known and cited by Ranstrand (1971, v) and others. Billanovich ([1956] 1958) considered all the derivative manuscripts as worthless for constituting the text, but with some success Parroni (1984) searched them systematically for useful emendations.

phy in any language. But these scholars focus on curiosities and expectations pertaining to technical subjects, and, as we have seen, the question of how to reconcile Mela's literary pretensions with his relative geographical naïveté has been left open.[49] To know what Mela was up to, it is necessary to examine and to understand his literary premises and the effect of melding the acts of writing, reading, and traveling in the ways that his narrative does, and this goal—to understand the literary program of this minor writer and popularizer—has been the focus of the argument here.

This discovery of Mela the littérateur does not make *The Chorography* great literature. It is not. Yet the book is engaging and very readable, and it represents an informative genre of Roman literature that is neither well known nor fully understood. In addition, the book's survival into and its influence in the European Age of Discovery enhance its historical importance and value. For all these reasons, as well as for the book's content, Pomponius Mela deserves a fresh translation today.

The present volume is the first published English version in more than four hundred years; none has appeared since that of A. Golding's *The Cosmographer* in 1585 (London), although an earlier sixteenth-century translation into English is preserved in the manuscript known as Lond. Hargr. 399 and now in the British Museum.[50] The existence of so many Latin copies and editions of *The Chorography* from the late Middle Ages through the early modern period and beyond shows the historical importance Mela's little book enjoyed for a very long time. Mela's fascination for the general reading public has waned, of course, and no one will be surprised at that fact, given the advances in the scientific study of geography, the smallness of the world as we now experience it, and the still-inchoate understanding of the world along the lines of a global community. Yet our fascination for the ancients flourishes, and just as Mela's miscellany addressed the needs of an ancient audience interested in history, literature, and mythology, so *The Chorography* continues to speak to a modern audience that shares those interests. Moreover, Mela's subject is unique among the surviving Latin writers of the

---

49. For the assessment of M. as a technical writer, see Gisinger 1952, 2360–2411; Goodyear in Kenney and Clausen 1982, 667–68; and Conte 1994, 391–93.

50. See Parroni 1984, 93. Bolgar (1954, 530–31) omits Lond. Hargr. 399 from his list of pre-1600 translations of classical authors, but this list is not exhaustive (see his p. 506).

classical period, and as a popularizer he represents a form of literary career that is dear to the hearts of our world, but one that is hard to document in detail for antiquity.

Multiculturalism also extends, or should extend, to geography and to ancient culture. After all, antiquity *is* a foreign country, and Mela casts his unique subject in the form of an intellectual tour of its territory. A modern audience shaped by the benefits of a world in which actual tourism is a major industry will be drawn to this work. *The Chorography* integrates geographical, historical, cultural, and mythological information, and it lets the modern reader appreciate the intellectual, as well as the physical, shape of the ancient world as the Romans experienced it. In the process of reflecting this physical world that educated Romans thought they inhabited, this manual also shows the curiously imperfect knowledge the Romans actually had of their own world.

Mela does not identify his intended audience, yet this handbook is an excellent textbook of Roman cultural ideas and attitudes. Our author neither defends nor rationalizes the Roman Empire, although he does write from within the perspective of his own culture. Mela remains basically nonjudgmental in his presentation and, from a political point of view, rather detached throughout.[51] As a miscellany *The Chorography* reflects its author's direct perception of his audience's psychology, which includes a certain anthropological gullibility mixed in with a rather skeptical attitude toward mythology and the interventions of the gods, all set off by a sense of place and a sense of history. Mela's motivation comes from a general curiosity, and his sense of it thus helps to acclimate the modern reader to the Roman world. His intellectual point of view is very much like our own—with its skepticism, curiosity about the other, tolerance for vagueness about far-off places, and broad interest in the past. Mela does make mistakes, but neither the introduction nor the notes in this translation are designed to point out *all* his errors. The reader is alerted to this aspect of *The Chorography* but, as indicated earlier in the reader's note, part of enjoying this work today lies in keeping a modern map at hand.

A number of curiosities throughout *The Chorography* will catch the modern reader's attention. The Black Sea is treated (correctly) as a gulf

---

51. His enthusiasm for Claudius' triumph (3.49), discussed earlier in this introduction (see also n. 37), is a patent exception, as is his brief remark about Carthage as a rival for the *imperium* now enjoyed by the Romans (1.34).

of the Mediterranean. Modern students tend to think of these two seas as separate and distinct bodies of water, but this perception is a problem of terminology more than anything else. Mela also knows of two different borders between Africa and Asia. Africa is described in one place as ending at the Catabathmos Valley in Cyrenaïca (1.40) but elsewhere as ending at the Nile (1.8, 1.20, 1.22) and at Alexandria (1.60), the latter of which is virtually the same as saying the Nile. Mela envisions Egypt (Aegypt in the translation) as straddling both Asia and Africa (1.60), as indeed it does, but oddly treats it as more geographically Asiatic than African (1.40, 1.49). The data about Africa and Egypt do not argue against Mela's map literacy but instead reflect issues of geographic theory that were still under debate (see book 1, n. 39).[52] A careful reading, however, does urge that Mela conceived continental Africa as more or less trapezoidal in shape, and such a geometric impression may reflect cartography (see, in this introduction, n. 31). Although Mela treats the Caspian Sea wrongly as a gulf of Ocean, an idea that became canonical after its acceptance by Eratosthenes (ca. 275–194 B.C.E.), it is still curious that he describes the Caspian breaking "into the land like a river, with a strait as long as it is narrow" (3.38). This description may mark the dawning awareness that the imagined northern inlet actually was just a river.[53] On these and other topics, *The Chorography* will reward a careful reading.

And now it is time to turn to what Pomponius Mela wrote.

---

52. Other problems of theory also exercised ancient scholars. One such question was the problem of the Nile's source, a problem known to Strabo (17.1.52 and 17.3.4) and addressed twice by M. (1.53–54 and 3.96). Two decades after M., Seneca probably reviewed relevant theories in the lost part of *Natural Questions* 4a ("On the Nile"), and he reported elsewhere that Nero had sent an expedition to discover the origin of the Nile (*QNat.* 6.8.3; cp. Pliny *HN* 6.181). Nero's interest no doubt helps to explain Lucan's fascination with the question (Luc. 1.19–20, 10.39–40, and 10.193–331).

53. Bunbury (1883, 2:363) takes the phrase "like a river" as pointing to an increased and increasing knowledge of these regions.

Book 1: Around Our Sea—from the Pillars of Hercules to the End of Asia

1. A description of the known world is what I set out to give, a difficult task and one hardly suited to eloquence, since it consists chiefly in names of peoples and places and in their fairly puzzling arrangement. To trace this arrangement completely is a time-consuming, rather than a welcome, subject, but nevertheless a very worthwhile thing to consider and understand. It repays the effort of those who give it attention—at least by the very act of contemplating it, if not by the richness of this supplicant's natural talent.

2. I should, however, say more elsewhere and with greater preciseness.[1] Now let me address the things that are most unambiguous, as they all certainly will be, even in a summary treatment. To start with, in fact, let me untangle what the shape of the whole is, what its greatest parts are, what the condition of its parts taken one at a time is, and how they are inhabited; then, back to the borders and coasts of all lands [a] as they exist to the interior and on the seacoast, [b] to the extent that the sea enters them and washes up around them, and [c] with those additions that, in the nature of the regions and their inhabitants, need to be recorded. So that this outline can be known and grasped more easily, its full extent will be revisited[2] in a little more depth.

---

1. That is, from 1.24 to the end of book 3. See the following note and the table of correspondences in my introduction, for how this paragraph relates to the rest of the work.

2. The last clause (in Latin, . . . *paulo altius summa repetetur*) echoes the first sentence of this paragraph, reinforces M.'s plan for the work as a whole (although that plan is only touched on here), and virtually assures the interpretation of that plan as argued in my introduction. *Repetetur* [will be revisited] plays on the ideas of motion (going back to), reconsideration (seeking again), and reinspection (repeating), all of which are inherent both in *repetere* and in *revisit*. In effect, *repetetur* glosses *alias* [elsewhere], and *paulo altius* [a little more in depth] both glosses *alias . . . et exactius* [elsewhere and with greater preciseness] in this paragraph's first sentence and reinforces the interpretation of *exactius* [with greater preciseness] at 1.24. Both *repetere* and *revisit* play on the idea that the text is the reader's journey.

The Shape of the Whole

3. Whatever all this is, therefore, on which we have bestowed the name of world and sky, it is a single unity and embraces itself and all things with a single ambit. It differs in its parts. Where the sun rises is designated formally as east or sunrise; where it sinks, as west or sunset; where it begins its descent, south; in the opposite direction, north. **4.** In the middle of this unity the uplifted earth is encircled on all sides by the sea. In the same way, the earth also is divided from east to west into two halves,[3] which they term hemispheres, and it is differentiated by five horizontal zones. Heat makes the middle zone unlivable, and cold does so to the outermost ones. The remaining two habitable zones have the same annual seasons, but not at the same time. The Antichthones[4] inhabit one, we the other. The chorography of the former zone is unknown because of the heat of the intervening expanse, and the chorography of the latter is now to be described.[5]

The Three Continents

5. This zone stretches from east to west and, because it is situated this way, is somewhat longer than it is wide at its widest point. It is entirely surrounded by Ocean, and from Ocean it allows four seas to enter—one from the north, from the south two, a fourth from the west.[6] Those

---

3. *Latera*, the word for "halves," usually means vertical sides but can be used as here to designate the surfaces of any geometric solid. That M. conceives the whole as a sphere is clear from the term *hemispheres* used to describe these two halves. Since the dividing line runs "from east to west," these halves are most likely the northern and southern hemispheres, and this orientation appears to be confirmed by the subsequent mention of the Antichthones (see the following note). The zones are belts etymologically, and they run horizontally too.

4. *Antichthones* is M.'s regular word for the people who live in the inhabitable zone of the southern hemisphere. The *antichthôn*, or counterworld, is conceived as being like our world (*orbis*) but with a different sequence of seasons from ours (1.54). M. avoids the word and idea of *Antipodes* (see my introduction, n. 13), perhaps because his limited sense of a spherical earth keeps him from thinking in terms of people whose feet are literally opposite to ours.

5. For the translation *chorography* here, see my introduction, n. 15.

6. In the north, the Caspian Sea, discussed at 3.38 (see n. 17 there); in the south, the Persian and Arabian (Red) Seas, described at 3.73–74 (see book 3, n. 52); and in the west, the Mediterranean, which M. describes here (see book 1, n. 8).

other seas will be recounted in their own places. **6.** This last one, at first narrow and not more than ten miles wide,[7] breaks into the land mass and penetrates it. Then, spreading in length and width, it pushes back the shores, which recede to an impressive degree, but when those same shores almost come together at the opposite end, the sea is reduced to a space so constricted that the opening is less than a mile wide. From there it spreads out again, but very moderately, and again it proceeds into a space even more constricted than the previous one. After the sea is received by this space, its size increases greatly again, and it is connected to a huge swamp, but only by a tiny aperture. The whole sea, both where it comes in and as far as it reaches, is called by a single name, Our Sea.[8]

7. We call the narrows and the entranceway of the incoming water the Straight [Lat. *fretum*], but the Greeks call it the Channel [Grk. *porthmos*].[9] Wherever that sea extends, it gets different names in different places. Where it is constricted for the first time, it is called the Hellespont [Dardanelles]; then Propontis [Sea of Marmara] where it spreads out; where it compresses itself again, the Thracian Bosphorus [Karadeniz Boğazi/Bosporus]; where it widens again, the Pontus Euxinus [Black Sea].[10] Where it comes into contact with the swamp, it is called the Cimmerian Bosphorus [Kerchenskiy Proliv/Strait of Kerch]. The swamp itself is called Maeotis [Sea of Azov].

---

7. In the text *mile* always means the Roman mile, which is slightly shorter than the English mile. The Roman mile (*mille passuum*) is one thousand Roman paces, i.e., what we would call a double pace, or two steps. Each pace (*passus*) was calculated as five Roman feet, and one Roman foot (*pes*) is 11.65 English inches. Thus one Roman mile equals about 4,854 feet 2 inches English.

8. In fact, what moderns call the Mediterranean Sea is composed of sections also called seas—the Aegean, the Ionian, and the Libyan Seas, for example: see M.'s remarks in the next paragraph. In general, the Romans called the Mediterranean *Mare Nostrum* (Our Sea), but they sometimes called it—logically enough—by the plural, *Maria Nostra* (Our Seas), as M. does too (cp. 1.13, 1.54, 1.81, et al.). (M. sometimes substitutes *pelagus* for *mare*.) M. uses the word *mediterraneus -a -um* once only (2.88) and there in its ordinary Latin sense, to describe an inland region that is at a distance from the coast.

9. The Strait where M. begins is the Strait of Gibraltar.

10. *Pontus Euxinus* is the Greek name for the Black Sea, which is perhaps the most important gulf of the Mediterranean Sea. The Romans borrowed this name from the Greek, and like the Greeks they regularly shortened it to *Pontus*. For the derivation of the name *Euxinus* (Euxine in its Anglicized form), see 1.102.

8. By this sea and by two famous rivers, the Tanaïs [Don] and the Nile, the whole earth is divided into three parts. The Tanaïs, descending from north to south, flows down almost into the middle of Maeotis, and from the opposite direction the Nile flows down into the sea. Those lands that lie from the Strait to those rivers, on the one side we call Africa, on the other Europe. Whatever is beyond those rivers is Asia.

Asia

9. Ocean, differing by name as by position, abuts Asia from three directions: the Eastern Ocean from the east, from the south the Indian, from the north the Scythian Ocean. Asia itself, reaching eastward with a huge and continuous coastline, empties its rivers on this end over a coast as wide as Europe, Africa, and the sea that extends between them. Then, after its coastline has advanced uninterrupted for some distance, it lets in the Arabian [Red] and the Persian Seas from what we call the Indian Ocean, and from the Scythian Ocean it lets in the Caspian. Therefore, being narrower where it lets them in, Asia expands again and becomes as wide as it had been. Then as soon as it arrives at its own limit and the boundaries it shares with other lands, the middle of the western edge is received by our waters; the rest of it goes by one horn to the Nile, by the other to the Tanaïs. **10.** Asia's coast descends in banks with the bed of the Nile River into the sea, and for a long time it stretches out its shores in conformity with that sea's advance. Then the coastline directly confronts the sea as the sea approaches. The shoreline extends, for the first time, in a curve with a huge sweep. After that, it again curves obliquely back to the Bosphorus. After repeatedly curving to the Pontic side, Asia stretches in a crosswise line as far as the entrance of the Maeotis,[11] and, hugging the edge of the very Maeotis all the way to the Tanaïs, it becomes the riverbank where the Tanaïs is located.

11. We are told that the first humans in Asia, starting from the east, are the Indians, the Seres [Lat., Silk People], and the Scyths. The Seres

---

11. The Maeotis (Sea of Azov) is alternately called a lake (cp. 1.14, *lacus*) or a swamp (cp. 1.15, *palus*). At 1.112, and perhaps at 1.15, Maeotis is referred to simply as the Swamp. It is a relatively shallow sea with a maximum depth of ca. 50 feet, as opposed to a maximum depth of ca. 7,364 for the Pontus and ca. 14,435 for the Mediterranean off Cape Taenaros (Matapán). Cp. 1.36 for the swamp called Lake Triton.

inhabit more or less the middle of the eastern part.[12] The Indians and the Scyths inhabit the extremities, both peoples covering a broad expanse and spreading to the ocean not at this point only. For the Indians also look south and for a long time have been occupying the shore of the Indian Ocean with continuous nations, except insofar as the heat makes it uninhabitable. The Scyths look north too, and they possess the littoral of the Scythian Ocean all the way to the Caspian Gulf,[13] except where they are forestalled by the cold. **12.** Next to the Indians is Ariane, then Aria and Cedrosis and Persis up to the Persian Gulf. The Persian peoples surround this gulf; the Arabs surround the other one named earlier.[14] After these peoples, what remains up to Africa belongs to the Aethiopians. In the former place the Caspiani, next to the Scyths, surround the Caspian Gulf. Beyond them, the Amazons are said to be found, and beyond them, the Hyperboreans.

13. Many different nations[15] inhabit the interior of the land. The Gandari, Pariani, Bactri, Sugdiani, Pharmacotrophi, Chomarae, Choamani, Propanisadae, and Dahae are found beyond the Scyths and the Scythian deserts. On the shores of the Caspian Gulf are found the Comari, Massagetae, Cadusi, Hyrcani, and Hiberi. Beyond the Amazons and Hyperboreans are found the Cimmerians, Cissianti, Achaei, Georgians, Moschi, Cercetae, Phoristae, and Arimphaei. Where its expanse protrudes into Our Seas are found the Matiani, Tibarani, and—

---

12. See also M. 3.60 and n. 37 there.

13. M. refers here to his middle bay, or gulf, of the Caspian Sea. At 3.38, he explains that the Caspian Sea has three bays, the Scythian, Caspian, and Hyrcanian. The middle one has the same name as the whole. (See the following note for the interchangeability of *sinus* and *mare* in M.'s usage.) The Caspian's first gulf is called Scythian because M. thinks of it as receiving the Scythian Ocean, and because Scythians inhabit its right bank as one supposedly enters the Caspian Sea from the Scythian Ocean. For M.'s conception, see book 3, n. 17.

14. That is, the Arabian Gulf (Red Sea) named at 1.9, where he calls it the Arabian Sea. Here the Latin demonstrative pronouns underline the geographic relationships and connect the present reference to its somewhat remote grammatical antecedent. That said, it is clear that M. sometimes uses the terms *sinus* (gulf, bay) and *mare* (sea) interchangeably: for example, in 1.9 he speaks of the Arabian and Persian Seas, but he later calls the same bodies gulfs (see 1.13 for his reference to the Persian Gulf and by implication the Arabian Gulf; see 3.73 for his reference to the Persian and Arabian Gulfs).

15. *Nation* [gens] is here used as we in the United States speak of the Onandaga Nation or the Sioux Nation or as Canadians now speak of First Nations.

better-known names—the Medes, Armenians, Commagenes, Murimeni, Eneti, Cappadocians, Gallo-Greeks, Lycaones, Phrygians, Isaurians, Lydians, and Syro-Cilicians.

14. Again, of these latter nations that face south, the same ones that hold the interior hold the shores all the way to the Persian Gulf. Beyond the Caspian Gulf are the Parthians and Assyrians, beyond the Persian Gulf are the Babylonians, and beyond the Aethiopians are the Aegyptians. The Aegyptians likewise possess the lands adjacent to the banks of the Nile River and Our Sea. Then Arabia, with its narrow coastline, is contiguous with the shores that follow. From there, as far as that bend we described above, is Syria. On that very bend is Cilicia, but, in addition, Lycia and Pamphylia, Caria, Ionia, Aeolis, and the Troad all the way up to the Hellespont. From there the Bithynians are found up to the Thracian Bosphorus. Around the Pontus are a number of peoples, with one boundary or another, but all with one name, the Pontici. Beside the Maeotic Lake are found the Maeotici; beside the Tanaïs, the Sauromatae.

Europe

15. For terminal points Europe has the Tanaïs, the Maeotis, and the Pontus in the east; in the west the Atlantic; to the north the Britannic Ocean. Its coastline is the form of the littoral from the Tanaïs to the Hellespont. Europe is not only opposite to the facing shores of Asia but also similar to them [a] where it is a bank of the aforesaid river, [b] where it brings the bend of the Swamp back to the curve of the Pontus, and [c] where it lies beside Propontis and Hellespont with its shore. 16. From there to the Strait, now sweepingly receding, now protruding, the European littoral makes three very large gulfs and projects into the sea with the same number of long extensions. On the other side of the Strait,[16] the Atlantic coast runs up quite irregularly to the west, particularly its middle portion. To the north it extends, practically speaking, as if in a straight line, except where once or twice it is pulled back in by means of a deep recess.

17. The sea that it takes in with its first gulf is called the Aegean. The one it takes in through the next opening is called the Ionian Sea, but its

---

16. That is, the Strait of Gibraltar. Note that after completing his description of Europe's general outline in 1.16, M. returns in a clumsy transition (1.17) to the subject of the first sentence in 1.16.

interior part is the Adriatic. Finally, the one that we regard as the Tuscan Sea, the Greeks regard as the Tyrrhenian Sea.

18. The first nation, from the Tanaïs more or less to the middle of the Pontic littoral, is Scythia (not the one already mentioned).[17] From here Thrace stretches into part of the Aegean, and Macedonia is joined to it. Then Greece protrudes and divides the Aegean from the Ionian Sea. Illyria occupies the coast of the Adriatic. Between the Adriatic itself and the Tuscan Sea Italy juts out. In the innermost part of the Tuscan Sea is Gaul; on the farther side is Spain. **19.** Spain stretches, with differently situated coastlines, to the west and also for a long time to the north. Then Gaul again extends for a long way, and it reaches from our shores all the way up to this point. After Gaul the Germans reach as far as the Sarmatae, and they to Asia.

Africa

20. Africa, terminated to the east by the Nile and everywhere else by the sea, in fact has a less extensive coast[18] than Europe, because it never extends opposite to Asia, and because it does not extend directly opposite to all of Europe's coastline. Nevertheless, Africa is actually longer than it is wide, and it is widest where it abuts the Nile. As far as Africa extends from that point, it goes uncurved to the west, rises—mainly in its middle reach—into mountain chains, and gently hones itself to a point.[19] Because of that point, Africa becomes gradually more con-

---

17. At 1.11–14 the eastern Scyths are discussed.

18. Here the reference seems to be to the east-west line of Africa's Mediterranean coast, although Strabo (17.3.1) does make Africa the smallest of the three continents despite the theories that divide the world into three equal continents.

19. M. seems to be following an Ionian tradition here because he makes Africa seem more or less triangular in this passage. Elsewhere (3.100) he specifies that the Atlantic Coast has a distinct seaboard of its own, and thus Africa appears there more like an irregular trapezoid, whereas Greek writers like Strabo (17.3.1–3) continue to regularize its form and depict it as an inverted right triangle. See Nicolet 1991, 86, on Roman exploration in northern Africa and the Sahara: in 20 B.C.E. Cornelius Balbus reached the Fezzan (Lat. *Phazania*), about 910 Roman miles south of Oea (Tripoli), as Agrippa knew (see Pliny *HN* 5.36–38; cp. 6.209, for the distance). Greek and Roman geographers tended to be vague about sub-Saharan Africa and especially vague about its Atlantic coast (conceived by Greek writers as the hypotenuse of the right triangle), but Agrippa was retailing what was new information in his own time.

tracted from its original width and is narrowest right where it ends. **21.** As much as is inhabited is remarkably fertile. Since most of it, however, is not cultivated and is a desert (either because covered by unproductive sand or because of climatic or regional aridity) or else is infested by many a harmful species of animal, Africa is huge but not populous. The sea by which it is surrounded we call to the north the Libyan Sea, to the south the Aethiopian Sea, and to the west the Atlantic.

22. In that part adjacent to Libya, next to the Nile, is the province they call Cyrene; next is Africa, the province designated by the name of the continent as a whole.[20] The Numidians and Moors hold the remainder, but the Moors are exposed to the Atlantic Ocean. Beyond these coastal peoples, the Nigritae[21] and the Pharusii are found all the way to the Aethiopians. These Aethiopians possess both the rest of this eastern coast and the whole coast that looks south, all the way to the frontier with Asia. **23.** On those shores washed by the Libyan Sea, however, are found the Libyan Aegyptians, the White Aethiopians, and, a populous and numerous nation, the Gaetuli. Then a region, uninhabitable in its entire length, covers a broad and vacant expanse. At that point we hear of the Garamantes as the first people to the east; after them, the Augilae and Trogodytae;[22] and farthest to the west, the Atlantes. In the interior—if one wants to believe it—at this point the scarcely human and rather brutish Goat-Pans, Blemyes, Gamphasantes, and Satyrs possess, rather than inhabit, the land. They roam freely everywhere, with no houses and no fixed abodes.

Restatement of Method

24. This is the full extent of our world. These are its largest parts, its shapes, and the nations of its parts. Now for me, as I begin to describe its coastlines and regions with greater preciseness, it is most convenient [a] to begin from that point where Our Sea enters into the land mass and preferably to begin with these lands that are on the right side of the inflow, then [b] to skirt the shores in the order they lie in, and [c], when

---

20. This section of the continent was known also as Africa Provincia or Africa Proconsularis. The Greeks called the continent as a whole Libya (Strabo 17.3.1).

21. The Nigritae live on the banks of the Nigris (Niger) River, probably south of Timbuktu.

22. For the common etymology, see 1.44 and n. 43 there.

all the places that abut that sea have been traversed, to coast along those places, too, that Ocean girds, until [d] the course of the work now begun sails around both the inside and the outside of the known world and returns to that place whence it began.

Mauretania

25. It has been stated earlier[23] that the Atlantic is the ocean that girds the earth on the west. From here—for those traveling into Our Sea—Spain is on the left, Mauretania on the right. The former is the first part of Europe, the latter of Africa. The eastern end of the Mauretanian coast is the Mulucha [Moulouya] River. Its head (and starting point), however, is the promontory that the Greeks call Ampelusia [Cape Spartel]; the Africans call that promontory by another name, but one that means the same thing.[24] **26.** On it is the sacred Cave of Hercules,[25] and beyond the cave is Tinge [Tangiers], a very old town founded, as they say, by Antaeus.[26] A proof of their claim exists, a huge shield cut from elephant hide, one that, because of its size, is not easy to wield if anyone today were to use it. The locals consider it as true that the shield was made by

---

23. See 1.15 and 21.
24. *Ampelusia* means "viny." The Greeks and Romans believed strongly that names conveyed essential characteristics of persons, places, and things. See 1.112 on the name of the Pontus, and see 2.56 with nn. 51–52 there on the *nomen/omen* phenomenon.
25. The Phoenician Melqart, or Melkart, and perhaps to be associated also with Melikertes in Greek mythology, has been assimilated to Hercules (Grk. Herakles). The importance of Hercules in this area once dominated by Phoenicians from Carthage is marked by the Columns of Hercules and the attendant miracle (1.27) and, across the Strait of Gibraltar on the island of Gades (Cádiz), by the wealthy temple and burial place of Hercules, which was founded by Phoenicians from Tyre to honor the Aegyptian Hercules (3.46). Mark Morford and Robert Lenardon, *Classical Mythology*, 4th ed. (New York and London: Longman, 1991), 480, observe, "Since the mythology of Melkart is virtually unknown, the similarities between him and Herakles remain unclear; nor can we establish the exact relationship between Herakles and the other Oriental figures with whom he shares many similarities—the Jewish hero Sampson, the Mesopotamian Gilgamesh, and the Cilician god Sandas."
26. M. gives more information about Antaeus at 3.106. The work as a whole is structured, like any round-trip voyage, to begin and end at the same place, as M. boasts in the final line of the last book: Point Ampelusia "is the terminus both of this work and of the Atlantic coastline" (see book 3, n. 74).

the famous giant.[27] They pass the story down, and for that reason they pay him cult in an exceptional way. **27.** Next comes a very high mountain, facing the one that Spain raises up on the opposite shore. The one on this side they call Abila [Jabal Musa], the one on the far side Calpe [Gibraltar];[28] they call them together the Pillars of Hercules. Oral tradition goes on to give the story of the name: Hercules himself separated the mountains, which had once been joined in a continuous ridge, and Ocean, previously shut out by the mole of the mountains, was let into those places that it now inundates. On this side of the Strait, the sea already pours in over a rather broad area, and with its great rush it bends back rather far the lands it has cleared from its path.

28. Moreover, the region, not well known, and scarcely endowed with anything illustrious, is populated with small towns and gives passage to small rivers. It is of better quality in its soil than in its men;[29] and it is obscure because of the inactivity of its people.[30] **29.** Nevertheless, of the things here that are not embarrassing to mention, there are tall mountains that spread—on purpose, as it were—in an unbroken line, and that are called the Seven Brothers [Ceuta] because of their number and likeness to one another, then the Tumuada [Martil] River, the small

---

27. The giant is Antaeus. I follow Brodersen's text here, *quam [parmam] locorum accolae ab illo gestatam pro vero habent,* where Silberman reads the unlikely noun *gestatem* for the participle *gestatam.*

28. M. begins his trip on the African coast (see my introduction, n. 17). Throughout the work, references to the "near side" and "far side" or to "this side" and "that side" are to be appreciated from the point of view and location of the imagined traveler at any given moment: see Silberman 1988, xvi–xvii.

29. M. uses the plural of *vir* (plural, *viri*), the word that designates a *man* in all his male capacities. *Homo* (plural, *homines*) means "man" in the sense of human being or person.

30. These last two ethnocentric sentiments appear to be among M.'s strongest reflections of cultural imperialism. In other places, and especially when identifying female behaviors among non-Greek and non-Roman peoples (see 1.41–42 and nn. 40 and 42 there), M.'s interest may be evoked by specific practices that he considers unusual, but he does not judge them. In contrast, heavy judgment is implicit in his observations about "barbarian" sounds that cannot be rendered conveniently into the Greek or Roman alphabets (see 3.15 and 3.31 on certain Cantabrian and German names, respectively) or about the Aethiopians' supposed mispronunciation of *Nilus* (the Nile) as *Nunc* (3.96). (For Greeks *barbaros,* "barbarian," meant "non-Greek"; for Romans the loanword *barbarus* meant "non-Greek and non-Roman.")

towns of Rusigada [Russadir/Melilla] and Siga [Takembrit]; and Portus Magnus [Lat., Great Port; Bettioua], so called because of its expanse. That river, which we called the Mulucha, is nowadays the boundary of tribes, but once it was the boundary of kingdoms, those of Bocchus and Jugurtha.[31]

Numidia

30. Numidia, which spreads from there to the banks of the Ampsacus [Kabir] River, is actually narrower in expanse than Mauretania, but it is both more widely cultivated and richer. Of the cities that it contains, the largest are Cirta [Constantine] and Iol [Chercell]. Cirta is far from the sea and is now a colony of the Sittiani, but once it was the home of kings, at its wealthiest when it belonged to Syphax.[32] Iol, on the seaside, was once unknown but is now famous because it was the royal residence of Juba[33] and because it is referred to now as Caesarea.

---

31. King Bocchus of Mauretania was the father-in-law of Jugurtha, the illegitimate grandson and heir of Masinissa, king of the Massyles (the easternmost Numidians). Dynastic infighting and international militarism plagued Jugurtha. Although King Bocchus joined Jugurtha's fight against the Romans, later the king betrayed Jugurtha to them in 106 B.C.E. He was received by Sulla, then serving as Marius' quaestor. Jugurtha was paraded before the people of Rome in Marius' triumph on 1 January 104 B.C.E. and shortly thereafter was starved to death in a Roman prison. Sallust's *Bellum Iugurthinum* (The war against Jugurtha) has most of the details. See the next note.

32. Syphax, another Numidian chieftain, was king of the westernmost Numidians, the Masaesyles, and he was a rival of Masinissa (see the preceding note), part of whose kingdom he overrode in a dynastic brawl. Syphax rose up against Carthage ca. 212 B.C.E. and received help from the Roman commanders in Spain during the Second Punic War (218–201 B.C.E.). Eventually Syphax married the Carthaginian Sophonisba (Saphanba'al in Phoenician), returned to the Carthaginian fold, was defeated and captured by the Romans in 203 B.C.E., and subsequently died a prisoner in Italy.

33. King Juba II was brought to Rome as a child by Julius Caesar. In 30 B.C.E. Augustus restored him as king of Numidia, but in 25 B.C.E. Numidia became a Roman province and Juba received Mauretania as his kingdom. He died there ca. 19 C.E. or a little later. Juba was a *comes* of Augustus (cp. Dio 51.15.6), probably a *comes* of C. Caesar Aug(usti) f(ilius) in the East (cp. Pliny *HN* 6.141), and much involved in the dynastic politics of the eastern Mediterranean. He wrote on historical and geographical topics. See also book 3, n. 72, and F.E. Romer, "A Case of Client-Kingship," *American Journal of Philology* 106 (1985):97–98.

31. On the near side of this city—it is situated more or less in the middle of the coast[34]—are the towns of Cartinna [Ténès] and Arsinna, the garrison town of Quiza, Laturus Gulf [Gulf of Arzew], and the Sardabale River. On its far side is the common tomb of the royal family, then the cities of Icosium [Algiers] and Ruthisia and, flowing between them, the Aucus [Harrach] and Nabar [Hamiz], as well as other things, which it is no loss, either of fact or fame, to pass over in silence. **32.** Farther inland, and quite far from shore, there reportedly exist and are found—amazingly, if their reality is credible—the spines of fishes, pieces of murex and oyster, rocks smoothed (as they are supposed to be) by waves and no different from rocks in the sea, anchors set in reefs, other indications of the same kind, and even traces, in fields that nourish nothing, of a sea that once poured right up to those locations.

Africa Provincia

33. The following region, from Point Metagonium [Cape Bougaroun] to the Altars of the Philaeni, usurps for itself the name of Africa.[35] In it are the towns of Hippo Regius [Annaba], Rusiccade [Skikda], and Thabraca [Tabarka]. **34.** Then three promontories—White Point [Cap Blanc], Point Apollo [Ras Si Ali Mekki], and Mercury Point [Cap Bon]—projecting an impressive distance into the sea, make two large gulfs. They call the one right after Hippo Diarrhytos [Bizerte] the Gulf of Hippo, because the town is located on its shoreline. In the other gulf are Castra Delia, Castra Cornelia, the Bagrada [Mejerda] River, Utica, and Carthage. Both Utica and Carthage are famous, and both were founded by Phoenicians. The former is marked by the death of Cato.[36] The latter is marked by its own fate: now it is a colony of the Roman people, but

---

34. M. means that Iol is located in the center of the Numidian coastline, not in the center of the entire North African coastline.

35. See 1.38 on the Philaeni, and see 1.22 and n. 20 there on the name of Africa.

36. The younger Cato (95–46 B.C.E.) was strongly anti-Caesarian. He committed suicide in 46 B.C.E. at Utica as Caesar's forces were closing in. He became a kind of Stoic saint, because Stoic doctrine authorized suicide when individuals could no longer discharge to the fullest the obligations incumbent on their station in life. Illuminating in regard to the philosophical contemplation of suicide are two letters of the younger Seneca, one in which he recalls his own potential suicide as he tries to dissuade another person from committing that act (*Ep.* 78), and another on the role of philosophy in living (*Ep.* 90).

it was once their determined rival for imperial power.[37] In fact, Carthage is now wealthy again, but it remains more famous for the destruction of its ancestors' claims than for the wealth of its present inhabitants. Hadrumetum [Sousse], Leptis [Lemta], Clupea [Kelibia], Habromacte, Phyre, and Neapolis [Nabeul], the most widely known cities vis-à-vis other obscure places, lie one after another from here to Syrtis.

35. Syrtis is a gulf almost one hundred miles wide where it receives the open sea and three hundred miles wide where it encloses the sea. It has no ports and is frightening and dangerous because of the shallowness of its frequent shoals and even more dangerous because of the reversing movements of the sea as it flows in and out. 36. On its shoreline a huge swamp receives the Triton River; the swamp itself is Lake Triton [Chott Jerid], that is, the lake of Minerva, who, as the locals think, was born there, whence it was given her epithet. They give some credibility to that legend, because they celebrate the day they think is her birthday with contests of virgins, who compete among themselves.

37. Farther on is the town of Oea [Tarābulus/Tripoli] and the Cinyps [Khāne] River, which descends through the lushest fields; then a second Leptis and a second Syrtis, equal in name and nature to the first, but approximately twice as large both where it remains open and where it curves. Its first promontory is Borion [Grk., North Point; Ras Taiùnes], and, from there on, the shore (which the Lotus-Eaters are said to have occupied) reaches its farther promontory on a coast with no ports all the way to Phycon [Ras Sem].

38. The actual Altars have taken their name from the brothers Philaeni, who were sent from Carthage to meet certain Cyrenaeans in order to end by treaty a border war that had been waged for a long time with great losses on both sides.[38] Later the agreement failed, by which the representatives of the two sides were to be dispatched from both

---

37. The Romans destroyed Carthage at the end of the Third Punic War (149–146 B.C.E.). For a general history of Carthage, see David Soren, Auba ben Khader, and Hedi Shin, *Carthage* (New York: Simon and Schuster, 1990).

38. The Altars were previously identified (1.33) by their full name, the Altars of the Philaeni. The Carthaginians considered the Altars of the Philaeni, as Sallust indicates (*BJ* 19.3), to be the eastern boundary of their *imperium*. Sallust's excursus at *BJ* 79 gives the story of the Philaeni in more intelligible detail. Parroni (1984, 45–46) sees similarities between M.'s and Sallust's accounts and suggests that Sallust serves as a stylistic model for M.

directions at a prearranged time, and by which the boundary was to be established right where the two sides met. They renewed from scratch the agreement that everything on the nearer side fell to their respective countrymen, and the brothers allowed themselves—an amazing deed and most worthy of memory!—to be buried alive on the spot.

Cyrenaïca

39. From there to Catabathmos [Senke on the Gulf of Salûm] is the province of Cyrenaïca, and in it are the famously reliable oracle of Ammon, the spring they call the Fountain of the Sun, and a particular cliff sacred to Auster [Lat., the Southwind]. When this cliff is touched by human hands, that wind springs up wildly and, whipping the sands like seas, rages the same way it does on water. The fountain boils up in the middle of the night, and then, gradually changing to lukewarm, at dawn it passes to cold; then, in proportion to the sun's rising, it gets colder and actually becomes solid ice at midday; then it turns lukewarm again, it is steaming at sundown, and the more night advances, the hotter the spring gets. In the middle of the night, it is boiling hot again. **40.** Along the shore are found Zephyr [Grk., West Wind] Point and Naustathmos [Grk., Anchorage; Ra's el Hilāl], Port Paraetonius [Marsa Matrûh], the cities of Hesperia, Apollonia [Sūsah], Ptolemaïs [Tulmaythah], and Arsinoë [Tūkrah]; and also Cyrene [Shahhāt] itself, from which the region takes its name. The Catabathmos Valley, sloping down into Aegypt, is the boundary of Africa.[39]

Peoples of Africa

41. That being so, the shores are inhabited by people socialized according to our custom,[40] except that particular ones differ in language and

---

39. See M. 1.49 and Pliny *HN* 5.38: the Catabathmos Valley is considered to be in Cyrenaïca, and the Nile is considered the eastern border of continental Africa (cp. also 1.8, 1.20, and 1.22, on the Nile as the boundary of Africa). The view that the Nile is the continental border reflects an old Ionian tradition (see Silberman 1988, 128 n. 7), but Strabo (1.2.25–26) argues that Egypt lies on both sides of the Nile and that the eastern border of Africa is the Red (Arabian) Sea. According to Manilius (*Astronomica* 4.627) the Nile bounds Asia and Africa. See also M. 1.60; cp. Pliny *HN* 3.3, 5.62.

40. This kind of reasonably detached point of view typifies M.'s own outlook. Nevertheless, its unexamined premises reflect the cultural imperialism of the age. See book 1, n. 30.

in the cult of the gods whom they worship as ancestral and venerate in the traditional way. No cities, in fact, arise in neighboring areas, but nevertheless there are groupings of nomads' huts called *mapalia*.[41] Their way of life is crude and lacks amenities. The chiefs dress in rough woolen cloaks, the people in skins of wild and domestic animals. Sleeping and banqueting are done on the ground. Containers are made of wood and bark. They drink milk and the juice of berries. Their food is most often the meat of game animals. Indeed, the flocks are spared as much as possible because that is their only wealth. **42.** The nomads to the interior also follow their flocks in a rather uncouth way of life. As the flocks are drawn on by pasturage, the nomads move forward and move their shelters too, and when daylight fails, there they spend the night. Although, being scattered all over in family groups and without law,[42] they take no common counsel, still, because individual men have several wives and for that reason more children than usual (both those eligible to receive an inheritance and those not eligible), they are never few in number.

43. Of the people here who are recorded as being beyond the desert, the Atlantes curse the sun, both while it rises and while it sets, on the grounds that it is disastrous to them personally and to their fields. Individuals do not have names; they do not feed on animals; nor is it granted to them to visit and see in their sleep things like those granted to all other mortals. **44.** The Trogodytae [Grk., Cave Dwellers][43] own no

---

41. According to the *Oxford Latin Dictionary* (Oxford: Clarendon, 1982), *mapalia -ium*, n., which exists only in the plural, appears to be of Semitic, and specifically of Phoenician, origin (cp. Hebrew *mappâlâh*, "ruin").

42. M. does not consider different kinds of law—clan law versus statute law, for example, or the *ius gentium*. He thinks of law as an active part of the state machinery. These people have no law because they have no state. (For a countercultural view of law's role in Roman history, see Tac. *Ann.* 3.25–28.) These people have no state because they have no fixed abodes and no cities. Here ethnocentrism and the Roman sense of manifest destiny do come across (cp. book 1, n. 30), and we are reminded of the moment in Vergil's *Aeneid* when Trojan Aeneas becomes Roman (with the dual Trojan and Roman burden). At that point (*Aen.* 6.851–53), his father Anchises says to Aeneas in the underworld, "Remember, Roman, to rule the peoples with *imperium* (these skills will be yours), to impose the way of peace, to spare the vanquished, and to make war against the arrogant."

43. Cp. the alternate spelling *Troglodytae*, from Greek *troglê* (cave) and *dytês* (one who enters). The name is applied to various peoples both in Africa and elsewhere. However, the Trogodytae of Aethiopia cannot be "cave-dwellers"

resources, and rather than speak, they make a high-pitched sound. They creep around deep in caves and are nurtured by serpents. **45.** There are also herd animals among the Garamantes, and those animals feed with their necks bent at an odd angle since their horns, when directed at the ground, get in their way as they bend down. No one has one specific wife. Out of the children, who are born here randomly from such indiscriminate sexuality on their parents' part, and who are not clearly identified, the adults recognize by their similar looks those whom they are to raise as their own.

46. The Augilae think only the Manes[44] are gods. They swear by them; they consult them as oracles. They pray to the Manes for what they want, and, after they have thrown themselves on burial mounds, the Manes bring dreams as oracular responses. On their wedding night, the women have a religious obligation to be available for sexual intercourse with every man that comes bearing a gift. On that occasion, it is a very great honor to sleep with many men, but the rest of the time chastity is manifested.[45] **47.** The Gamphasantes go naked and have no knowledge of any weapons. They know neither how to duck away from spears nor how to hurl them. For that reason they run away from anyone they meet and do not endure either meetings or conversations with anyone who does not have the same kind of nature. **48.** The Blemyes lack heads; their face is on their chest. The Satyrs have nothing human except their superficial appearance. The form of the Goat-Pans is celebrated in their name. So much for Africa.

(there are no natural cave systems in their region), and the name Trogodytae, which has the authority of Vat. lat. 4929, must be considered—despite M.'s etymology here—separate and distinct from the similarly named Troglodytae, a term that may be applied literally to cave-dwellers in other parts of Africa or beyond.

44. In Roman religion the Manes are the spirits of the dead and are generally considered to be lesser supernatural beings. They are evoked during festivals of the dead and in curses. Under the empire, the Manes are identified specifically as the souls of the dead that have been raised to divine status, as shown by numerous funerary inscriptions dedicated to them by the abbreviation *D.M.* (= *Dis Manibus*, "To the Divine Manes").

45. M. is not judgmental about cultural differences in women's various roles, although he is fascinated by them, as is shown by his interest in Augilae women here, in the topos of men's and women's roles among the Aegyptians (1.57), in martial and marital practices among both the Ixamatae (1.114) and the Sarmatae (3.34), and in the variant of sati practiced among Thracian women (2.19; see n. 18 there).

Aegypt

49. The first division of Asia is Aegypt between Catabathmos and the Arabs. From this shore Aegypt extends far to the interior and runs back southward, until it borders on Aethiopia with its back. The land is devoid of rain but is an amazingly fertile and very prolific producer of both human beings and other animals. The Nile causes this fertility, since it is the largest river that makes its way into Our Sea. **50.** The Nile reaches out from the deserts of Africa and at this point is neither easily navigable at once nor called the Nile at once. After it descends in a single, rushing torrent, the river spreads wide around Meroë, an island covering a broad expanse on the border of Aethiopia; and on one side of Meroë the river is called Astabores, on the other Astape. Where it comes together again, it takes this name, the Nile. **51.** From there, sometimes rough, sometimes capable of supporting ships, the river descends into a tremendous lake, from which it rushes out in steep cataracts, then embraces a second island, Tachempso, and runs down, still rough and seething, all the way to Elephantine [Gesiret Aswân], a city in Aegypt. Then at last, more peaceful and now quite navigable, it begins for the first time to have three streams near the town of Cercasorum [El Arkas]. Then, dividing again and again at Delta and Melys, it moves freely and broadly through all of Aegypt. The river divides itself into seven mouths, but still it rolls on in ample individual beds. **52.** It does not, however, spread over very much surface, but it does overflow its banks under the summer sky and also irrigates the land. Its waters are so efficacious for procreation and sustenance that—besides swarming with fish and producing huge beasts like hippopotamuses and crocodiles—the river even pours out the breath of life in clumps of silt and from the very soil fashions living creatures. This process is plain from the fact that when it has stopped flooding and returned to itself, certain organisms that are not yet completely formed are seen again and again. These organisms, however, take their first breath when they are still partially formed and still earthen in part.

53. The Nile increases, furthermore, either [a] because snow, melted under great heat, flows down from the immense mountain ridges of Aethiopia more abundantly than can be held by the riverbanks, or [b] because the sun, being nearer the earth in winter, and thereby evaporating the river's head, then retreats to a higher point and allows the river's head, unaffected by the sun and at its fullest, to raise the river's level, or else [c] because the Etesian winds, which blow throughout that period, either [i] drive in clouds that move from north to south as rain directly above the river's starting points, or [ii] block the advancing water with an adverse wind and forestall the course of the descending water, or [iii] choke the river's mouths with the sand they drive onto the shore right along with the waves. The Nile becomes greater either because it loses nothing from itself, or because it receives more water than usual, or because it loses less than it should.

54. If, however, there is a second world, and if there are Antichthones located directly opposite to us in the south, that first explanation will not have departed too far from the truth. The river, originating in those Antichthonian lands, emerges again in ours, after it has penetrated beneath Ocean in an unseen channel, and it therefore increases at the summer solstice because at that time it is winter where the river originates.

55. Other amazing things also exist in these lands. In one particular lake floats the island of Chemmis, which supports sacred groves, a wood, and a large temple of Apollo; and it is driven in whatever direction the winds push it. The pyramids are built with rocks of thirty feet; the largest of these structures—there are three—occupies almost four *iugera*[46] of ground at its base and is erected to an equivalent height. Moeris [Birket Qârûn], once a plain, now a lake accommodating a circumference of twenty miles, is deeper than necessary to sail in heavy freighters. **56.** The Labyrinth is a work of Psammetichus; it embraces a thousand homes and twelve palaces within its continuous enceinte. It is built of marble and roofed and has one passageway down into it but almost countless paths inside; many confusing paths turn back on themselves this way and that but extend in both directions with a continuous winding and with porticoes that are often circular; with these paths promptly making one circle on top of others, and with the curve of a circle promptly bending back as far as it had advanced, the Labyrinth is puzzling with its long, yet solvable, wandering path.

---

46. One *iugerum* is just under two-thirds of an English acre. Technically, one *iugerum* is a surveyor's measurement (= 2 *actus*) equivalent to a notional farmer's field 240 x 120 feet Roman (233 feet x 116 feet 6 inches English). One Roman foot (*pes*) equals approximately 11.65 English inches. Four *iugera* amount to under two and two-thirds acres. As a unit of linear measure (cp. 3.40), one *iugerum* should equal one side of the notional farmer's field, but it is unclear whether it should be the short side or the long.

57. The cultivators of Aegypt's districts live much differently from everyone else. They smear themselves with dung when they lament their dead; they consider it unholy to cremate or to bury them; but they place the dead, skillfully embalmed, in the inner rooms of a building. They write backward. They pulverize dirt between their hands but grind flour under their heels. Women take care of the forum and business; men take care of spinning and the home. Women carry bundles on their shoulders; men do so on their heads. It is mandatory for women to nurture their parents when they are in need, and for men it is a choice. They take food in the open air and outdoors; they consign their bodily functions to the inner recesses of the house.

58. They pay cult to the images of many animals and even more to the animals themselves (but different people to different animals)—to such an extent that it is a capital offense to kill certain animals, even through inadvertence. When those animals have been killed by disease or by chance, it is a religious obligation to bury them and grieve over them. Apis—a black bull, marked by particular spots and different from other bulls in his tail and in his tongue—is the divinity of all the Aegyptian peoples. He is born only rarely, conceived not from mating cattle, as they say, but miraculously in a celestial fire. The day of his birth is particularly festive to the whole people.[47]

59. The Aegyptians themselves are, as they declare, the oldest human beings, and they refer in unambiguous annals to 330 pharaohs before Amasis and to a history of more than thirteen thousand years. They also preserve a written tradition that, for as long as there have been Aegyptians, the stars have changed their course four times, and the sun has set twice already where it now rises. 60. They inhabited twenty cities when Amasis ruled, and now they inhabit numerous ones. The most famous of those cities far from the sea are Saïs [Sa el-Hagar], Memphis [Mit Rahina and Saqqâra], Syene [Aswân], Bubastis, Elephantine [Gesiret Aswân], and, in particular, Thebes, which, as stated by Homer,[48] has one hundred gates or, as others say, one hun-

---

47. Notice M.'s allusiveness; he clearly expects his readers to have a general knowledge to which he appeals and lends order. Apis is the sacred bull of Memphis, where he lived in a lavish sacred residence. His birthday was celebrated annually all over Aegypt. When one earthly incarnation of Apis died, Aegypt entered mourning until his successor was found and identified by his special markings.

48. Hom. *Il.* 9.381.

dred palaces, the homes, once, of one hundred important chiefs, each house accustomed to send out ten thousand armed soldiers when trouble had driven them to it. On the coast is Alexandria, bordering on Africa, and Pelusium, which borders on Arabia. The mouths of the Nile—the Canopic, Bolbitic, Sebennytic, Pathmetic, Mendesian, Cataptystic, and Pelusiac mouths—cut into those very shores.

Arabia

61. From here Arabia reaches to the Red Sea [Arabian Sea], but on the far side, being richer and more productive, it abounds in incense and perfumes. On this side, except where it is heightened by Mt. Casius [El Kas], Arabia is flat and barren and admits Port Azotus [Ashdod] as a trading place for their own wares. On this side Arabia rises to a great height, being so elevated that, from the mountaintop, sunrise is visible from the fourth watch on.[49]

Syria

62. Syria holds a broad expanse of the littoral, as well as lands that extend rather broadly into the interior, and it is designated by different names in different places. For example, it is called Coele, Mesopotamia, Judaea, Commagene, and Sophene. **63.** It is Palestine at the point where Syria abuts the Arabs, then Phoenicia, and then—where it reaches Cilicia—Antiochia, which was powerful long ago and for a long time, but which was most powerful by far when Semiramis held it under her royal sway. Her works certainly have many distinctive characteristics. Two in particular stand out: Babylon was built as a city of amazing size, and the Euphrates and Tigris were diverted into once dry regions.

---

49. The Romans divided the individual day (*dies*) into daylight (*dies*) and night (*nox*), each made up of twelve hours (*horae*), with noon (*meridies*) and midnight (*media nox*) defined as the sixth hour of day and night, respectively. The length of an hour varied by day and night as well as by geographic location (cp. M.'s remarks at 3.36) and by time of year. Daybreak was defined as the beginning of the day's first hour, and nightfall as the beginning of the night's first hour. The night also was divided, on the military model, into four watches (*vigiliae*), each lasting for three of the night's twelve *horae*. At the vernal or autumnal equinox, then, the fourth watch would correspond to a notional period from 3 to 6 A.M. on our clock.

Book 1

64. In Palestine, however, is Gaza, a mighty and very well fortified city. This is why the Persians call it their treasury (and from that fact comes the name): when Cambyses headed for Aegypt under arms, he had brought here both riches and the money for war.[50] Ascalon [Ashqelon] is no less important a city. Iope [Tel Aviv-Yafo] was founded, as they tell it, before the flood. Iope is where the locals claim that Cepheus was king, based on the proof that particular old altars—altars with the greatest taboo—continue to bear an inscription of that man and his brother Phineus. What is more, they even point out the huge bones of the sea-monster as a clear reminder of the event celebrated in song and legend, and as a clear reminder of Andromeda, who was saved by Perseus.[51]

Phoenicia

65. The Phoenicians are a clever branch of the human race and exceptional in regard to the obligations of war and peace, and they made Phoenicia famous. They devised the alphabet, literary pursuits, and other arts too; they figured out how to win access to the sea by ship, how to conduct battle with a navy, and how to rule over other peoples; and they developed the power of sovereignty and the art of battle. 66. In Phoenicia is Tyre [Soûr], once an island, but now tied to the mainland, because siegeworks were thrown up by Alexander, who at one time assailed it.[52] Villages occupy the upper coast, along with still-

---

50. The Latin word *gaza* (treasure) refers especially to the treasure of Eastern rulers. The word is apparently Persian in origin, as this anecdote suggests. The story of Cambyses (second king of Persia, 529–522 B.C.E.) and of his conquest of Aegypt (525 B.C.E.) is told at Hdt. 3.1–38. M. appears to be using a source that antedates the destruction of the city by Alexander the Great (cp. Strabo 16.2.30). The idea that Gaza was Cambyses' treasure-house apparently is retailed by M. and later writers.

51. Iope was formerly Joppa or Jaffa. Ovid (*Met.* 4.604–803) gives the whole story of Andromeda and Perseus. Cepheus, the king of Aethiopia, was Andromeda's father, his brother Phineus her uncle. Queen Cassiopea was her mother. In the early imperial period, tourists could still see the traces of Andromeda's travail. Perhaps M.'s "huge bones of the sea-monster" refers to a mass of coral, hardened after being exposed to the air, since for Ovid (*Met.* 4.740–52) this legend is an etiological myth to explain the creation of coral.

52. Alexander the Great (356–323 B.C.E.) besieged the city from January to July (possibly August) 332 B.C.E. (On Tyre and earthquakes, see book 2, n. 87.)

wealthy Sidon [Saïda], the most important of the maritime cities before it was captured by the Persians. **67.** From it to Point Theuprosopon [Grk., Face of God; Cape Madonna/Ras es-Saq'a] there are two towns, Byblos [Jbail] and Botrys [Batroûn]. Farther on there were once three towns, each separated from the next by a single stade;[53] now the place is called Tripolis [Grk., Three-Cities; Trâblous] from the number of those towns. Then comes Simyra, a military post, and Marathos, a not obscure city.

68. From there on, Asia is no longer sideways to the sea but runs directly into it. Asia forms a tremendous gulf [Iskenderun Körfezi] with the unbent extension of its littoral. Wealthy peoples live around the gulf, and the location makes them rich, because the fertile district, perforated by frequent navigable riverbeds, exchanges and combines, in a ready traffic, the diverse riches of sea and land. **69.** On the gulf is the remainder of Syria, to which the name of Antiochia applies, and on its shore are the cities Seleucia [Kabousi], Hypatos, Berytos [Beyrouth/Beirut], Laodicea [Al Lādhiqīyah/Latakia], and Rhosos, as well as the rivers that go between these cities, the Lycos [Kelb], the Hypatos, and the Orontes [Asi]; then comes Mt. Amanus [Elma Daği] and, right after it, Myriandros and the Cilicians.

Cilicia

70. In the gulf's deepest recess, however, is the site of a great historical turning point long ago. This place observed and witnessed both the Persians routed by Alexander and Darius in flight.[54] Now it is marked not even by the most insignificant city, but then it was famous because of its mighty city. The place was Issos, and that is why the gulf is called

---

53. A stade (*stadium*) = 125 Roman paces (*passus*) or 625 Roman *pedes*. One Roman pace (a double pace as we reckon paces) is 5 *pedes* (about 4 feet 10 inches English). Thus a stade of 625 Roman feet is approximately 606 feet 9 inches English, calculated on a *pes* equal to 11.65 English inches.

54. In early November 333 B.C.E., Alexander the Great defeated King Darius III of Persia on the plains of Issus. (Darius III is the royal name of the Achaemenid prince Codomannus.) Caught in a thoughtless strategical dilemma, Darius fled, abandoning even his wife and mother. Here Alexander founded one of his namesake cities—Alexandria ad Issum, long known as Alexandretta (Iskenderun). The little nook of sea on which it is located (M.'s "the gulf's deepest recess") is called by the same name. (The Gulf of Iskenderun is here to be distinguished from the little Bay of Iskenderun.)

the Gulf of Issos. At a distance from there lies Point Hammodes, between the Pyramus [Ceyhan] and Cydnus [Tarsus] Rivers. The Pyramus, the river nearer to Issos, flows beside Mallos; the Cydnus, farther on, goes through Tarsus. **71.** Next is a city once occupied by Rhodians and Argives, later occupied by pirates when Pompey allotted it to them; now called Pompeiopolis, then called Soloe.[55] Beside it, in a small mound, the funerary monument of the poet Aratus must be mentioned for this reason: because—no one knows why—rocks that are hurled on it burst apart. Not far from here the town of Corycos [Korghoz], which is tied to the continent by a narrow ridge, is surrounded by a harbor and by the open sea.

72. Above the town is the so-called Corycian Cave [Çenet Deresi], a cave of unique nature, too extraordinary to be easily describable.[56] For in fact it gapes wide with a tremendous maw and makes an opening, right at the very top, into the mountain, which is located alongside the shore, and which is quite steep with a path of ten stades.[57] Then, going down deeply—the more impressive the farther down it goes—the cave is alive with hanging growth everywhere, and it is encircled completely by the shady embrace of its sides. The cave is so wonderful and beautiful that, at first sight, it boggles the minds of those who approach it, but it will not gratify them when they have steeled themselves to observe it better. **73.** There is one descent into it, narrow, rough, a mile-and-a-half long, through lovely shadows and the shade of a forest that resonates with a tinge of rusticity, while streams continually flow from one direction or another. When the bottom is reached, again a second cave is opened up, but this one is now to be described for entirely other reasons. It terrifies those who enter with its miraculous roar of cymbals and the great uproar of things rustling around. **74.** After that, it is visible for some time, but then—where it goes down farther—it becomes darker. It draws deep down anyone who dares, and it lets them in deep as if through a rabbit hole. There a mighty river rising from a mighty spring shows just a glimpse of itself, and, after it has drawn great force

---

55. In 67 B.C.E. a *lex Gabinia* bestowed on Pompey the Great (Gnaeus Pompeius Magnus, 106–48 B.C.E.) his unprecedented command (*imperium*) against the pirates of the eastern Mediterranean. In the following year, Soloi, the city that gave its name to solecism, became Pompeiopolis.

56. This Corycian Cave is to be distinguished both from its namesake on Mt. Parnassus (an important cult site of the nymphs) and from the Cave of Typhon described at 1.76.

57. See book 1, n. 53, for the conversion scale.

in its short channel, again it plunges down and disappears. Inside, there is a space too hair-raising for anyone to dare to go forward, and for that reason it remains unknown. 75. The whole cave, however, being narrow and truly sacred, both worthy of being inhabited by gods and believed to be so, reveals nothing that is not venerable, and it reveals itself as if with some kind of numinous power.

76. Farther on is another cave, which they call the Cave of Typhon, with a narrow mouth and a very tight squeeze, as those who have experienced it have reported. That is why the cave is permeated by an unending night and never easy to investigate. Because this cave was once the bedchamber of Typhon, however, and because now it instantly deprives of life anything and everything that goes down into it, it is worth recording for its nature and its legend.[58] 77. Next, there are two promontories: Sarpedon [Incekum Burun], once the boundary of the kingdom of Sarpedon, and Anemurium [Anamur Burun], which separates Cilicia from Pamphylia. Between them lie Celenderis and Nagidos, colonies of the Samians, but Celenderis is the one nearer to Sarpedon.

Pamphylia

78. In Pamphylia are the navigable Melas River, the town of Sida [Selimiye/Side], and a second river, the Eurymedon. Beside the latter

---

58. Hundred-headed Typhon (or Typhoeus or Typhaön), son of Gaea (Earth), is described either as a deadly hurricane or as a fire-breathing giant. (The English word "typhoon" is an alteration of Greek *typhōn*, "whirlwind," after it merged with the Cantonese Chinese word *taaî fung*, "big wind," through Arabic *tūfān*, "hurricane.") He contested the rule of Zeus, who suppressed him with a lightning bolt (Hes. *Theog.* 820–80). A late source, Apollodorus (1.6.3), gives further details, some of which are relevant here: (a) Typhon was born in Cilicia; (b) with outstretched arms he could reach from horizon to horizon; and (c) in hand-to-hand combat on Mt. Casius (Jabal al-Aqra) in Syria, Typhon subdued Zeus, cut out the tendons from his hands and feet (he saved them in a jar), and brought the enervated Zeus and the jar back to the Corycian Cave, whence he was reassembled by Hermes and Aegipan. Corycus has long associations with the Luwian Weather God whose shrine was located there; the territory of Cilicia and northern Syria points to the Hittites; and the Greek story of Typhon also is linked to Hittite mythology. In Greek myths, Typhon also is the father of the storm winds and various monsters, including Cerberus, the watchdog of the underworld. He was imprisoned in Tartarus and, according to one legend, right beneath Hephaestus' workshop in the bowels of Mt. Aetna.

river the great naval battle took place against the Phoenicians and Persians, as well as the great victory of Cimon, the Athenian general.[59] From a moderately high hill, Aspendos looks out on the sea where the battle was fought. Argives had founded Aspendos, but their neighbors came to possess it. **79.** After that, there are two other very strong rivers, the Cestros [Ak] and the Catarhactes [Düden]. The Cestros is easy to navigate, but the latter gets its name because it makes waterfalls. Between those rivers are the town of Perga [Perge] and the temple of Pergaean Diana, whom they name after the town. Across those same rivers are Mt. Sardemisos and Phaselis, which was founded by Mopsus and marks the boundary of Pamphylia.

Lycia

80. Moving right along, Lycia, named for King Lycus, the son of Pandion, and, as they say, once unsafe because of the Chimaera's fiery breath, terminates the tremendous gulf with the harbor of Sida and a spur of the Taurus range. **81.** The Taurus range actually rises over an immense distance starting from the shores of the Eastern Ocean and reaches quite an elevation. Then, turning with its right flank to the north, its left to the south, the range goes straight west, and with its unbroken chain, where it separates the lands from one another, it is the boundary of great peoples wherever it drives its ridge. The range ends by extending into the sea. Even where it looks east, the Taurus is called by the same name as the whole (as just indicated). Then it is called Haemodes and Caucasus and Propanisus [Paropamisus]; after that, the Caspian Gates, the Niphates, the Armenian Gates; and, where now it abuts Our Seas, the Taurus again. **82.** After the Taurus promontory come the Limyra River and the city that is its namesake. Except for Patara, the towns are as unresplendent as they are numerous. The temple of Apollo, once similar to Delphi in wealth and in oracular credibility, makes Patara well known. Farther on are the Xanthus River [Koca Çayi], the town of Xanthos, Mt. Cragus [San Dagh], and the city that bounds Lycia, Telmesos [Fethiye].

---

59. The reference is to Cimon's expedition against the Persians ca. 468 B.C.E. The battle is frequently described as a great naval victory, but it was a double battle fought on both land and sea. Cimon ultimately destroyed two hundred Phoenician ships and essentially broke the Persians' grip on this Mediterranean littoral.

Caria

83. Caria follows, and peoples of uncertain origin inhabit it. Some writers hold the opinion that they are indigenous peoples, others that they are Pelasgians, still others that they are Cretans. The nation was once so enamored of weapons and fighting that they used to fight other peoples' wars for pay. There are some forts here; then two promontories, Pedalion and Crya; and after the Calbis River, the town of Caunus, infamous for the ill health of its inhabitants.[60] 84. From there to Halicarnassos [Bodrum] the following places are located: a few Rhodian colonies and two harbors, Gelos and the one called Thyssanusa after the city it surrounds. Between those harbors are the town of Larumna and the Hill of Pandion, which extends into the sea; then three gulfs, in order, Thymnias, Schoenus, and Bubassius. Thymnias' promontory is Point Aphrodisium; Schoenus surrounds Hyla; Bubassius surrounds Cyrnos. Then comes Cnidus on the tip of a peninsula, and between it and the Ceramicus Gulf, located in a secluded place, is Euthana. 85. Halicarnassos is an Argive colony, and there is a reason, apart from its founders, why it is memorable: it produced the Mausoleum, that is, the funerary monument of King Mausolus, one of the Seven Wonders and the work of Artemisia.[61] Beyond Halicarnassos are the following

---

60. There are a number of variants, but the familiar story of Caunus and his sister Byblis is told by Ovid at *Met.* 9.454–665. Caunus fled their home in Miletus on discovering his sister's incestuous desires and founded his namesake town in southwestern Caria (cp. *Met.* 9.633–34). The town was located in the Rhodian *Peraea* [Grk., Overseas Territory] on the mainland. Strabo 14.2.3 reports that the Caunians were pale as the walking dead and suffered in summer and fall from stale air because of heat and overabundance of fruit.

61. The Mausoleum (Grk. *Mausoleion;* Monument of Mausolus) at Halicarnassus has given its name to all grand-scale funerary monuments. The Mausoleum was one of the seven wonders of the ancient world. It was completed ca. 351 B.C.E. and built for King Mausolus of Caria (the Persian governor, or satrap, ca. 377–353 B.C.E.) and Queen Artemisia, who continued the work after her husband's death. The structure has not survived, but the damaged colossal statue of Mausolus has. The personalized representation of the satrap is the earliest surviving original of a Greek portrait, and the style of both the structure and the statue is considered to be pre-Hellenistic, i.e., transitional from the classical style to the full Hellenistic style, which is conventionally dated after the death of Alexander the Great in 323 B.C.E. In general, see Simon Hornblower, *Mausolus* (Oxford: Clarendon, 1982).

places: the coast of Leuca; the cities of Myndos, Caruanda, and Neapolis; the Iasian and Basilic Gulfs. Bargylos is on the Iasian Gulf.

Ionia

86. After the Basilic Gulf, Ionia winds around with several twists and turns. Beginning its first bend from Point Poseidon, it goes around the oracle of Apollo, who in the old days was called Branchidian but nowadays is called Didymaean Apollo. Then comes Miletus, once the leading city of all Ionia because of its skill in war and in peace, and the birthplace of the astronomer Thales, the musician Timotheus, and the natural philosopher Anaximander; and whenever they talk of Ionia, Miletus is also justly renowned for the celebrated talents of its other citizens.[62] The city of Hippis is the outlet of the Maeander River, and Mt. Latmus is known for the legend of Endymion, deeply loved, as they report, by the Moon.[63] **87.** After that, bending in again, the coastline goes around the city of Priene and the mouth of the Gaesus River, and then, the bigger its circuit, the more it embraces. The Panionium [Grk., Pan-Ionian Sanctuary] is there. It is a sacred district and, for that reason, is so designated because the Ionians tend it in common. **88.** There, founded by fugitives, as they say (and the name agrees with the report), is Phygela.[64] Ephesus is there, and the most renowned temple of Diana, which the Amazons, rulers of Asia, are reported to have dedicated. The Caÿster River is there. Lebedos is there, and the shrine of Apollo, which

---

62. Thales (ca. 636–ca. 546 B.C.E.) was a famous Ionian philosopher and one of the Seven Sages; he died, traditionally, in his ninetieth year. Anaximander (ca. 610–ca. 547) was another great name in the Ionian school of philosophy; he was associated with a radical new theory of the earth's sphericity. Timotheus (ca. 450–ca. 360) was a radical modernist and innovator in dithyrambic poetry at Athens; he too died, according to tradition, in his ninetieth year.

63. The sources are elusive and scattered, but among the more important are Theoc. *Id.* 3.49–50, 20.37–39; and Apollod. 1.56. Paus. 5.1.4–5 adds that at Elis they believed that the Moon bore fifty daughters to Endymion.

64. That is, Greek *phyg-* equals Latin *fug-*. On ancient etymology and wordplay, Frederick Ahl's *Metaformations: Soundplay and Wordplay in Ovid and Other Classical Poets* (Ithaca: Cornell University Press, 1985) is important and useful but should be used with care. His introduction (17–63) provides a good overview of ancient practice. Various contributors have attended to the more technical developments in ancient linguistic theory in E.F.K. Koerner and R.E. Asher, eds., *Concise History of the Language Sciences from the Sumerians to the Cognitivists* (Tarrytown, N.Y.: Pergamon, 1995).

Manto, Teiresias' daughter, founded when she was fleeing the Epigoni, the conquerors of Thebes. Colophon is there, which Mopsus, son of that same Manto, founded. **89.** By contrast, the promontory by which the gulf is defined projects like a peninsula, because with its other side it makes another gulf, which they call the Gulf of Smyrna [Izmir], and because it extends its remaining portions over a wider expanse after a narrow neck of land. On that isthmus, Teos to the south side and Clazomenae to the north are tied together by a common boundary where they press their backs together, and they look out on different seas with different coastlines. On the peninsula itself is Coryna. On the Gulf of Smyrna are the Hermus River and the city of Leuca; beyond is Phocaea, the last city of Ionia.

Aeolis

90. The next region became Aeolis from the time when it began to be cultivated by Aeolians. It was previously called Mysia, however, and where it adjoins the Hellespont, with the Trojans in possession, it was the Troad. They call the first of its cities Myrina after its founder Myrinus. Pelops established the following city when he returned from Greece after his victory over Oenomaüs; the leader of the Amazons, Cyme, called it Cyme, once those who had dwelt there were driven out. Above it, the Caïcus runs down between Elaea and Pitane, the city that bore Arcesilas, a very renowned head of the Academy when its doctrine was the suspension of judgment.[65] **91.** At that point, on a promontory, comes the town of Cyna. This promontory receives gulfs that are not detailed here; they are not small gulfs but long and gentle bends that gradually carry the shoreline all the way back to the foot of Mt. Ida

---

65. Arcesilas (ca. 316/5–242/1 B.C.E.) founded the Middle (Second) Academy at Athens ca. 266 B.C.E. Arcesilas is not the only *philosophus* named in this work, but he is the only one characterized by his chief doctrine. G.F. Schoemann writes (in *M. Tulii Ciceronis de natura deorum libri tres*, ed. and trans. A. Stickney [Boston, 1885], 174–75, ad 1.11): "Socrates was thought to be the predecessor of the Academic scepticism and the opposition to the dogmatism of the other schools because of his assertion: That he knew only one thing, namely that he knew nothing; and because of the reasoning he used to convict of ignorance those who boasted of knowing something.—Arcesilas of Pitane ... went farther than Socrates." Cicero (*Acad.* 1.12.45) is explicit: Arcesilas "said [a] that nothing could be known, not even the very thing that Socrates had reserved for himself; and [b] that everything is concealed in being unknown."

[Kaz]. The mountain range is sprinkled at first with small cities, of which the most renowned is Cisthena. On the inner fold the plain, Thebe by name, contains the adjacent towns Adramytion, Astura, and Chrysa (in the same order as named), and it contains Antandrus on the other side. 92. A dual explanation of that last name is in circulation. Some claim that Ascanius, the son of Aeneas, was captured by the Pelasgians when he ruled there, and that he ransomed himself in exchange for that city. Others think that it was founded by people here, whom civil war had driven from the island of Andros. The latter want the name *Antandrus* to be accepted as meaning "in exchange for Andros," the former as "in exchange for a man."[66]

93. The following stretch of coast reaches Gargara and Assos, colonies of the Aeolians. Then, not far from Troy, a second gulf, Achaeôn Limen [Grk., Achaean Harbor], curves its shores, which are very renowned because of the city, the war, and the destruction. Here was the town of Sigeum, here the camp of the warring Achaeans. Descending to this place from Mt. Ida, the Scamander makes its outlet, and the Simoïs too, rivers more important because of tradition than because of their physical character. 94. The mountain itself, remembered on account of the old struggle for booty and because of the judgment of Paris, reveals the rising sun differently from the way it is usually viewed in other lands. In fact, for people watching from the very peak, more or less from the middle of the night on, scattered fires appear to shine. The nearer the light draws, the more those fires appear to come together and to fuse with one another, until, as a result of being gathered closer and closer together, fewer fires are burning, and until, at the end, they burn with a single flame. 95. After that light has blazed brilliantly, like a fire, for a long time, it compresses itself, becomes round, and turns into a huge sphere. For a long time that sphere appears sizable and tied to the earth. Then it decreases little by little, becoming brighter the more it decreases. Last of all, it dispels the night, and, turning into the sun now, it rises along with the day.

96. Outside the gulf is the Rhoetean coast, with the renowned cities of Rhoeteum and Dardania, but the coast is particularly important for the tomb of Ajax. From here the sea narrows down and no longer washes onto the mainland. Instead, it divides the land again, and it

---

66. The Greek *anêr, andros,* m., "man," exactly parallels the Latin *vir* in meaning (see book 1, n. 29).

splits, by means of the narrow strait of the Hellespont, the shore that blocked its path. The sea causes the lands where it flows to be its sides again.

Hellespont, Propontis, Pontus, and Maeotis

97. Farther in are the Bithynians and the Mariandyni; on the coast are the Greek cities Abydos, Lampsacum, Parion, and Priapos. Abydos is famous because of the circulation of a great love story long ago.[67] Lampsacum, as the Phocaeans call it, got its name from the fact that, when they inquired where it would be best for them to head out for, an oracular response told them to make their home on the very spot where daylight had first struck.[68]

98. Then the sea widens as the Propontis, into which flows the Granicus, the river known for the very first battle between the Persians and Alexander.[69] On the other side of the river, Cyzicum is located on the isthmus of a peninsula. We have learned that Cyzicus, its namesake, died in battle, slaughtered by the unthinking Minyans when they were invading the Colchians.[70] Later on come Placia and Scylace, small Pelasgian colonies over which, from the back, hangs Mt. Olympus, or Mt. Mysius as the locals call it. 99. The Rhyndacos River goes through those places that follow. All around it are generated monstrous snakes, remarkable not only because of their size but also because, after they have fled from the sun's heat into the riverbed, they in fact emerge, open their mouths wide, and swallow birds that fly above them, even if they are flying high and fast. On the far side of the Rhyndacus are Dascylos and Myrlea, the city the Colophonians settled.

---

67. Simply the name of Abydos is enough to recall the love story of Hero and Leander, although at 2.26 M. does name Leander. For the story, Verg. *G.* 3.258–63 and Ov. *Her.* 18 and 19, together with Strabo 13.1.22, are the earliest surviving sources. In the fifth century C.E. Musaeus Grammaticus wrote an appealing short epic poem called "Hero and Leander" (343 lines).
68. The name of Lampsacus is explained as an etymologizing pun on the Greek verb *lampein* (= M.'s *fulgere*).
69. The Battle of the Granicus took place in May 334 B.C.E.
70. The allusion is to the legend of Jason and the Argonauts, who sailed to Colchis to retrieve the Golden Fleece. The story of Jason, the Argonauts, and Medea is told at length by Apollonius Rhodius in his *Argonautica*, and that of Jason and Medea is reported selectively by Euripides in *Medea* and in more traditional form by Ovid at *Met.* 7.1–452.

100. After that, there are two moderate-sized gulfs. One without a name embraces Cion, the most convenient trading town for Phrygia, which lies not too far away; the other one, the Gulf of Olbia, bears on its promontory a shrine of Neptune and in its bosom Astacos, a city founded by Megarians. **101.** Next, the continents again lie rather close to one another, and the channel, where the sea narrows as it is about to enter the Pontus, separates Europe from Asia by five stades. This channel is the Thracian Bosphorus, as previously indicated.[71] In the very jaws of this Bosphorus is a town, and at its mouth is a temple. The name of the town is Calchedon, its principal founder Archias the Megarian. The divinity of the temple is Jupiter, its founder Jason.

102. Here now the mighty Pontus opens out, and it extends to both the near and far sides in a long and straight line (except where there are promontories), even though the coast winds everywhere else. However, because the shoreline recedes less on the opposite side than it does to the left or the right, it curves around with soft points until it makes narrow angles on both ends and is rounded very much like the shape of the Scythian bow.[72] The sea is brief, cruel, and cloudy; its stopping-off places are few and far between; it is surrounded by a shore that is neither soft nor sandy; it borders on the north winds; and it is billowy and tempestuous, because it is not deep. In the olden days the sea was called the Axenus [Grk., Unfriendly] Sea from the vicious disposition of the inhabitants, but later it was called the Euxinus [Grk., Friendly] Sea because of traffic with somewhat gentler nations.[73]

103. On the Pontus, first off, the Mariandyni inhabit a city founded,

---

71. See 1.7 and 1.14.

72. M. works from books and perhaps directly from a map or maps (see my introduction, n. 31), and he is caught using his sources here. The image of the Pontus as bow-shaped was established by the time of Augustus (see Strabo 2.5.22; cp. Man. *Astronomica* 4.755). M.'s description of the opening into the Pontus is in error. The description of the bow shape works only loosely, and only if the observer is stationed, as Strabo says, at Point Carambis (M. 1.104, 2.3), in the center of the southerly coast of the Pontus: from there, Strabo says, and not from the Thracian Bosphorus, the shore extends in almost straight lines to either side.

73. The word *xenos -ê -on* (foreign), which has the alternate form *xeinos -on*, is the root of both *Axenus* (Grk. *a* + *xenos*) and *Euxinus* (Grk. *eu* + *xeinos*). The Latin forms here are each derived from an alternative form of the Greek base, but the alternative Greek forms *axeinos* and *euxenos* also existed. Strabo (7.3.6) gives a similar account of the sea's name except that he adds winter storms to human savagery as a factor (cp. book 2, n. 84).

as they say, by Argive Hercules. It is called Heraclea [Ereğli], and that name adds credibility to the tradition. Next to it is the Acherusian Cave, which goes down, as they tell it, to the Manes, and they believe that Cerberus was hauled up from there.[74] **104.** After that comes the town of Tios, in fact a colony of the Milesians, but now belonging to the land and people of Paphlagonia. More or less in the middle of their littoral is Point Carambis [Kerempe Burun]. On its nearer side is the Parthenius River; the cities of Sesamus, Cromnos, and Cytorus (founded by Cytisorus, the son of Phrixus);[75] then Cinolis, Collyris, and Armene, which marks the end of Paphlagonia. **105.** Next, the Chalybes occupy two very renowned cities, Amisos and Sinope [Sinop], the latter being the birthplace of Diogenes the Cynic.[76] As to rivers, they have the Halys [Kizil Irmak] and the Thermodon [Terme]. Beyond the Halys is the city of Lycastos; a plain lies beside the Thermodon. On that plain was the town of Themiscurum, and there was an encampment, too, of Amazons, which they call Amazonius for that reason.

106. The Tibareni, for whom the highest good lies in playing and laughing, extend to the Chalybae. Farther on, the Mossyni take shelter under wooden towers, completely mark their whole bodies with tattoos, eat in the open air, recline with the sexes mixed and without concealing it,[77] and choose kings by vote. They keep their kings in chains and under the closest guard, and when the kings have earned blame for

---

74. That is, hauled up by Hercules. According to Hom. *Il.* 5.395–97, Hercules entered the underworld, fought with Hades, and wounded him "among the dead." Entering the realm of death and fighting with Death himself are stock folktale motifs whereby in his quest the hero overcomes death and wins immortality. Hercules is the only major Olympian deity to have a human origin (cp. Hom. *Od.* 11.601–4). In the *Odyssey* (11.617–26) the poet also knew the tradition of the labors imposed on Hercules by Eurystheus, king of Tiryns (or of Mycenae in some versions). Later the many traditions about Hercules' labors were reduced to a canonical twelve. In some versions Hercules entered the underworld at Cape Taenaros in the Peloponnesus. On Hercules, see book 1, n. 25.

75. For Phrixus, see book 1, n. 78.

76. Diogenes (ca. 400–325 B.C.E.) was nicknamed "the dog" (Grk. *kuôn;* hence derives English *cynic*) from his antisocial asceticism and extreme unconventionality. He is famous for having lived in a barrel, actually a storage jar, at Athens. Another anecdote records that at Corinth once, when Alexander the Great announced his presence and offered to do Diogenes a favor, the Cynic merely asked Alexander to stop blocking the sunshine.

77. The reference here is to unconcealed sexual activity. Cp. also M.'s remark at 1.29 about embarrassment.

exercising some power wrongfully, the people punish them by depriving them of a whole day's food. Otherwise, the people are rough, crude, and absolutely vicious to those who put in to shore there.

107. After them come the less savage Macrocephali [Grk., Long-Heads], Bechiri, and Buxeri, but even these peoples are of unruly disposition. Cities are rare; particularly renowned, though, are Cerasunta and Trapezos [Trabzon]. **108.** Next is that place where the stretch of coastline coming from the Bosphorus terminates, and from there the bend of the opposite shore, becoming more elevated on the gulf, forms the narrowest angle of the Pontus. Here are the Colchians; the Phasis [Rioni] bursts into the sea here; here is the town colonized by Themistagoras the Milesian; here are the grove and temple of Phrixus, who is well known from the old legend of the Golden Fleece.[78] **109.** Rising from here, the mountains stretch in a long ridge until they connect to the Riphaean [Grk., Gusty] Range.[79] These mountains, on one end, face the Euxine, the Maeotis, and the Tanaïs, and on the other they face the Caspian Sea. They are called the Ceraunians but are elsewhere called the Taurus Mountains, the Moschic, the Amazonian, the Caspian, the Coraxic, the Caucasus—called by as many different names as there are peoples beside them.

110. On the first bend, however, of the now curving shore, there is a town that Greek merchants founded, and they reportedly called it Cycnus because the voice of a swan [Grk. *kyknos*] had given a sign to them when, while being tossed around in a blinding storm, they did not know where land was. Wild, uncivilized nations living beside the vast sea occupy its remaining coastline: the Melanchlaeni,[80] theToretici, and six Colician peoples (the Coraxici, the Phthirophagi, the Heniochi, the

---

78. Phrixus and his sister, Helle, were the children of Athamas and Nephele. When Phrixus was to be sacrificed to Zeus because of his wicked stepmother, Ino, Nephele rescued both children by mounting them on the ram with the Golden Fleece, and the ram flew them to safety. Unfortunately, Helle fell into the sea that is named for her (the Hellespont or Sea of Helle). Phrixus was carried to Colchis, where he sacrificed the ram, gave its fleece to King Aeëtes (from whom Jason eventually retrieved it), and married one of Aeëtes' daughters.

79. The Riphaean Mountains are variously located to the far north of Europe and Asia. Strabo (7.3.1; cp. 7.3.6) knew that both these mountains and the Hyperboreans were mythical. By contrast, Pliny (*HN* 4.79, 4.88) treats the Riphaeans as real but hesitates (*HN* 4.89) over the happy Hyperboreans. M. blinks at neither the mountains (1.109, 1.115, 1.117, 2.1, 3.36) nor the people (1.12, 1.13, 3.36–37).

80. Discussed further at 2.14.

Achaeans, the Cercetici, and, at this point, the Sindones, on the boundary of the Maeotis).

111. In the territory of the Heniochi, Dioscorias was founded by Castor and Pollux,[81] who came to the Pontus with Jason; and Sindos, in the territory of the Sindones, was founded by the actual cultivators of the land. **112.** Then a region, situated sideways to the sea and moderately wide, runs between the Pontus and the Swamp[82] to the Cimmerian Bosphorus. The Coracanda, which drains in two riverbeds to the lake and to the sea, makes this region a peninsula. Four cities are located there: Hermonassa, Cepoe, Phanagorea, and, on the very shore, Cimmerium. **113.** On the near side, the Maeotic Lake receives those who enter it. It spreads in all directions where it touches broad land, but it is surrounded by an uncurving shore nearer to the sea. Maeotis is enclosed, as it were, by a border except where it has its opening, and at the nearer end it is virtually similar to the Pontus in size. **114.** The Maeotici cultivate the shore that curves from the Cimmerian Bosphorus all the way to the Tanaïs, as do the Thatae, the Sirachi, the Phicores, and—next to the mouth of the river—the Ixamatae. Among them, women practice the same skills as men, so much so that women are not free even from military service. Men serve in the infantry and fight with bows; women enter battle on horseback and do not fight with swords but kill their captives by dragging them off with lariats. Still, women do marry, but there is no predictable age at which to be considered marriageable: women remain virgins except for those who have killed an enemy.

115. The Tanaïs itself, falling from the Riphaean Mountains, rushes so precipitously that it alone endures both summery heat and wintry cold in close proximity, yet it runs down always the same, unchanged and fast-moving, even when neighboring rivers, the Maeotis, the Cimmerian Bosphorus, and certain parts of the Pontus are all frozen by winter's cold.[83] **116.** The Sauromatae occupy its banks and the places that are contiguous with them. They are one nation but have as many peoples as they have names. First, the Maeotid Gynaecocratumenoe [Grk., Ruled By Women]—the kingdoms of the Amazons—occupy plains that are rich in pasture but barren and bare for other things. The

---

81. Castor and Pollux are also known as the Dioscuri.
82. The Swamp is the Maeotic Lake (cp. 1.10 and n. 5 there).
83. An exaggeration: the Pontus is well known for not freezing, but see book 2, n. 84.

Budini inhabit the city of Gelonos. Next to them the Thyssagetae and Turcae occupy endless forests and feed themselves by hunting. **117.** The next region is deserted and rough, with uninterrupted cliffs over a wide stretch; it extends all the way to the Aremphaei. These people enjoy customs that are very much based on fair treatment; they have sacred groves for homes and berries as food; and both men and women keep their heads bare. Therefore these people are regarded as consecrated, and no one from nations as savage as those here profanes these people, which results in the custom that other people flee to them for asylum. Farther on, the Riphaean Mountains rise up, and beyond them lies the shore that faces Ocean.

Book 2: Around Our Sea—from the End of Asia to the Pillars of Hercules

1. That is the boundary, as I have said, and the layout of Asia where it verges on Our Sea and the Tanaïs [Don]. If people travel by the Tanaïs into the Maeotis, Europe is situated to the right, but to the left if sailing upriver. In Europe, constantly falling snow makes those places contiguous with the Riphaean Mountains (which actually reach even this far) so impassable that, in addition, they prevent those who deliberately travel here from seeing anything. After that comes a region of very rich soil but quite uninhabitable because griffins, a savage and tenacious breed of wild beasts, love—to an amazing degree—the gold that is mined from deep within the earth there, and because they guard it with an equally amazing hostility to those who set foot there.

Scythia

2. The first human beings are Scyths, and first of the Scyths are the so-called one-eyed Arimaspoe; after them the Essedones are found all the way to Maeotis. The Buces [Nogaïka] River cuts the Maeotis' bend, and the Agathyrsi and Sauromatae surround it. The Hamaxobioe [Grk., Wagon Dwellers] are called that because they use their wagons as homes.[1] Then a strip, now running sideways to the Cimmerian Bosphorus, is enclosed both by the Pontus and by the Maeotis. **3.** The Satarchae occupy the area that goes toward the Swamp;[2] beside the Cimmerian Bosphorus are the Cimmerian towns of Murmecion, Panticapaeon [Kerch], Theodosia [Feodosiya], and Hermisium, while the Taurici live beside the Euxine Sea. Beyond them, a bay full of harbors and therefore called Calos Limen [Grk., Beautiful Harbor] is enclosed by two

---

1. *Hamaxobios* is a Greek word meaning "living in wagons." As an adjective it is roughly equivalent in English to *nomadic*. The substantive Hamaxobioi, however, does not refer to the people called Nomads in 2.4–5 (see n. 5 there).

2. The Swamp (Lat. *Palus*) is the alternate name for the Maeotis, that is, the Maeotic Lake (see book 1, n. 11).

promontories. One promontory they call Criu Metopon [Grk., Ram's Brow; Ay Todor], and it is equal and opposite to Point Carambis, which we have said[3] is in Asia. The other one is Point Parthenion [Grk. Maidenshead]. The town of Cherronesus[4] [Sevastopol] lies beside this promontory and was founded—if this is believable—by Diana. The town is particularly famous for a nymphaeum in the form of a cave, which was dedicated on its citadel to the nymphs.

4. Then the sea encroaches on the bank, and it follows all the way along the receding coastlines until it is five miles distant from the Maeotis, where it renders them into a peninsula [Krym/Crimea]. One of these coasts the Satarchae occupy, the Taurici the other. What lies between the Swamp and the bay is called Taphrae [Perekop]; the bay is called Carcinites [Karkinitskiy]. In it is the city of Carcine [Skadovsk], flanked by two rivers, the Gerrhos [Malochnaya] and the Hypacaris [Kuban], which make their outlet to the sea through a single mouth, although they flow down from different springs and from different directions. For the Gerrhos rolls along between the territory of the Basilidae and that of the Nomads, the Hypacaris right through that of the Nomads.[5]

5. Then come the vast forests that these lands bear, as well as the Panticapes [Ingulets] River, which separates the Nomads and the Georgians. At that time the land, which pulls back for a long stretch, is tied to the shore by a slender base; subsequently, where it is moderately wide, the land fashions itself gradually into a point. Just as if it were collecting its long sides into a sword point, the land affects the appear-

---

3. At 1.104.

4. Greek *khersonêsos* (Lat. *chersonesus;* cp. 2.25 and 49 for the spelling), sometimes showing rhotacism as here (*cherronêsos*), is the ordinary Greek noun meaning "peninsula." Latin sometimes doubles the medial -s- (-*nessus*) in this transliteration. *Khersonêsos* is used in the same way as San Franciscans designate the location of Stanford University "on the Peninsula," i.e., on the San Francisco Peninsula. Locals apply the noun to the obvious regional referent, and from that practice a number of prominent peninsulas received the familiar name *Chersonesus* but require an adjective for precision. The peninsula in question is the Cimmerian Chersonese, the modern Crimea. Here the name spelled *Cherronesus* is transferred to the nearby town.

5. These Nomads are not the Hamaxobioi mentioned at 2.2. The term *Nomadae* was often used to name specific peoples in Africa and Scythia. See 2.11 for more about these Nomads and 3.38 for an eastern Scythian group called Nomads as well. Book 3, n. 20, treats a related problem of terminology.

ance of a drawn sword. Achilles entered the Pontic Sea with a hostile fleet, and it is remembered that he celebrated his victory there with competitive games and that there he routinely exercised himself and his men when there was a respite from the fighting. Therefore the land is called Dromos Achilleos [Grk., Achilles' Racecourse; Tendrovskaya Kosa].

6. Then the Borysthenes [Dnepr] River washes up on the territory of the nation that bears its name. The loveliest among Scythia's rivers, it flows down the most smoothly (the others are turbulent), and it is calmer than the others and absolutely delicious to drink. This river feeds the most prolific pastures and sustains big fish with the best flavor and no bones.[6] The Borysthenes comes from a long way off and rises from unidentified springs. With its bed the river skims through a path of forty days' hiking, is navigable over the same route, and debouches between the Greek towns of Borysthenida and Olbia. 7. The Hypanis [Yuzhny Bug/Southern Bug] River borders the territory of the Callipidae. It rises from a vast swamp, which the locals call its Mother, and for a long while flows down exactly as it was born.[7] Finally, not far from the sea, it takes in from a small spring (the name of which is Exampaeus) waters so bitter that from this point on the very river still continues to flow but is now changed completely. The Asiaces [Tiligul], the next river, descends between the territories of the Callipidae and the

---

6. This entire passage owes a good deal to Herodotus, who also asserts that the river's source (like the Nile's) is unknown to him (4.53). The Dnepr rises in the hills west of Moscow and extends for about 1,420 miles to the Black Sea. Historically it has been the Ukraine's most important river. Pliny (*HN* 9.45) also records these "spineless" fish, which are identified with the still-famous sturgeon of the Dnepr River. Sturgeon, especially those of the beluga type, are prized for their roe today, and if we understand Herodotus right, caviar was known in antiquity too.

7. The description of this river is indebted to Hdt. 4.52. M. has several ways to express the sources of rivers. Here he calls on the verb *natus est* [was born] and plays on the local imagery of the swamp as "mother" of the river. The Hypanis is identified with two rivers, the Yuzhny (Southern) Bug and the Kuban, which M. knows by the name Hypacaris (see 2.4). In any event, M. would mean the Yuzhny Bug in the Ukraine if he is following Herodotus or the Herodotean tradition here. On M.'s direct and indirect debts to Herodotus, see Bunbury 1883: Bunbury maintains that M. is behind Herodotus in some data (2:356), elsewhere copies "to a great extent from Herodotus" (366), and still elsewhere uses an intermediary source that is dependent on Herodotus (367).

Asiacae. The Tyra [Dnestr] separates the people here from the Istrians.[8] That river rises among the Neuri, and where it makes its outlet to the sea, it runs beside a town of the same name.

8. The river that separates the peoples of Scythia from their neighbors, however, begins—its sources in Germany are known—with a name different from the one with which it finishes. In fact, through immense lands belonging to great nations, it is for a long time the Danube; then with the local peoples using another name, it becomes the Ister.[9] After receiving several more rivers, it then becomes a mighty river. Of those rivers that debouch into Our Sea, the Ister is no smaller than the Nile and has the same number of mouths as that river, but it flows into the sea with three shallow mouths and four that are navigable.

9. The temperaments and cultures of the nations differ. The Essedones celebrate their parents' funerals joyfully and with a festive gathering of family members. In the feast, they devour the actual corpses, once they have been ripped apart and stirred in with the innards of slaughtered cattle. After they have smoothed and polished them skillfully, the skulls are bound with gold, and they use them for drinking cups. These are, among them, the last rites of their religion. **10.** The Agathyrsi tattoo their faces and limbs, each more or less in proportion to the prominence of their ancestors, but they all do so with the same marks and in such a way that they cannot be washed off. The Satarchae have no experience of gold and silver (the worst pestilences), and they conduct business by barter. They even inhabit caves and dugouts, with their homes sunk into the ground because of the savage and virtually unending winter; they cover their whole bodies and even their faces except where they look out. **11.** The Taurians, well remembered for the arrival of Iphigenia and Orestes, are monstrous in character and have the monstrous reputation that they slaughter newcomers as sacrificial offerings. The Basilid nation began with Hercules and Echidna. Their character is regal,[10] and only arrows serve them as weapons. The wandering Nomads follow the pastures of

---

8. These people share their name with the region and the local river. The river is the Danube; cp. its Latin name, *Danuvius*. The lower Danube was called Ister in Greek, and one of its adjacent regions was therefore Istria and its people the Istrians. See 2.8.

9. See the preceding note. The Danube is about 1,750 miles long. It rises in the mountains of Germany and flows east to the Black Sea, where it debouches through six of its seven supposed mouths.

10. M. gives an etymological explanation by using *regius -a -um* here, which like the Greek *basilidês -es* means "kingly, regal, royal."

the flocks, and as long as those pastures last, they pass the time in a fixed abode. The Georgians cultivate and work the fields.[11] The Asiacae do not know what stealing is, and for that reason they neither protect their own property nor touch anyone else's.

12. To the interior the ritualistic behavior of the inhabitants is cruder and the territory less tilled. They love the bloodshed of war, and it is customary for warriors to drink blood from the very wounds of the first man they ever killed. The more a man kills, the more valued he is among them. Among the marks of shame, by contrast, surely the worst is to have no experience of shedding blood. Not even their peace treaties are without blood. The negotiators all cut themselves and sip the drawn blood after they have mixed everybody's together. They think that drinking it is the surest guarantee of a lasting good faith. **13.** At their banquets, the happiest and most frequent topic of conversation is to tell how many men each one has killed. Those who have reported the most chug from double cups. Among the carousers, that is a special honor. These people smooth out their drinking cups from the skulls of their greatest personal enemies, the same way the Essedones do from their parents' skulls.[12] **14.** Among the Anthropophagi,[13] even ordinary banquets are provided with human entrails. The Geloni cover themselves and their horses with the skins of their enemies—their horses with the flesh from the rest of the body, themselves with the skin from the heads. The Melanchlaeni [Grk., Black-Robes] have coal black clothing, and from that they get their name. There is a preordained time for each of the Neuri at which, if they so desire, they metamorphose into wolves and back into who they were.[14]

---

11. M.'s sentence, *colunt Georgi exercentque agros,* plays on the Greek verb *geôrgein,* which in turn explains the Greek etymology of the name given to the agricultural tribes of this region (Lat. *Georgi* from Grk. *geôrgoi,* "farmers").

12. The practice of the Essedones is given earlier, at 2.9.

13. Their name means "Human-Eaters," or "Cannibals," in Greek. At 3.59 (see n. 36 there) M. speaks of Androphagoi (Grk., Man-Eaters). Many Scyth names are simply fantastic, as are many of the stories told about these peoples and others of the extreme north (see book 3, nn. 15, 16, and 20).

14. So too writes Herodotus (4.105.2). The werewolf, a stock figure of European and world folklore, appears in both Greek and Roman folktales. On the human origin of the wolf, cp. Ov. *Met.* 1.211–43, where Ovid reports how King Lycaon of Arcadia served human flesh to Zeus and was punished by having himself and his descendants changed into wolves. The story probably reflects early human sacrifice in honor of Zeus Lycaeus (Zeus of Mt. Lycaeus), but the

15. Mars is the god of all these peoples. To him they dedicate swords and sword belts instead of images and sacrifice human beings instead of animals. The lands cover a broad expanse, and because the rivers often overflow their banks, they are never barren of pasture. Yet in some places the lands are so completely infertile for any other growth that the inhabitants, who are short of wood, feed their fires with bones.

Thrace

16. Thrace is next to these lands, and it extends far inland from its front on the Pontic end all the way to the Illyrians. Where it extends its lateral borders, Thrace is contiguous with the Ister and Our Sea. The region is favorable neither in its climate nor in its soil, and except where it is closer to the sea, it is infertile, cold, and quite intolerant of cultivated plants. It rarely ever sustains a fruit-bearing tree but rather commonly sustains the vine. The fruit of the vine, however, does not ripen and soften except where the cultivators have stopped the cold by heaping leaves around them. It nourishes men[15] in more kindly fashion, but not for their physical appearance. Indeed, their bodily condition is rough and unbecoming but is especially conducive to fierceness and population size, since they are both numerous and merciless. **17.** It lets few rivers go through to the sea, but the most famous ones it lets through are the Hebrus [Merica], the Nestos [Nestos/Mesta], and the Strymon [Struma]. The interior throws up mountains—Mt. Haemos [Stara Planina], Mt. Rhodope [Rodopi Planina/Despoto dagh], and Mt. Orbelos [Vihren/Belasitza], all very well known for the sacred rituals of Father Liber and for the gathering of maenads that Orpheus instituted.[16] Of

---

Greeks later used *lycaôn* as a common noun meaning "werewolf" (derived from *lukos*, "wolf") and equivalent to *lukanthrôpos* ("wolfman"; hence derives *lycanthropy*). The Romans borrowed the word *lycaôn* from the Greeks but used it to designate unfamiliar wolflike animals found in Aethiopia, according to M. at 3.88 (see book 3, n. 59 there). *Lycaones* is the name of a people at 1.13.

15. Here M. speaks not of people in general (*homines*) but of males (*viri*).

16. These mountains are associated with ecstatic religious worship (see the following note). Liber is often identified with Dionysus (see book 3, n. 45); the maenads (Grk. *maenades*, "maddened ones") are the worshipers who become frenzied in the worship of Dionysus; Orpheus, the most renowned poet before Homer, has a mythical life of his own but is sometimes linked to Dionysus (see book 2, n. 29).

these three, the Haemos rises so high that it gives views of both the Euxine and the Adriatic Seas from its very peak.

18. The Thracians inhabit the land, one people, although they are furnished with a variety of names and customs. Some Thracians—and certainly the Getae—are wild and absolutely prepared to die. A range of belief brings this readiness into being. Some individuals think that the souls of the dead will return; others think that even if they do not return, souls still are not obliterated but go to a happier place; still others think that souls do perish absolutely but that dying is better than living. Therefore childbirth is mourned among certain Thracians, and newborns are wept over. Funerals, in contrast, are festive and are celebrated, just like their sacred rites,[17] with singing and gamboling.

19. Not even in the case of women does the mind shirk its duty. They consider it the greatest obligation to be killed over the corpses of their dead husbands and to be buried along with them.[18] Because individual men have several wives at once, their wives compete in a great contest to be the one to have this honor, and they compete before those who will make the decision. It suits their mores and is a special source of joy when there is a struggle to be supreme in this contest. **20.** Other women raise the lament with their keening and raise their voices in the most bitter lamentations. But those who have a mind to console them bring their weapons and wealth to the funeral pyre, and these same individuals are prepared, as they say over and over again, either to bargain with or to fight with the destiny of the dead man in case it is up to them;

---

17. M. probably has in mind the exuberance of the local Dionysiac worship, which is often considered by scholars to have entered Greece chiefly from Thrace. The idea of the soul (Grk. *psychê*) is widely thought to have entered the Greek world from the shamanistic cultures of Scythia and Thrace. Herodotus refused to tell the story of the Hyperborean shaman-figure Abaris (Hdt. 4.36) but gives more details—and curious ones at that—about Salmoxis of Thrace (Hdt. 4.94–96). In general, see E.R. Dodds, *The Greeks and the Irrational*, Sather Classical Lectures 25 (Berkeley and Los Angeles: University of California Press, 1951), 135–78. For various aspects of Dionysus, see T.H. Carpenter and C.A. Faraone, eds., *Masks of Dionysus* (Ithaca: Cornell University Press, 1993).

18. These women practice a variant of what is called sati, or suttee, in English; that term, however, is a misnomer. The word is borrowed from Hindu culture, where, as noted by A.L. Basham, "the word *satî* (written *suttee* by older English writers) means 'a virtuous woman,' and the word was erroneously applied by early officials and missionaries to the satî's self-immolation": see Basham, *The Wonder That Was India* (New York: Grove Press, 1954), 187. For a related act of self-sacrifice at death, see M.'s report at 3.19.

when there is no room for fighting or money, < . . . >. **21.** Virgins worthy of marriage are not given to their husbands by their parents. Instead, they either are publicly displayed as ready for marriage or else are put up for sale. The explanation for the choice of procedure rests on appearance and character. Upright, beautiful women are prized; men with money seek out all the others for a price. The use of wine is unknown to some Thracians, but a hilarity like drunkenness comes over them from the smoke at banquets when certain seeds are thrown onto the fires as they sit around them.[19]

22. On the seacoast, Istropolis [Istriya] lies beside the Ister; next Callatis [Mangalia], colonized by the Milesians; then Tomoe [Constanta], the Carian Port [Shabla], and Point Tiristis [Kaliakra Burun]. The second angle of the Pontus receives those who go past this promontory—that is, the angle opposite to the one by the Phasis River and like it but fuller. Here was Bizone [Kavarna], which collapsed in an earthquake. Here are the port of Crunos and the cities of Dionysopolis [Balchik], Odessos [Varna], Messembria [Nesebŭr], and Anchialos [Pomoriye], as well as the great Apollonia [Sozopol] in the deepest part of the bay, right where the Pontus finishes its second bend with an angle. **23.** From here the shoreline is straight except that more or less in the middle it extends into a promontory, which they call Thynias [Iğneada Burun]. In contradistinction, the coast continues with its uncurved shores, and it supports the cities of Halmydesos [Midye], Philiae, and Phinopolis. That is as far as the Pontus goes.

24. After that come the Thracian Bosphorus and Propontis; on the Bosphorus is Byzantion [Istanbul], and on the Propontis, Selymbria [Silivri], Perinthos [Marmaraereğlisi/Ereğli], and Bytinis [Vize]. The rivers that flow among these places are the Erginos [Ergene] and Atyras [Karasu]. At that point comes the part of Thrace once ruled by Rhessus,[20] then Samian Bisanthe [Tekirdağ], and once-mighty Cypsela

---

19. Herodotus (4.59–75) describes various beliefs and practices of the Scyths in some detail. As so often, Herodotus' influence, although much filtered, can be seen in M.'s account (see book 2, n. 7).

20. King Rhesus of Thrace was the hope and salvation of Troy, which could not fall if his white horses drank from the Xanthus River and fed on the Troad, but before this could happen, Rhesus was killed in the famous night raid by Odysseus and Diomedes. See Hom. *Il.* 10.432–502 and Eurip. *Rhesus*. (Note again the doubling of the Greek medial -s-, where Latin has *Rhessus* for Greek *Rhêsos*; cp. *khersonêsos*, discussed in book 2, n. 4.)

[İpsala]. Farther on is the place the Greeks call Macron Teichos [Grk., Long Wall], as well as Lysimachia, sitting at the base of the great peninsula.[21] **25.** The land that follows never runs to much width and is very constricted here between the Hellespont and the Aegaean. They call the narrow part Isthmos, its forward part Mastusia, and the whole Chersonessus [Gelibolu/Gallipoli], which is famous for many reasons. **26.** On it is the river Aegos [Grk., Goat], remarkable because of the destruction of the Attic fleet.[22] Sestos [Nara] is there too, opposite Abydos [Maltepe], and is very well known for the love of Leander.[23] That is also the region where the Persian army dared to join by bridges lands that were separated by space and sea. An amazing and mighty deed! It crossed from Asia to Greece on foot and crossed the sea without sailing on it.[24] The bones of Protesilaüs have been consecrated there with a shrine.[25] Here too is Port Coelus [Kilya], remarkable for the destruction of the Laconian fleet when the Athenians and Lacedaemonians clashed in naval battle.[26] Here is Cynos Sema [Grk., Tomb of the Dog], the tomb of Hecuba, acquiring this humble name either from the figure of the

---

21. Macron Teichos is named for its defenses. Lysimachia has a similarly apotropaic name (meaning, roughly, "undoer of battle") but actually is named for one of Alexander's successors (Grk. *diadouchoi*), Lysimachus, who relocated the inhabitants of nearby Cardia there in 309 B.C.E. Lysimachus was one of several successors who competed for Alexander's position. None was successful, and they divided his domain.

22. Called Aigospotamoi, a plural, by the Greeks, but rendered either as *Goat-Rivers* or *Goat River* in English. Xenophon's contemporary account (*Hell.* 2.1.20–32) gives the details of this battle in 405 B.C.E. that paved the way for a Lacedaemonian victory in the Peloponnesian War (432–404 B.C.E.). The much later account of Diodorus Siculus (13.105.1–106.7) differs as usual in important details.

23. Sestos [Nara] is about seven or eight miles from Eceabat. For Leander, see 1.97 and n. 67 there.

24. M. refers to the crossing of Xerxes' army in 480 B.C.E. Herodotus (7.33–36 and 7.54–56) gives the story in detail.

25. Protesilaüs, the first Greek ashore, was also the first Greek slain in the Trojan War (see Hom. *Il.* 2.695–709)—killed by an unnamed Dardanian, says Homer, but by Hector according to legend. By Hermes' special dispensation, according to Roman writers, Protesilaüs returned from the dead to meet briefly with his widow, Laödamia, but on his return to the dead she went with him.

26. Thucydides (8.99–107) treats events surrounding this naval battle off the promontory of Cynossema in 411 B.C.E. and its immediate consequences. According to him (8.106), the victory heartened the Athenians after several years of naval setbacks against the Peloponnesian fleets.

dog into which she reportedly was changed or else from the misfortune into which she had fallen. Here is Madytos [Maydos/Eceabat] and here Eleus [Eski Hissarlik], which ends the Hellespont.

27. The long shore immediately thrusts along the Aegean Sea for a considerable distance, and in a great, gentle ambit from here to what is called Cape Sunium it goes around land that is swept back from its path. Those who sail this stretch and round Mastusia have to enter a gulf that flows onto the other side of the Thracian Chersonesus and is enclosed by a mountain ridge just like a valley. The gulf is called Melas [Grk., Black] after the river [Kavak] it takes in, and it embraces two cities, Alopeconnesus and Cardia [Karaköy], which is situated on the far side of the Isthmus.[27] **28.** Aenos [Enez], which was founded by Aeneas in exile, is an exceptional place. The Cicones are found around the Hebrus River, and on its far side is Doriscos, where they say Xerxes measured his troops by space, because he could not do so by number.[28] After that is Cape Serrhion [Mákri] and Zone [Tshoban], where even the groves, according to the story, followed the singing Orpheus.[29] At that point come the Sthenos River and Maronia lying on its banks.

29. The farther region bore Diomedes. He used to throw strangers to be eaten by his monstrous horses, and he was thrown, once and for all, to those same horses by Hercules.[30] What they call the Tower of

---

27. That is, the Isthmus of the Thracian Chersonnese.

28. Herodotus (7.59–60) describes Xerxes' technique and general result in 480 B.C.E. Because Xerxes' troops were too numerous to count individually, their number was estimated by the amount of space they occupied.

29. The legendary singer Orpheus is another shaman-figure associated with Thrace (see book 2, n. 17). Like the Thracian Salmoxis, Orpheus had a connection with the underworld, and his disembodied head even retained the magic power of his singing. In Greek tradition, Orpheus is the most famous singer before Homer. Legend says that he died dismembered by Bacchic maenads. Orphic traditions were also important in Greek religion, but the details are scattered and vague. Ovid (*Met.* 10.1–154 and 11.1–84) gives the main lines of the myths about Orpheus and his connection to Dionysus (Bacchus).

30. Again the importance of Hercules as a civilizing hero among the Greeks and Romans cannot be underestimated. In the traditional reckoning, the capture of these man-eating mares is the eighth of Hercules' great labors. This Diomedes is not the great hero of the *Iliad*, Diomedes Tydeïdes, but a brutish Thracian (Bistonian) king whose father was Ares. Apollodorus (2.5.8) indicates that Abdera was named for Abderus, Hercules' companion (and lover) in the campaign to take the mares. In some accounts it is uncertain whether Abderus founded the city before he died or Hercules did so in his honor. Some accounts also indicate that Hercules went alone on this mission.

Diomedes remains as evidence of the legend, and so too the city of Abdera, which his sister named after herself. That city, however, has something else to be remembered for, namely, that it gave birth to Democritus the natural philosopher, rather than that it was founded in this way.[31] 30. Farther on, the Nestos River flows, and between it and the Strymon are the cities of Philippi, Apollonia, and Amphipolis; between the Strymon and Athos is the Tower of Calarnaea, the port of Capru Limen [Grk., Boar's Harbor], and the cities of Acanthus [Hierissos] and Echinia; between Athos and Pallene are the cities of Cleonae and Olynthos. The Strymon, as we have said, is a river. It begins far away, where it is a rivulet, but becomes fuller now and then from waters that originate elsewhere. After the river forms a lake not far from the sea, it then rushes into the sea from a bed greater than the one it had come down with.

31. Mt. Athos is so tall that it is believed to be even higher than the place from which the rains fall. The idea gets credibility because ashes do not wash off the altars that it has on its peak but remain on the mound where they are left. The mountain, however, proceeds to the sea not by a spur, as some say, but with its whole long ridge. 32. Where it clings to the continent, it was excavated and then sailed across by Xerxes when he was invading Greece,[32] and it is still traversable by a navigable strait. Small colonies of Pelasgians occupy the foot of the mountain. On its summit was the town of Acrothoön, where, as they tell it, the life of the inhabitants was longer by half than it was in other lands.[33] 33. Pallene [Kassándra] has so much open land that it is the seat and territory of five cities; the whole

---

31. Democritus (ca. 460–ca. 360 B.C.E.) lived to be very old, but there is little evidence for his exact age at death. Democritus was a materialist and established the ancient atomic theory by building on the work of Leucippus (second half of the fifth century B.C.E.). It is not possible to separate neatly Leucippus' ideas from those of his younger contemporary.

32. The famous excavation of this peninsula in 480 B.C.E. and the reasons for it are described by Herodotus (7.22–24 and 37).

33. Information about Acrothoön is hard to come by. Thucydides (4.109) notes that Acrothoön and surrounding cities have mixed populations of Greek-speakers and non-Greek-speakers. In the lifetime of the elder Pliny, Acrothoön already had disappeared, but he noted that Macrobioi (Grk., Long-Lived) inhabited the present-day towns in the region. M. reserves the name Macrobioi, however, for certain Aethiopians living south of Aegypt, whose lifespans are half again as long as is usual (3.85).

peninsula extends into the sea even though it is quite narrow where it begins. Potidaea is located there, but where it is broader, Mende and Scione need mention. Mende was founded by the Eretrians, Scione by the Achaeans as they were returning after the capture of Troy.

Macedonia, Greece, and Illyricum

34. Then the Macedonian peoples inhabit a number of cities, of which Pelle is especially renowned. Its native sons create this reputation—Philip the conqueror of Greece and Alexander, too, the conqueror of Asia.[34] On the coast, Megyberna Bay, between Points Deris and Canastraeum, goes around both the port of Cophos and the cities of Torone and Myscella, as well as Megyberna [Grk. *Mekyberna*; Molivópyrgos] (whence the bay's name). **35.** Sane is next to Point Canastraeum; in the middle, where the land folds in, Megyberna Bay cuts moderately into the shoreline. However that may be, the huge Thermaïc Gulf, with its long sides, extends well into the sea. The Axius River [Vardar/Axios] runs through Macedon into this gulf, and at this point so does the Peneus through Thessalian territory. Thessalonice [Thessaloníki/Salonica] comes before reaching the Axius, and between these two places are Cassandria, Cydna, Aloros, and Itharis. From the Peneus to Point Sepias are Eurymenae, Meliboea, and Castanea, all equally famous except that Philoctetes, its native son, ennobles Meliboea.

36. The lands of the interior, famed for the names of its localities, produce almost nothing that is not well known. Not far from here is Olympus; Pelion is here; so is Ossa—all mountains remembered for the fabled War of the Giants. Here is Pieria, both the mother of the Muses and their home. Here is the ground last tramped by the Greek Hercules, the defile of Mt. Oeta. Here is Tempe, well known for its sacred grove, and Libethra [Litókhoron], the fountain of songs.

37. At that point Greece now projects very much on a grand scale. As far as it borders on the Sea of Myrtos, Greece, extending from north to south, faces the sunrise over the Aegean's waves and sunset over those of the Ionian Sea. Also, the land, quite wide at first and called Hellas, goes forward with a considerable coastline; then it is virtually cut more

---

34. Philip II (d. 336 B.C.E.) and Alexander III (the Great, 356–323 B.C.E.) of Macedon.

or less in half as both seas—but the Ionian Sea more—invade its lateral coastlines to the point that Hellas is four miles wide. **38.** From there again, with the land mass widening both to the near and the far side and going farther down into the sea, Greece is not as wide as it had begun, but nevertheless it is of great size again and extends as a virtual peninsula. It is called the Peloponnesos, and at the same time, because of the bays and promontories, by which it is incised as if by veins, it is similar to the leaf of a plane tree,[35] because it spreads rather widely from a slender stem.

39. After Macedonia, first comes Thessaly, and after it Magnesia, Phthiotis, Doris, Locris, Phocis, Boeotia, Atthis [Attica], and the Megarid; but most famous of all is Atthis. In the Peloponnesos are Argolis, Laconice, Messenia, Achaian Elis, and Arcadia; farther on are Aetolia, Acarnania, and Epiros, all the way to the Adriatic. **40.** Of the places and cities that the sea does not wash up on, the following are the ones especially worth remembering: in Thessaly nowadays Larissa is best known, but in the old days Iolcos was; in Magnesia, Antronia; in Phthiotis, Phthia;[36] < . . . >; in Locris, Cynos and Calliaros; in Phocis, Delphi, Mt. Parnassos, and both the shrine and the oracle of Apollo; in Boeotia, Thebes and Mt. Cithaeron, which is celebrated in song and legend; **41.** in Atthis, Eleusis, which is sacred to Ceres, and Athens, more famous than needs to be pointed out; in the Megarid, Megara, from which the region takes its name; likewise, in the Argolid, Argos, along with Mycenae and the temple of Juno,[37] which is very famous for its antiquity and for its cult; in Laconice, Therapnae, Lacedaemon, Amyclae, and Mt. Taÿgetus; in Messenia, Messenia and Methone; **42.** in Achaia-and-Elis, once the Pisa of Oinomaüs, Elis, still famous today,

---

35. This is the leaf of the mulberry fig. From the Middle Ages until relatively recent times, the Peloponnesos' ancient name, now restored, had fallen into disuse, and it was known as the Morea, because its outline resembles this leaf (Grk. *moron* and Lat. *morum* are translated into English as *mulberry*). See Robert Liddell, *The Morea* (London: Jonathan Cape, 1958). So inherently Greek was this image of the leaf that in the late nineteenth century the French poet Jean Moreas (né Ioannis Papadiamantopoulos) expressed his ethnicity by adapting his nom de plume from the Morea even though he was an Athenian by birth.

36. Silberman (1988) and Parroni (1984) print a lacuna after Phthia; Ranstrand (1971) does not.

37. The famous Heraeum was forty stades from Argos, ten from Mycenae (see Strabo 8.6.2). Pausanias (2.17.1–7) describes the sanctuary and its surroundings in some detail.

and the shrine of Olympian Jupiter, known mainly, in fact, for its athletic competition and unique inviolability but also for the actual statue that is the work of Phidias.

43. The Peloponnesian peoples ring Arcadia on all sides. In Arcadia are the cities of Psophis, Tegea, and Orchomenos, along with Mt. Pholoë, Mt. Cyllene, Mt. Parthenius, and Mt. Maenalus and the Erymanthus and Ladon Rivers; in Aetolia, the town of Naupactos; in Arcanania, that of Stratos; in Epirus, the temple of Jupiter Dodonaeus and likewise the sacred spring. Although this spring is cold, and although like all other springs it extinguishes burning torches that are immersed in it, it lights them up again when from afar they are moved, unlit, toward it.

44. When, however, one coasts along the shores, the course after Point Sepias lies beside Demetrias, Halos, Pteleon, and Echinos, to the Gulf of Pagasa. That gulf, embracing the city of Pagasa, takes in the Sperchios River and is remembered because the Minyans launched the Argo from there when they left for Colchis. **45.** The following places must first be passed by those sailing from there to Sunium: the sizable Gulf of Malia and equally sizable Opuntian Gulf, and on these gulfs the monument to the Laconian war-dead;[38] Thermopylae, Opoës, Scarphia, Cnemides, Alope, Anthedon, Larumna, and Aulis, the camp of Agamemnon's fleet and the Greeks who swore allegiance against Troy; Marathon, the witness of numerous heroic acts right from Theseus on but especially known for the slaughter of the Persians;[39] **46.** Rhamnus, small but still renowned, because in it is the shrine of Amphiaraüs and the Nemesis by Phidias;[40] then Thoricos and Brauronia, once cities,

---

38. This monument commemorated the battle of Thermopylae in 480 B.C.E. and still existed in the Augustan period (see Strabo 9.4.2 and 16): it was a group burial site (Grk. *polyandrion*) with five memorial *stelai*.

39. Herodotus (6.107–17) narrates both the preliminaries and the famous battle in 490 B.C.E. He concludes his account with the numbers of the dead on both sides (6,400 of the enemy, he says, and 192 Athenians). The tumulus (Grk. *sôros*) that covers the fallen Athenian heroes can still be seen today, but the epitaphs listing the dead by tribes (see Paus. 1.32.3) are lost. The mound is approximately thirty feet high and two hundred yards in circumference.

40. M. has mislocated the sanctuary of Amphiaraüs, which is actually located nearer to Oropos (cp. Paus. 1.34.2–3 with Silberman 1988, 188 n. 13). The legendary Amphiaraüs was celebrated at Argos both as a hero and as a prophet. He reconciled with Adrastus and joined him in the famous expedition to restore Polynices, one of Oedipus' sons, to the throne of Thebes (see Aeschylus *Sept.*

now mere names. Sunium is a promontory and terminates the coast of Hellas that faces east.

47. From there the land mass rotates to face south and goes back up as far as Megara; the land lies now with its front to the sea, the same way it did previously with its side.[41] Piraeus, Athens' port, is there, as well as the Scironian Rocks, infamous once upon a time (and even today) for Sciron's savage hospitality. **48.** Megara's territory runs up to the Isthmos, which gets its name because the Aegean Sea, being at a remove of four miles from the Ionian Sea, ties the Peloponnesos to Hellas by a narrow neck of land. On it is the town of Cenchreae; a temple of Neptune, which is renowned because of the so-called Isthmian Games; and Corinth, a city once famous for its wealth, better known later for its destruction, and now a Roman colony.[42] Corinth has a view of both seas from the peak of the acropolis they call Acrocorinth.[43]

---

for the story). Phidias (ca. 490–ca. 432) was the superintendent of art for Pericles' building project on the Acropolis at Athens. His most famous work was the Athena Parthenos (Paus. 1.24.5), which he sculpted himself; the statue of Nemesis (described at Paus. 1.33.3) is attributed to Phidias by M. and Pausanias but not by all witnesses.

41. M.'s description is a good example of the sweeping view he takes in describing landmasses, and this practice reflects the difference between chorography and geography as described by Ptolemy (*Geog.* 1.1). This technique also is consistent with the idea of M.'s map literacy, and a small-scale literary treatment cannot, by its nature, take in every nook and cranny on any important strip of coastline; M. is obliged to strike a balance that addresses the reader's ability to visualize what is being described at any given moment. M. describes Greece as having three fronts, almost as if it had three relatively straight sides. It comes as something of a surprise to discover that he considers Attica's western coast as part of Greece's southern front; the five promontories that face south (Attica and the four Peloponnesian ones) hardly seem to constitute a southern "front" to the untrained eye. On Roman maps, see book 2, n. 93.

42. The consul L. Mummius razed Corinth in 146 B.C.E., the same year that the Romans leveled Carthage. Julius Caesar refounded the city as a Roman colony in 44 B.C.E., with the official name Colonia Laus Julia Corinthiensis. The history of Corinth down to 338 B.C.E. has been examined critically by J.B. Salmon in *Wealthy Corinth* (Oxford: Clarendon, 1984), and its economic and social development in Roman times is explored by Donald Engels in *Roman Corinth: An Alternative Model for the Classical City* (Chicago: University of Chicago Press, 1990).

43. Acrocorinth is more or less an hour's hike from old Corinth to the top, and the climber is as likely as not to share the pinnacle with a wandering flock of sheep. Pollution is a problem in our time, but a clear day still affords a view of both seas from the peak.

49. Bays and promontories mangle the coast of the Peloponnesos, as we have noted:[44] from the east, Bucephalos, Chersonessus [Méthana], and Scyllaeon; to the south, Malea, Taenaros [Matapán], Acritas, and Ichthys; to the west, Chelonates and Araxos. The Epidaurians and Troezenians live between the Isthmos and Scyllaeon. The Epidaurians are famous for the temple of Aesculapius, the Troezenians glorious for their loyalty to an alliance with Athens.[45] **50.** The Saronic Gulf and the Gulfs of Schoenos and Pogon are located there, but on their shores are the towns of Epidaurus, Troezene, and Hermiona. Between Scyllaeon and Malea is the so-called Gulf of Argolis; between Malea and Taenaros, the Laconian Gulf; between Taenaros and Akritas, the Gulf of Asine; between Taenaros and Ichthys, the Gulf of Cyparissos.

51. On the Gulf of Argolis are the well-known Erasinus and Inachus Rivers and the well-known town of Lerne; on the Laconian Gulf are Gythium and the Eurotas; on Cape Taenaros itself is a temple and a cave of Neptune, similar in appearance and legend to what we called the Acherusian Cave on the Pontus;[46] in the Gulf of Asine is the Pamisum River; on the Gulf of Cyparissos is the Alpheus River. A city located on the shore gave its name to these gulfs—Cyparissos to the latter, Asine to the former. **52.** The Messenians and Pylians till the land, and Pylos actually lies beside the sea. Cyllene, Callipolis, and Patrae [Pátrai/Pátras] occupy that shore where the Chelonates and Araxos Rivers have their outlets, but Cyllene is distinguished because they think Mercury was born there.[47] After that, the Rhion—that is the sea's

---

44. Stated earlier, at 2.38.

45. The Troezenians remained loyal to Athens during the Persian War of 480–479 B.C.E. (see Hdt. 8.41–43, 72; 9.28, 31, 102, 105). Their loyalty underlies the now well known Decree of Themistocles (see R. Meiggs and D. Lewis, eds., *A Selection of Greek Historical Inscriptions*, rev. ed. [Oxford: Clarendon, 1988], 48–52, no. 23) and its attendant historical and interpretive difficulties. When Athens was abandoned in 480, some Athenians took refuge in Troezen.

46. See 1.103. The Acherusian Cave is associated with Hercules' labors.

47. Mercury was, in fact, called Cyllenian, but M. has confused the city of Cyllene on the coast of Elis with Mt. Cyllene (Grk. Kyllênê) in Arcadia (mentioned at 2.43). Mercury's birth was associated with Mt. Cyllene, as Vergil shows (*Aen.* 8.138–39). Perhaps the mistake occurred because M. knew that Mercury's birth was associated with a place called Cyllene, and because in Latin the onomastic adjective for Mt. Cyllene (*mons Cyllenius*) might have made the mountain seem to be a different place and led M. to mistake the town for the birthplace.

name there—cuts, by means of a narrow passage like a strait, into the side of the remaining shoreline and breaks in between the Aetolians and the Peloponnesians as far as the Isthmos.

53. There the Peloponnesian littoral starts to face north. On these shores are Aegion, Aegira, Olyros, and Sicyon, but on the opposite shores are Pagae, Creusis, Anticyra, Oeanthia, Cirrha [Itéa], Calydon (somewhat better known by name),[48] and Evenos beyond Rhion. In Acarnania, which is especially famous, are the town of Leucas and the Acheloüs River [Aspropótamo]. **54.** In Epiros nothing is better known than the Ambracian Gulf. The gulf, which lets in a great sea through its narrow jaws (less than a mile wide), makes it well known, as do the cities that line its shore—Actium, the Amphilochian Argives, and Ambracia [Árta], the royal seat of the Aeacids and of Pyrrhus in particular.[49] Beyond is Butroton, then the Ceraunian Mountains [Mali i Çikës with Kara Burun], and after these places a bend toward the Adriatic.

55. The Adriatic Sea is formed by a great retraction of the littoral and in fact covers a considerable breadth, although it reaches considerably farther in. It is surrounded by Illyric peoples as far as Tergeste [Trieste] but then by the Gallic and Italic peoples. The Partheni and Dasaretae occupy its first places; the Taulantii, Encheleae, and Phaeaces occupy what follows. **56.** After that come the Illyrii proper, then the Piraeans, Liburnians, and Istria.[50] The first city is Oricum [Eriko], the second

---

48. Calydon, in Aetolia, was famous in legend but not so much in history. Meleager's legendary boar hunt took place in the surrounding mountains (see Hom. *Il.* 9.529–99), and Augustus relocated its inhabitants at Nicopolis, which he founded to celebrate his victory over Anthony and Cleopatra in 31 B.C.E. at nearby Actium (see Strabo 7.7.5–6). Later accounts of Meleager (one of the Argonauts) extend his story to provide an etiological account of the term for guinea hens (Grk. *meleagrides*). B. Powell (*Classical Myth* [Englewood Cliffs, N.J.: Prentice Hall, 1995], 535–36) provides useful guidelines for interpreting the legend of the Calydonian boar hunt.

49. The Aeacids claimed to be descended from Aeacus, the grandfather of Achilles. Pyrrhus (318–272 B.C.E.), king of Epirus, is best known because in 280 B.C.E. he agreed to aid the Tarentines in their war against Rome. Fighting with his elephant corps, he defeated the Romans in that year and advanced within twenty-four miles of Rome. He suffered such heavy losses at Beneventum in 276 B.C.E. that he fled from Italy thereafter. In general, Pyrrhus achieved his military successes at too great a cost, and his accomplishment still lives on infamously in the phrase "a Pyrrhic victory."

50. On the name *Istria*, see book 2, n. 8.

Dyrrachium [Durazzo/Durrës], where Epidamnus used to be. (The Romans changed the name, because travelers headed there thought of the name as an omen,[51] as if they were going "to damnation.")[52] **57.** Farther on are Apollonia [Polan], Salona [Solin], Iader [Zadar], Narona, Tragurium [Trogir], the Gulf of Pola, and Pola, which was once inhabited, as they tell it, by Colchians. How much things change! Now Pola is a Roman colony. Moreover, the rivers are the Aeas [Vijosë], the Nar [Neretva], and the Danube (which here is called the Ister); but the Aeas comes after Apollonia, and the Nar comes between the Piraeans and the Liburnians, while the Ister runs through the territory of the Istrians.[53] Tergeste, located in the deepest part of the Adriatic Gulf, is the boundary of Illyricum.

Italy

58. About Italy a few things will be said, more because the order requires it than because it needs to be described. All its places are well known.[54] From the Alps it begins its extension into the sea, and as it proceeds it is elevated down the middle by the continuous ridge of the Apennines. Italy runs down solid for a long time between the Adriatic

---

51. The wordplay is clear, and M. echoes the old Latin tag about names being omens, *nomen atque omen* (Plautus *Persa* 625). In general, the ancients believed that a name revealed the essence, good or bad, of the thing named. A name was considered to be intrinsic to the character of its bearer. As here, the omen is not always favorable: Cicero (*Pro Rosc. Amer.* 16.47) says that "names are hateful things" [nomina sunt odiosa]; cp. Ov. *Her.* 13.53–54.

52. The ominous pun is bilingual. The Greek preposition *epi* means "to" or "toward" when it takes the accusative case. *Damnus* in the Greek word merely sounds like Latin *damnum* (loss, damage, harm, forfeiture).

53. See 2.7–8 and nn. 8 and 9 there. The idea that the Danube/Ister has another mouth in the Adriatic (cp. 2.63) is erroneous, but for this canonical error, see Parroni 1984, 320, ad loc.; and Silberman 1988, 196 n. 10. This mythical branch of the river was the route taken by the Argonauts from the Black Sea to the Mediterranean (cp. Ap. Rhod. 4.282–96). In any case, the imagined Adriatic debouchment is counted among the river's seven mouths. The other six mouths are located on the Black Sea.

54. Let the reader beware. Despite his confidence, M. makes a number of errors in his account of Italy. For example, see book 2, nn. 47, 53, and 63, on obvious geographical errors; and M. can always make historical ones (see book 2, n. 89).

and Tuscan Seas (also known as the Upper and Lower Seas). But when it is far removed from its beginning, it divides into two horns, and it looks off toward the Sicilian Sea with one horn, toward the Ionian Sea with the other. Italy as a whole is narrow, and in some places much narrower than where it had begun.

59. Various peoples cultivate its interior. The Carni and Veneti cultivate the left part up to Gallia Togata; then come Italic peoples—Picentines, Frentani, Dauni, Apulians, Calabri, and Sallentines. To the right, at the foot of the Alps, are the Ligurians; at the foot of the Apennines, Etruria; after that, Latium, the Volsci, Campania, and, below Lucania, the Bruttii. **60.** Of the cities that are inhabited far from the sea, the wealthiest are, to the left side, Antenor's Patavium [Padova/Padua], Mutina [Modena], and Bononia [Bologna], colonies of the Romans; to the right, Capua, founded by the Tuscans, and Rome, long ago founded by shepherds, now a second book in itself if there is to be discussion on the topic.[55]

61. On the shores, by contrast, Concordia[56] is next after Tergeste. Between them flows the Timavus [Timavo], which rises from nine heads but debouches through a single mouth.[57] Then, not far from the sea, the Natiso [Natisone] River runs beside rich Aquileia. Farther on is Altinum [Altino]. **62.** The Padus [Po] occupies the upper coast over a considerable expanse. In fact, where it rises from the very roots of Mt. Vesulus [Monte Viso], it first gathers itself from small springs and is somewhat scant and meager. Then the river increases and is fed by other rivers so much that at the end it lets into the sea through seven mouths. One of these mouths they call the Great Padus. **63.** Once it begins, the river rushes forward with such speed that for a long time it drives, with waves breaking, the same waters it began with and preserves its own bed even in the sea until the Ister River, flowing in with the same force from the opposite shore of Istria, meets it.[58] Because of

---

55. This is, to my way of thinking, M.'s firmest clue to what he *may* have intended as his next work (see my introduction, n. 37).

56. Roman and modern practice coincide: Pliny's Concordia is Concordia Sagittaria, and the modern village also goes by both names.

57. Vergil (*Aen.* 1.245) also specified nine fountainheads; Polybius said seven (see Strabo 5.1.8). For the dangers and problems of the Timavus (Timavo) at its estuary, see R.R. Dyer, "Timavus and the Supine at Vergil *Aen.* 1.246," *Classical World* 89, no. 5 (May/June 1996): 403–8.

58. See book 2, n. 53.

this phenomenon, for those sailing through that vicinity, where the rivers meet from both sides, a drink of fresh water is possible in the midst of salty sea.[59]

64. The route from the Padus to Ancona crosses Ravenna, Ariminum [Rimini], Pisaurum [Pesaro], the colony of Fanum [Fano], the Metaurus River, and the Aesis River. And in fact, the terminus sits in the narrow joint—like a bent elbow [Grk. *ankôn*]—of those two famous promontories that meet there from opposite sides, and thus it was called Ancon by the Greeks; Ancona lies between the Gallic and Italic peoples like a boundary stone. 65. The shores of Picenum welcome travelers beyond this point. On these shores are the cities of Numana [Umana], Potentia [Santa Maria di Potenza], Cluana, and Cupra[60] [Cupramarittima] and, moreover, the strongholds of Firmum [Fermo], Adria [Atri], and Truentinum (the adjacent river [Tronto] is also its namesake). After that, the Frentani hold the mouths of the Matrinus and Aternus [Pescara] Rivers, as well as the cities of Buca [Termoli] and Histonium [Vasto]. The Daunians, however, have the Tifernus [Biferno] River and the towns of Cliternia [Campomarino], Larinum [Larino], and Teanum, as well as Mt. Garganus [Gargano]. 66. A bay by the name of Urias [Lago di Varano], moderate in size but often harsh of access, is surrounded by the continuous Apulian shore. It is above both Sipontum [Santa Maria di Siponto]—or, as the Greeks said, Sipiuntum—and the river contiguous with Canusium [Canosa di Puglia], the Aufidus [Ufente] as they call it; after that are Barium [Bari], Gnatia [Torre d'Egnazia], and Rudiae [Rugge], renowned for Ennius; and at this point in Calabria[61] are Brundisium [Brindisi], Valetium [Valeso], Lupiae [Lecce], and Mt. Hydrus, then the Sallentine Fields, the coast of Sallentum, and the Greek city Callipolis [Gallipoli].

67. The Adriatic reaches this far; so does one side of Italy. Its coast-

---

59. It always amuses the modern reader to confront M.'s gullibility even in simple matters.

60. Cupra is a local goddess who may be the same as Bona Dea among the Romans. In nearby Grottamare are the remains of a temple of Cupra.

61. Since today's Calabria is located in the "toe" of the Italian "boot," students and tourists are surprised to find Roman Calabria on the "heel." In the Middle Ages, when Lombard invaders occupied Roman Calabria in the early eighth century, Byzantine bureaucrats shifted the name to the "toe," where ancient Bruttium had been located.

line breaks into two horns, in fact, as we have said.[62] It lets the sea enter between both horns, however, and divides it several times by slender promontories. The coast does not go around, then, with a uniform edge, and it receives the sea not spread out and wide open but in bays. 68. The first one is called the Gulf of Tarentum, between Point Sallentum and Point Lacinium [Capo Colonna], and on it are Tarentus [Taranto], Metapontum [Metaponto], Heraclea, Croto [Crotone], and Thurium. Second is the Bay of Scyllaceum [Gulf of Squillace], between Point Lacinium and Zephyr [Grk., West Wind] Point, and on this bay is Petelia [Strongoli], Carcinus, Scyllaceum [Squillace], and Mystiae. The third one, between Zephyr Point and Bruttium, passes around Bruttium, Consentia [Cosenza], Caulonia, and Locri. In Bruttium are Columna Rhegia, Rhegium [Reggio], Scylla, Taurianum, and Metaurum.

69. From here there is a bend to the Tuscan Sea and the second side of the same land. On this side of Italy are Medma, Hipponium (or Vibo), Temesa, Clampetia [San Lucido], Blanda, Buxentum, Velia, Palinurus [Capo Palinuro] (once the name of a Trojan helmsman, now the name of a place), the Gulf of Paestum [Gulf of Salerno], the town of Paestum, the Silerus [Sele] River, Picentia [Vicenza], Petrae (which the Sirens once inhabited), Point Minerva [Punta della Campanella]—all places in Lucania;[63] 70. then the Bay of Puteoli [Bay of Naples], Syrrentum [Sorrento], Herculaneum, a view of Mt. Vesuvius, Pompeii, Neapolis [Naples], Puteoli [Pozzuoli], the Lucrine Lake and Avernus, Baiae,

---

62. See 2.58. Again moderns sometimes are surprised to find that in antiquity Italy was not conceived of as boot-shaped. Instead, ancient geographers considered—correctly—that the Italian peninsula simply ended in two distinct major promontories. Italy is painted with the same sweeping strokes as Greece (see book 2, n. 41)—as having three broad fronts on the sea, one each facing east, south, and west. Geometry (Grk. *geômetria*) was invented as a means to measure land with some precision. M.'s method leads to a loss of subtlety and geographic nuance, a universal fault of the handbook genre and also, it seems, of literary chorography (cp. Ptol. *Geog.* 1.1). Strabo (5.1.2–3) struggles to describe the Italian peninsula's angularity, and the beauty of Italy from a scientific point of view, as of other places, is lost on M.'s reader. Lucan (2.435–38) describes the separation of Sicily from Italy as resulting from the action of the sea.

63. In fact the Silerus River is the boundary between Lucania and Campania (see Pliny *HN* 3.71 and Strabo 6.255). Pliny spells the river's name *Silarus*, but M.'s spelling is probably better. Picentia, Petrae, and Point Minerva are already in Campania.

Misenum [Miseno] (the name of a place now, but once the name of a Trojan soldier),[64] Cumae, Liternum, the Volturnus River, the town of Volturnum [Volturno]—the lovely shores of Campania; **71.** then Sinoëssa, the Liris [Liri] River, Minturnae, Formiae [Formia], Fundi [Fondi], Tarracina [Terracina], Circeia (once the home of Circe), Antium [Anzio], Aphrodisium, Ardea, Laurentum, and Ostia on the near side of the Tiber. **72.** Above it are Pyrgi, the Minio [Mignone] River, Castrum Novum [Torre Chiaruccia], Graviscae [Porto Clementino], Cosa, Telamon, Populonia [Porto Baratti], the Caecina [Cecina] River, and Pisae [Pisa]—Etruscan localities and rivers; after that comes what belongs to the Ligurians, Luna [Luni], Tigula, Genua [Genova/Genoa], Sabatia, and Albingaunum [Albenga]; then come the rivers Paulo [Paglione] and Varum [Var], both descending from the Alps, but the Varum somewhat better known because it marks the boundary of Italy. **73.** The Alps themselves spread over a considerable expanse from these shores and run in a long stretch, first to the north; then, after they have reached Germany, they go forth with an eastward thrust; and after dividing savage peoples from one another, they penetrate all the way to Thrace.

Gaul

74. Gaul, which is divided by Lake Lemannus [Lake Leman/Lake Geneva] and the Cebennici [Cévennes] Mountains into two parts, and which abuts the Tuscan Sea on one side, the Ocean on the other, reaches all the way to the Pyrenees from the Varum River on this side and from the Rhenus [Rhein/Rhine] on the far side. The part located beside Our Sea—it was once Gallia Bracata, now it is Gallia Narbonensis—is more cultivated and more plentifully sown and therefore also more productive.[65] **75.** The wealthiest of the cities are Vasio [Vaison la Romaine]

---

64. A lively ride by bus and train from Naples confirmed that the headland of Cape Misenum was shaped naturally like a huge tumulus, and for that reason the site attracted the legend of Misenus, Aeneas' trumpeter, who died at Triton's hands after challenging the god to a hubristic musical contest (see Verg. *Aen.* 6.162–74). Topography probably explains other legendary burial sites, like that of Aeneas' helmsman Palinurus (2.69) or those of Menelaüs' helmsman (2.103) and Hannibal's (2.116). The principle certainly applies to the alleged tumulus of Antaeus at 3.106.

65. Gallia Narbonensis, one of four Augustan provinces in Gaul, is the region of modern Provence in southern France. Its territory included Massilia

(belonging to the Vocontii), Vienne (the Allobroges), Avennio [Avignon][66] (the Cavares), Nemausus [Nîmes] (the Arecomici), Tolosa [Toulouse] (the Tectosages), Arausio [Orange] (the veterans of Legion II), Arelate [Arles] (the veterans of Legion VI), and Beterrae [Béziers] (the veterans of Legion VII). The colony, however, of the Atacini and of the veterans of Legion X (who once brought help to these lands) leads the pack and is now an honored name, Martius Narbo [Narbonne].

76. On the littoral there are a number of places with names, but cities are rare, because harbors are rare. The whole strip is exposed to the south wind and to the southwest wind.[67] Nicaea [Nice] is immediately next to the Alps; so is the town of the Deciates and also Antipolis [Antibes]. 77. Then comes Forum Iulii [Frejús], a colony of veterans from Legion VIII; and at that point after Athenopolis [Saint-Tropez], Olbia, Tauroïs [Le Brusc?], and Citharistes [Ceyreste] comes Lacydon, the Port of Massilia, on which is Massilia [Marseilles] itself. This last city originated with Phocaeans, was long ago founded among violent peoples, but now borders on peoples as different as they are peaceful. It is amazing how easily these Phocaeans took up a foreign abode in those days yet still maintain their own tradition. 78. Between it and the Rhodanus [Rhône], Maritima Avaticorum sits beside a marsh, and the Marian Canal[68] empties part of its river into the sea by means of a navigable channel. In general, the shore, Litus Lapideum [Lat., Rocky Beach; the Crau] as they call it, is undistinguished. Here, they report, while Hercules was fighting Alebion and Dercynos, the sons of Neptune, and when his arrows had run out, he

---

(Marseilles), which was founded as a trading post by Phocaean Greeks ca. 600 B.C.E. The Romans began their conquest ca. 125 B.C.E., and the region became a province (*provincia*) in 121 B.C.E. The Romans referred to the area simply as Provincia (hence the modern name). Gallia Bracata (Lat., Trousered Gaul) was an informal term that distinguished the area from Gallia Comata (Lat., Longhaired Gaul). The image distinguished civilized (trousered) Roman Gaul from wild, uncivilized (longhaired) Gaul. In general, Narbonensis was commercially and agriculturally prosperous for a long time.

66. At Avignon in 1335 C.E. Petrarch saw Heiric's codex of M.'s work (Vat. lat. 4929). Petrarch's copy has been lost, but a copy of it has survived, together with Petrarch's own marginal note ("Avinio, ubi nunc sumus 1335").

67. The south wind, Auster, may be identified with the sirocco, and the southwest wind is Africus, so named because it blows into Italy from Africa.

68. To counter a silting problem on the lower Rhone, Gaius Marius had the canal dug between 105 and 103 B.C.E., as he prepared for the imminent invasion of Italy by the Teutones and Cimbri. The canal went from Arles to the sea at Fos-sur-Mer, where there was a Roman port (now under water). See also Pliny *HN* 3.34 and Strabo 4.1.8.

was helped by a rain of rocks at the hands of Jupiter, whom he had invoked. You would believe that it had rained rocks—so numerously and so widely do they lie scattered all over![69]

79. The Rhodanus rises not far from the sources of the Ister and the Rhenus. It is then received by Lake Lemannus, retains its force, keeps itself intact through the middle of the lake, and emerges as powerful as it arrived. Then, on the opposite side, heading to the west, the river divides the Gauls for some distance; and later, with its course drawn southward, it enters Gallia Narbonensis. At this point it is voluminous, and it is now and then even more voluminous from the entrance of other rivers; and it debouches between the Volcan and Cavaran peoples. 80. Farther on are the marshes of the Volci, the Ledum [Les] River, the fort of Latara, and Mesua Hill, which is surrounded almost completely by the sea, an island except where it is tied to the continent by a narrow mound. Then, descending from the Cebennae [Cévennes] Mountains, the Arauris [Hérault] flows beside Agatha [Agde], the Orbis [Orb] beside Beterrae. 81. The Atax [Aude], descending from the Pyrenees, is slight and shallow wherever it comes with its original waters. At this point it retains its otherwise huge bed but is never navigable except when it reaches Narbo. When it is swollen from winter storms, however, this river routinely rises so high that it actually cannot contain itself. Lake Rubraesus, relatively spacious but slight of access where it lets the sea in, becomes the river basin.

82. Farther on is Leucata (the name of the coast) and the spring of Salsula [Fontaine de Salses],[70] which flows down with waters that are not sweet but saltier than the sea's. Beside Salsula is a plain that is bright green from a slight and slender marsh grass but supported atop the swamp that passes under it. Its middle section makes that clear, since it is cut off from the surrounding parts, floats like an island, and

---

69. The Crau is a broad plain and was usually called *Lapideus Campus* or *Lapidei Campi* in Latin sources, and only much later *Campus Cravensis*. Also, Alebion's name is given as Ialebion in the canonical versions of the story.

70. Salsula seems to have been a salt marsh sacred to the Celtic water divinity Sulis, who was often identified with Roman Minerva (as at Aquae Sulis [Bath] in Britain). Her worship centered around springs and apparently served in most places as a healing cult. In addition to healing, like Minerva, Sulis was renowned for wisdom and in all probability for military expertise too. Sulis may also be connected to the sun, to judge from the fragmentary pedimental sculptures at Aquae Sulis; and the following etymology has been proposed for her name: *sul-* = Lat. *sol* = Eng. *sun*.

allows itself to be driven and pulled.[71] **83.** What is more, indeed, where these surrounding parts are dug all the way through to the bottom, the sea is revealed because it rises up from below. As a result, Greek writers, and even our own, thought it right, either from ignorance of the truth or else from the pleasure of lying (even for sensible writers), to pass on to posterity the story that in this region a fish was pulled from deep within the earth, because after the fish had penetrated from the sea to this place, it was killed by a blow from its captors and brought up through those holes. **84.** Next is the coast of the Sordones and the small Telis and Ticis Rivers (both quite violent when swollen), the colony of Ruscino [Castel Rousillon], and the village of Eliberrae [Elne], which is the slender vestige of a once-great city and its once-great wealth. Then, between spurs of the Pyrenees, come the saltless Port Venus and the district of Cervaria [Cerbère], the boundary of Gaul.

Spain

85. The Pyrenees, to begin with, extend from here to the Britannic Ocean. Then, after shifting direction, the range bursts into the lands of Spain, and excluded from its smaller division to the right, it protracts its continuous sides in an uninterrupted path until it reaches the western shores after going across the entire province in a single dividing line.

86. Spain actually is girt by the sea except where it is contiguous with Gaul,[72] and it is especially narrow at the places of contact. Spain extends gradually into Our Sea and Ocean, and becoming increasingly wider the farther west it goes, it becomes widest right there.[73] Spain is also teeming with men,[74] horses, iron, lead, copper, silver,

---

71. See 1.55 on the floating island of Chemmis in Aegypt. The younger Pliny (*Ep.* 8.20) evinces scientific curiosity about a similar phenomenon in Lake Vadimo, which is now much smaller as Lago di Bassano. He begins his letter by observing how willingly people travel long distances to see such wonders, even though they do not appreciate similar phenomena nearer to home. In a paragraph devoted to floating islands (*HN* 2.209; cp. also Seneca *QNat.* 3.25.8), the elder Pliny lists those of Lake Vadimo but does not mention this marsh on the Gallic coast. In any case, the nephew does not seem to know his uncle's discussion.

72. See 2.74, where M. describes the geographic division of Gaul into two parts or "sides" [latera]. See also book 1, n. 3.

73. M. is describing Spain's northernmost width more or less along the line of the Pyrenees. See 2.85 and also Pliny *HN* 4.110.

74. *Viri* again (see book 1, n. 29). M. treats men here as a commodity.

and gold, and it is so fertile that wherever it changes and is barren for lack of water, it still supports flax or esparto.[75] **87.** It is, however, distinguished by three names. Part of it is called Tarraconensis, part Baetica, and part Lusitania [Portugal]. Tarraconensis borders on the Gauls at one extreme, on Baetica and Lusitania at the other. Where it looks south, it thrusts its sides along Our Sea; where it looks north, along Ocean. The Anas [Guadiana] River separates the other two regions there, and thus Baetica faces both seas—the Atlantic to the west, Our Sea to the south—while Lusitania is situated only along the Atlantic, but with its lateral extension to the north, its front to the west.

88. The most renowned of the inland[76] cities in Tarraconensis were Palantia [Palencia] and Numantia (nowadays it is Caesaraugusta [Saragossa]); in Lusitania, Emerita [Mérida]; and in Baetica, Astigi [Ecija], Hispal [Seville], and Corduba [Córdova].

89. If, however, you coast along the shores, right after Cervaria comes the cliff that thrusts the Pyrenees out into the sea, next the Ticis River near Rhoda, next Clodianum near Emporiae, and then Mt. Jupiter. They call its western face the Stairs of Hannibal, because outcroppings of cliffs rise up from below, stepwise, between small spaces. **90.** Then, near Tarraco, are the small towns of Blande, Iluro [Mataró], Baetulo [Madalona], Barcino [Barcelona], Subur, and Tolobi; small rivers, the Baetulo [Besos] beside Mt. Jupiter, the Rubricatum [Llobregat] on the shore of Barcino, and the Maius between Subur and Tolobis. Tarraco [Tarragona] is the city on these shores that is wealthiest in maritime resources. The moderate Tulcis [Francoli] River runs beside it, and on the farther side, the mighty Hiberus [Ebro] runs beside Dertosa [Tortosa].

91. From there the sea winds its way into the land, and then as soon as it is let in with a great sweep, it is divided into two bays by the promontory they call Ferraria [Cabo de la Nao]. **92.** The first is called the Bay of Sucro. It is the larger one and admits the sea with quite a large mouth, but the farther one enters it, the narrower it gets. This bay takes in the unimportant Sorobis [Serpis], Turia, and Sucro [Júcar] Rivers. It includes some cities too, in fact, but the best-known are Valentia [Valencia] and that famous city, Saguntum, which is renowned for

---

75. Esparto is a wild field grass that requires no cultivation. Mela's regional pride has surfaced here (see my introduction, n. 2).

76. The word for "inland" is *mediterraneis* (see book 1, n. 8).

its loyalty as well as its troubles.⁷⁷ **93.** Next, the Bay of Ilice holds Allo [Allone], Lucentia [Alicante], and Ilice [Elche] (whence its name). Here now the land goes farther into the sea and makes Spain broader than it had been.

94. At the same time, though, from the places mentioned in this vicinity to the starting point of Baetica, nothing needs to be reported except Carthage [Cartagena], which the Carthaginian general Hasdrubal founded.⁷⁸ On Baetica's coast there are obscure towns, of which mention is relevant only for proper sequence. There is Urci on the Bay of Urci, as they call it; outside the bay are Abdera [Adra], Suel, Ex, Maenoba, Malaca [Málaga], Salduba, Lacippo, and Barbesula. **95.** Then the sea becomes very narrow, and mountains constitute the closest shores between Europe and Africa. The Pillars of Hercules, as we said at the beginning,⁷⁹ Abila and Calpes, each jut into the sea in fact, but Calpes more so and almost totally. Calpes is hollowed out to an amazing degree, and on its western face its side opens more or less halfway. From there, for those who enter, the whole grotto is reasonably passable for almost its whole width. **96.** There is a bay beyond that point, and on it is Carteia. Carteia, some think, used to be Tartessos.⁸⁰ Tingentera, which Phoenicians who crossed from Africa still inhabit—and where we're from too—is located there. Then Melaria, Bello, and Baesippo [Barbate] occupy the shore of the Strait all the way to Point Juno. At this stage that promontory runs to the west and to Ocean with a sidewise ridge, and it faces that promontory in Africa

---

77. In 220 B.C.E. Hannibal began the siege of Saguntum, which remained loyal to Rome and held out until it fell in November 219 B.C.E. The siege is considered to be the immediate cause of the Second Punic War (218–201 B.C.E.).

78. This city was founded as Mastia but then refounded by Hasdrubal ca. 228 B.C.E. as Carthago Nova (Cartagena). It is near the famous silver mines that enriched first the Carthaginians and then the Romans. It quickly became a center of activity and was the North African Carthaginians' most important port in Spain until it was captured by Scipio Africanus Maior in 209 B.C.E., during the Second Punic War (218–201). The Romans exploited Iberian mineral wealth mercilessly during the next century.

79. See 1.27.

80. On the name and the problem of Tartessos, see Silberman 1988. Tartessos, a Phoenician settlement, is the biblical Tarshish, although it is not entirely clear whether Tarshish applies to the settlement (Tartessos) or to Tartessis, the entire littoral west of Gibraltar.

that we had said was called Ampelusia.[81] It terminates Europe where Our Seas are situated.

Islands

97. The island of Gades [Cádiz], which meets travelers as they exit the Strait, is a reminder to mention all the other islands before the narrative proceeds, as we promised at the beginning,[82] to the shores of Ocean and the earth's periphery. There are a few islands in Maeotis—it seems easiest to begin there—but they are not all under cultivation, since they do not produce even range grass generously. That is the reason the meat of huge fish is dried by the inhabitants in the sun and ground to a powder for use as flour.[83]

98. There are a few islands in the Pontus also. Leuce is thrust up opposite the mouth of the Borysthenes. It is relatively small and, because Achilles is buried there, has the eponym of Achillea. Not far from the Colchians is Aria, which was dedicated to Mars, as told in legend, and which produced birds that hurled their feathers like spears— along with the greatest carnage of newcomers. There are six islands among the mouths of the Ister, of which Peuce [Piczina] is the best known and most important. Thynias [Kefken Adasi], next to the land of the Mariandyni, has a city that they call Bithynis because Bithynians live there. **99.** Opposite the Thracian Bosphorus, two islands that are small and scarcely removed from one another were once believed, and said, to crash together: they are called Cyaneae and Symplegades.[84] In the Propontis, only Proconnesos is inhabited.

81. That is, the headland of the Iberian Peninsula runs sideways to the Mediterranean at the Strait of Gibraltar. On Ampelusia, see 1.25 and n. 24 there.

82. See 1.2. M. returns later to Gades, which he describes in greater detail at 3.46.

83. This practice is not attested otherwise for peoples in this region, but it is associated elsewhere with Ichthyophagoi (Grk., Fish-Eaters), a vague term applied to different coastal peoples in Africa and Asia. Strabo (15.2.2) describes an Asian people of this name who use a ground-fish flour like the one described here. Fish, in any case, provided the main source of protein in the Mediterranean diet, as it does generally for coastal peoples and islanders.

84. The Symplegades (Grk., Crashing Rocks) were two islands near the entranceway to the Pontus. *Cyaneae* and *Symplegades* are both plural nouns. M.'s point is that these two islands together could be called by either name. According to legend, these islands originated as rocks that crashed together and crushed any ship sailing between them. After Jason and the Argonauts suc-

100. Outside the Hellespont, of the islands adjacent to the Asiatic regions, the most renowned are Tenedos, opposite the coast of Sigeum, and—in the order listed—those islands that spread out near the spur of the Taurus Mountains, and which some authors thought were called the Macarôn [Grk., (Islands) of the Blessed], either because they were moderately blessed in climate and soil,[85] or because Macar had held them under his own sway and that of his descendants: **101.** in the Troad, Lesbos and on it once the five towns of Antissa, Pyrrha, Eresos, Methymna, Mytilene; in Ionia, Chios and Samos; in Caria, Coös [Kos/Cos]; in Lycia, Rhodes. On the latter islands there are individual cities of the same name, and on Rhodes in the past there were, as well, the three cities of Lindos, Camiros, and Ialysos. **102.** Those islands that lie—unluckily for those sailing by—directly opposite the spur of the Taurus Range are called Chelidonian.[86] Cyprus runs in an east-west direction into the biggest gulf that Asia takes in, and it lies more or less in its center. It stretches in a straight ridge between Cilicia and Syria, and as an island that at one time held nine kingdoms and now sustains a number of cities (the most renowned being Salamis, Paphos, and Old Paphos, where they claim Venus first emerged from the sea), Cyprus is huge.

103. Arados [Rûad] is a small island in Phoenicia, and the whole island is coast-to-coast town, but it is a crowded town, because it is legal to build apartment buildings.[87] Canopos is small and lies before

---

ceeded in negotiating them, the rocks became fixed in place as islands. Storms, high winds, and shoals were familiar dangers to Mediterranean sailors, but the ice floes off the northerly shores of the Pontus would have surprised them and may have been preserved in a cultural memory that underlies the legend of the Symplegades: see L. Casson, *The Ancient Mariners*, 2d ed. (Princeton: Princeton University Press, 1991), 59–60. The story of these cruel Crashing Rocks near the mouth of the Black Sea is related, as cause or effect, to the tradition about the Pontus' old name (see book 1, n. 73).

85. The inhabitants of these islands are considered blessed (Grk. *makares*) by the soil's fertility (if that is the origin of their name). The islands themselves are not to be confused with the Fortunate Isles (Fortunatae Insulae) in the Atlantic, which are so lush that plants reproduce spontaneously (3.102).

86. This spur is the promontory of Chelidonia (Grk., Swallow Point), on the southern coast of Lycia, and these small islands mark the dangerous shallows that surround it.

87. Strabo (16.2.13) describes the small island and its crowded conditions, and he later says (16.2.23) that Tyre, another island city, is almost as built-up as Arados, adding that "they say the high-rise domiciles here [Tyre] have more floors than those at Rome. . . ." Fire, collapse, and the demands of the real estate

the so-called Canopic mouth of the Nile. Menelaüs' helmsman Canopus died there accidentally, and he gave his name to the island, which then gave its name to that mouth. **104.** Pharos is linked to Alexandria by a bridge now, but once upon a time, as transmitted in the Homeric epic,[88] it was removed from those shores by a whole day's sail. If that was the case, it seems possible to researchers that the Nile provided the cause for such a great change. As long as the river dredges silt from its bed, and especially during the period while the river is dredging it up, the Nile adds the silt to the shoreline, increases the land mass, and extends the area of the increasing land mass into the neighboring shallows. **105.** In Africa, opposite the greater Bay of Syrtis, is Euteletos; opposite the promontories of the lesser Syrtis are Menis [Jerba] and Cercina [Kerkenah]; opposite the Gulf of Carthage are Chyarae, Thylae, and Aegatae, memorable for the bloody Roman defeat.[89]

106. Several additional islands are located off the shores of Europe: in the Aegean Sea near Thrace are Thasos, Imbros, Samothrace, Scandile, Polyaegos, Sciathos, Halonessos, and—opposite Mt. Athos—Lemnos, where at one time only women are said to have lived, after all the men had been slaughtered. The Gulf of Pagasa looks on Scyron and encloses Cicynethon. **107.** Euboea causes Point Geraestos and Point Caphereus to protrude southward and Point Cenaeum northward. Euboea is never wide and has a breadth of two miles where it is narrowest, but it is long and lies along the whole of Boeotia, separated from its coastline by a narrow strait. **108.** They call that strait Euripos. It has a swift current and flows in alternating directions seven times a day

---

market no doubt created dangers at Arados and Tyre as at Rome (cp. Strabo 5.3.7), and Strabo noted the destruction caused by earthquake at Tyre. (Tyre was *instabilis*, according to Lucan [3.217], and renowned for its earthquakes, according to the younger Seneca [*QNat.* 6.1.13 and 6.26.4].)

88. Hom. *Od.* 4.354–57. Strabo (1.2.23) defends Homer—somewhat speciously, by our standards—against the charges of the ignorant.

89. M. is simply wrong. The Aegatae, more familiarly known in Latin as the Aegates, are the Goat Islands, now called the Aegadian Isles, off the western coast of Sicily between Drepanum and Lilybaeum. The phrase *Romana clades* [the bloody Roman defeat] must mean that the Romans lost the battle, not that they inflicted a defeat on their enemy—cp. the familiar phrases *clades Variana* and *clades Lolliana*, as well as M.'s description of Marathon at 2.45, *Persica maxime clade pernotus* [especially known for the slaughter of the Persians]. But the battle of Aegatae was the Roman victory that ended the First Punic War (264–241 B.C.E.). A shortcoming of M.'s narrative technique also makes these islands appear much closer to Africa than they are.

and seven times a night, with its waves changing direction too. It flows so unusually that it frustrates even the winds as well as ships with the wind to their backs.[90] There are some towns on the island, namely, Styra, Eretria, Pyrrha, Nesos, and Oichalia, but the wealthiest cities are Carystos and Chalchis.

109. In Atthis, Helene is the isle known for the adultery of Helen,[91] and Salamis is even better known for the destruction of the Persian fleet.[92] In the vicinity of the Peloponnesos, but still at this point on the Aegean side, are Pityussa and Aegina; off the coast of Epidaurus, among other obscure islands, Calauria, famous for Demosthenes' demise at Troizene; **110.** in the Myrtoän Sea, Cythera opposite Malea, as well as Theganusa and the isles of Oinussae opposite Mt. Acritas; on the Ionian Sea, Prote, Asteria, Cephallania, Neritos, Same, Zacynthos, Dulichium, and, among those not obscure, Ithaca, which is mainly illustrious for the name of Ulysses; in Epiros, the Echinades group and another group formerly called the Plotae, now called the Strophades;[93] opposite the Ambracian Gulf, Leucadia [Leucas] and, bordering on the

---

90. There are no true tides in the Mediterranean, but the Greek term *euripos* is the generic designation of any place where the water's natural ebb and flow was unusually violent. *Euripus* is also the proper name of the narrow strait between Euboea and the mainland, and a medieval story from the Arabic tradition claims that Aristotle drowned himself there, because he could not explain its current. On the Euripus, see Pliny *HN* 2.219.

91. The isle of Helene, just off the southeastern Attic coast, is named for Helen of Troy, who took refuge there (cp. Eurip. *Hel.* 1673). On the legends of Helen, see Norman Austin, *Helen of Troy and Her Shameless Phantom* (Ithaca: Cornell University Press, 1994).

92. The main narrative for the battle of Salamis in 480 B.C.E. is Hdt. 8.83–96, but other references are spread throughout the account. The messenger's description of the battle in Aeschylus' *Persians*, produced in 472 B.C.E., may contain important elements of an eyewitness account (see *Pers.* 249–514).

93. Roman maps did not look like modern ones, and they made more glaring errors than ours do. Thus it is difficult for modern readers to imagine what a Roman map looked like in general—for example, to imagine one that shows the Echinades and the Strophades as being located off the coast of Epirus. Throughout antiquity the geographic tradition required, and was built on, the systematic correction of previous systems and explanations, and in principle it should not be surprising to find errors of this magnitude on maps or in technical discussions. Strabo (2.5.8) reflects the difficulties that persisted even during the Augustan period in calculating precise latitudes and longitudes. (See Ov. *Met.* 8.573–89 on the mythological origin of the Echinades.)

Adriatic Sea, Corcyra [Kérkira/Corfu]. These islands lie near the coasts of Thrace and Greece.

111. By contrast, farther out to sea are Melos, Olearos, Aegina,[94] Cothonius, Thyatira, Gyaros, Hippuris, Dionysia, Cyanos, Chalcis, Icaria, Pinara, Nyspiros, Lebinthos, Calymnia, and Syme. These islands are called the Sporades, because they are scattered, but Ceos, Sicinos, Siphnos, Seriphos, Rhenea, Paros, Myconos, Syros, Tenos, Naxos, Delos, and Andros are called the Cyclades, because they lie in a circle.[95]

112. Beyond these islands, in the middle of the sea at this point, huge and once inhabited by a hundred cities, Crete extends Point Samonium to the east, to the west Criu Metopon [Grk., Ram's Brow]. It is similar to Cyprus except bigger, and it is notorious for its many legends (the arrival of Europa, Pasiphaë's and Ariadne's loves, the Minotaur's savagery and his death, the works of Daedalus and his escape, Talus' lookout and his death), but especially because the locals point out as the virtually unambiguous indication that Jupiter was buried there the tomb on which his name is engraved. **113.** Its best-known cities are Gnossos, Gortyn, Lyctos, Lycastos, Olopyxos, Therapnae, Cydonea, Moratusa, and Dictynna. Among its hills,[96] because we are told that Jupiter was born there, Mt. Ida's tradition is preeminent. **114.** Off the coast of Crete are the islands of Astypalaea, Naumachos, Zephyre, Chryse, and Caudos; those three that they nevertheless call by one name, Musagorus; and Carpathos, from which the Carpathian Sea gets its name.

In the Adriatic are Apsoros, Dyscelados, Absyrtis, Issa, Titana, Hydria, Electrides, Black Corcyra [Korchula], Linguarum, Diomedia, Aestria, Asine, and Pharos, which lies beside the coast of Brundisium, just as that other Pharos lies beside Alexandria.

115. Sicily was long ago, as they report, part of the continent and tied to Bruttium, but it was severed at a later time by the strait that belongs to the Sea of Sicily. That strait is narrow and moves in two directions. With one current it flows through to the Tuscan Sea, with the other to the Ionian Sea. It is frightful, violent, and renowned for the savage

---

94. The sea here is the Aegean, but M. has confused two islands. Aegina, just mentioned at 2.109, does not belong here and has been confused with Aegialia. See Parroni 1984, 361–62.

95. The etymology of *Sporades* is derived from Greek *spora*, "scattered" or "strewn"; of *Cyclades* from Greek *kyklos*, "circle."

96. M. falls into a poetic turn of phrase here by using the Latin word for hill (*collis*) to describe the mountains of Crete.

names of Scylla and Charybdis. Scylla is a rock, Charybdis the sea. Both are deadly to those who are driven onto them. Sicily itself is huge, and running in different directions with its three promontories, it looks like the Greek letter called "delta." **116.** The promontory that looks toward Greece is called Point Pachynum [Capo Passero]; Lilybaeum [Capo Boeo/Capo Lilybeo], the one that looks toward Africa; and Pelorias [Punta del Faro], the one that turns toward Italy and is opposite Scylla. Its namesake is the helmsman Pelorus, who was buried there by Hannibal. When Hannibal, as a political refugee from Africa, was traveling through these regions to Syria, he had killed Pelorus because he thought Pelorus had betrayed him. His reason was that as he scanned the horizon from some distance, the shores seemed to him to be continuous, and the sea did not seem to be passable at all.[97]

117. The shore that extends from Pelorias to Pachynum, bordering on the Ionian Sea, produces these illustrious places: Messana [Messina], Tauromenium [Taormina], Catina [Catania], Megaris [Agosta], Syracusae [Siracusa/Syracuse], and—a marvel in this last city—Arethusa. The Fountain of Arethusa is the one where objects reappear that are thrown into the Alpheus, a river—as we have said[98]—that flows on the Peloponnesos. Because of this phenomenon, the fountain is believed not to be connected to the sea but to drive its bed this far and to rise again here after it has sunk below the surface of land and sea. **118.** Between Pachynum and Lilybaeum are Agragas [Agrigento], Heraclea, and Thermae; between Lilybaeum and Pelorias are Panhormus [Palermo] and Himera. Farther inland, to be sure, are Leontini [Lentini], Centuripinum [Centuripe], Hybla, and several other cities. Henna [Enna] has special fame because of the temple of Ceres. **119.** Of the mountains, Eryx [Erice] is mentioned mainly because of the sanctuary of Venus founded by Aeneas, Aetna because in olden times it bore the Cyclopes and nowadays burns with uninterrupted fire.[99] Of the rivers, the Himera needs to be mentioned, because it rises exactly in the mid-

---

97. M. gives the most detailed account of this event, which occurred during Hannibal's flight in 195 B.C.E. After the anecdote, M. returns abruptly to a discussion of the Strait of Messina and of how close Sicily lies to the mainland at this point.

98. At 2.51.

99. Aetna is the famous volcano in northeastern Sicily (near Catana), and its etiological myths are familiar: supposedly Hephaestus and the Cyclopes forged Zeus' thunderbolts there, and buried below their forge was the monster Typhon (see book 1, n. 58).

dle of the island and descends in opposite directions. On both sides that river divides the island. It comes down to the Libyan Sea on one side, to the Tuscan Sea on the other.

120. Near Sicily, in the Sicilian Strait, is the island of Aeaee, which Calypso reportedly inhabited;[100] toward Africa, Gaulos [Gozo], Melita [Malta], and Cossura [Pantelleria]; nearer Italy, Galata and those seven that they call the Isles of Aeolus [the Lipari Islands]—Osteodes [Ustica], Lipara [Lipari], Heraclea [Alicudi], Didyma [Salina], Phoenicusa [Filicudi], and the two like Aetna, Hiera [Vulcano] and Strongyle [Stromboli], which burn with uninterrupted flame.

121. But to move on, Pithecusa [Ischia], Leucothea, Aenaria, Sidonia, Capreae [Capri], Prochyta [Procida], Pontiae [Ponza], Pandateria, Sinonia, and Palmaria [Palmarola] lie on the Italic coast on this side of the Tiber's mouth. **122.** Farther on there are some small islands, Dianium [Giannutri], Igilium [Giglio], Carbania, Urgo, Ilva [Elba], and Capraria [Capraia], as well as two large islands divided by a strait. Of these two, Corsica is nearer to the Etruscan coast. It is narrow between its lateral extensions but long, and it is cultivated by barbarians except around the colonies of Aleria and Mariana. **123.** Sardinia, which also borders on the African Sea, is equal and squarish on all sides except that its western flank is narrower than its eastern, and it is nowhere any wider than Corsica is long. In other regards, Sardinia is fertile, has better soil than it does climate, and is almost as malarious[101] as it is productive. Of its peoples the most ancient are the Ilienses; of its cities, Caralis [Cagliari] and Sulci [San Antioco].

124. In Gaul, by contrast, the only islands fit to report are the Stoechades [Îles d'Hyères], which are scattered from the coast of Liguria all the way to Massilia. The Balearic Isles, located in Spain across from the coast of Tarraco, are not far from one another and are designated by size; some are the Greater Balearic Isles [Mallorca], others the Lesser

---

100. According to Homer (*Od.* 10.135 and elsewhere), Aeaea is the home of Circe, not Calypso. Only Hyginus (*Fab.* 125.16) gives the same tradition as M.— so Silberman 1988, 241–42 n. 11.

101. Sardinia was famous for malaria; cp. Strabo 5.2.7 and Paus. 10.17.11. Pausanias (10.17) and other sources confirm the island's productivity. In 57–56 B.C.E., when Pompey the Great was in charge of Rome's grain supply (*annona*), he sent Q. Cicero as legate to Olbia, Sardinia's chief port, to oversee things. The famous Marcus Tullius Cicero, unsure of his brother's itinerary in Sardinia, warned Quintus in a letter (*QFr.* 2.3.7) to take special care of his health, since Sardinia was malarious even during the winter.

[Menorca]. The forts of Iamno [Ciudadela] and Mago [Mahón] are on the Lesser Balearic Isles; on the Greater Balearics are the colonies of Palma and Pollentia [Pollenca]. **125.** Near the promontory they call Ferraria in the Bay of Sucro, the isle of Ebusos [Ibiza] has a city by the same name. Only for grain is it unproductive; it is rather bountiful for other crops. The island is so free of all harmful animals that it does not produce even those wild animals that are gentle, nor does it sustain them if they are imported. **126.** Facing Ebusos is Colubraria [Formentera], which it comes to mind to mention because, although the island is teeming with many a harmful breed of snake and is uninhabitable for that reason, it is still without danger and safe for anyone who enters within a space demarcated by a circle of dirt from Ebusos. Those same snakes that otherwise habitually attack people they meet stay far away from the sight of that dust—in terror—as if the sight were a kind of poison.

Book 3: Around the World—the Circle of Ocean from the Pillars of Hercules

1. The coastline of Our Sea has been described now, and the islands it includes too.[1] What is left is the periphery, as we said at the outset,[2] that Ocean encircles. The huge and boundless sea is in motion, being stirred by great tides (that is what they call its movements). Sometimes it inundates fields; other times it strips them and runs back—not one field and another in turn, and not going back and forth between opposite coasts in alternating advances with full thrust, now on these fields, now on those. Instead, after it floods out from its center point equally onto all the shores of land and island, even though they lie in different directions, Ocean gathers itself back into its center point from those shores and returns to its original condition. It always moves with so much force that it even drives back great rivers and either sweeps away the creatures of the earth or else strands marine life there.

2. It is, moreover, not quite understood [a] whether the world[3] causes that process by its own breathing and restores all around the water that has been pulled back with its breath—if, as pleases the more learned, the world is a single animate being—or [b] whether there are certain caves sunk below the surface where the returned waters reside and whence they rise up copiously again, or [c] whether the moon is the

---

1. The coastline in 1.24–2.96, the islands in 2.97–126.
2. Twice, at 1.5 and 1.24.
3. M. uses *mundus* (cp. Grk. *kosmos*). Both words address the orderliness and arrangement of the universe. *Mundus* may mean the heavens, the universe, the world, or the earth. Here it seems to mean earth in the full sense (i.e., land and sea taken as a unity), but it is not clear from what is stated whether the Earth is considered to be breathing as an independent entity or as an organic part of the animate universe. One limitation of ancient scientific thinking resulted from the fact that it always conceived the universe as animate. In general, see ps.-Aristotle *de Mundo* (On the universe). Cicero's *de Natura Deorum* (On the nature of the gods), especially book 2, depends in detail on a discussion of the animate universe. Lucan (1.412–19) suggests three theories about tides but leaves their investigation to more motivated individuals.

explanation of such great movements. The tides certainly vary with the moon's rising and setting, and we have ascertained that they ebb and flow, not regularly at the same moment, but as the moon waxes and wanes.

Iberian Peninsula

3. The Atlantic and the line of Baetica's oceanfront receive those who travel this way and follow the right-hand coast.[4] This coastline is virtually straight as far as the Anas River, except where it draws back gradually once or twice. The Turduli and Bastuli are its inhabitants. **4.** In the nearest bay is a harbor they call the Port of Gades and a woods they call Wild-Olive Grove; then a fort, Ebora, on the coast; and far from the coast the colony of Hasta [Mesa de Asta]. On the coast again there is an altar and a temple of Juno,[5] and on the sea itself, the Monument of Caepio,[6] which is set on a cliff rather than an island. **5.** The Baetis [Guadalquivir] River, coming from the Tarraconensis region more or less through the middle of this one, runs down for a long time in a single stream, just as it originates. Later on, after it has made a large lake not far from the sea, a twin rises up as if from a new source, and the river flows on in separate beds as sizably as it had arrived in its single bed. Then a second bay curves all the way to the province's boundary, and the small towns of Olintigi, Onoba [Huelva], and Laepa [Lepe] line it.

6. By contrast, on the other side of the Anas, where it faces the Atlantic Ocean, Lusitania at first goes on with a mighty thrust into the sea; then it stops and recedes farther than Baetica does. **7.** Where it juts

---

4. The right-hand or European coast, that is, for those traveling from the Mediterranean and exiting the Strait of Gibraltar.

5. Hercules/Melqart is important in this vicinity (see book 1, n. 25); so it is not surprising to discover that in this region once subjected to strong Carthaginian influence, the Carthaginian Juno/Tanit has been assimilated both to local goddesses and to the chief goddess of the Roman cultural superstructure. Tanit was originally a rather obscure Phoenician goddess whose importance was enhanced as the Carthaginians came into increasing contact with a local African fertility deity.

6. In 108 B.C.E., the year after he quashed the revolt of Viriathus and the Lusitanians (see App. *BHisp.* 70), Q. Servilius Caepio built a lighthouse, now identified, on an island in the mouth of the Baetis (Guadalquivir) River (see Strabo 3.1.9).

out, the coast spreads into three promontories, with the sea being received in two folds. The promontory beside the Anas is called Wedge Field [Cabo de Santa Maria], because it runs out from a wide base and gradually hones itself into a point; they call the second one Sacred Point [Cabo de Sâo Vicente] and the one beyond it Great Point [Cabo da Roca]. On Wedge Field are Myrtili [Mértola], Balsa [Torre de Tavira], and Ossonoba [Faro]; on Sacred Point, Laccobriga [Lagos] and Port Hannibal [Portimâo]; on Great Point, Ebora [Evora]. **8.** Bays lie between the promontories. Salacia is on the first one; on the second are Ulisippo [Lisboa/Lisbon] and the mouth of the Tagus [Tejo/Tajo], a river that generates jewels and gold. From these promontories to the part[7] that has receded, a huge bend opens up, and on it are the Old Turduli and the towns of the Turduli as well as the Munda [Mondego] River, which flows broadly more or less halfway up the coast of the last promontory, and the Durius [Duero] River, which washes the foot of the same promontory. **9.** The oceanfront there has a straight bank for a considerable distance and then protrudes a little bit where it takes a moderate bend. At that time, drawn back again and again and lying in a straight line, the coast extends to the promontory we call Celtic Point [Punta de Narija].

10. Celtic peoples—except for the Grovi from the Durius to the bend—cultivate the whole coast here, and the rivers Avo [Ave], Celadus [Cavado], Nebis [Neyva], Minius [Miño], and Limia (also known as the Oblivion) flow through their territory. The bend itself includes the city of Lambriaca [Lambre] and receives the Laeros [Lérez] and Ulla Rivers. **11.** The Praetamarici inhabit the section that juts out,[8] and through their territory run the Tamaris [Tambre] and Sars [Sar] Rivers, which arise not far away—the Tamaris next to Port Ebora, the Sars beside the Tower of Augustus,[9] which has the famous inscription. The Supertamarici and the Neri, the last peoples on that stretch, inhabit the remainder. This is as far as its western shores reach.

12. From there the coast shifts northward with its entire flank from Celtic Point all the way to Scythian Point. The shoreline, uninterrupted except for moderate recesses and small promontories, is almost straight

---

7. This part is Lusitania—roughly, modern Portugal.
8. See the description at 3.9.
9. Only M. mentions this monument, and its location is uncertain. Presumably the tower was built to celebrate Augustus' victory in the Cantabrio-Asturian War (29–19 B.C.E.).

until it reaches the Cantabri. **13.** On that shore, first of all, are the Artabri (actually a people of Celtic ancestry), then the Astyres. In the territory of the Artabri a bay admits the sea through a narrow mouth but encloses it with its not-so-narrow grasp; it rings the city of Adrobrica and the mouths of four rivers. Two mouths are little known even among locals; through the other two the Mearus and the Iubia Rivers make their outlets. On the coast that belongs to the Astyres is the town of Noege, and on the peninsula sit the three so-called Altars of Sestius. These altars are dedicated in the name of Augustus, and they make famous a land previously undistinguished.[10]

14. From what they call Salia River, though, the coast begins to recede gradually, and the breadth of still-wide Spain begins to contract more and more. The land narrows so much that where it abuts Gaul, its breadth is less by half than where it extends its western shore. **15.** The Cantabri and Vardulli occupy this stretch; there are several peoples and rivers among the Cantabri, but their names cannot be couched in our language. The Saunium [Saja] descends through the territory of the < . . . > and of the Salaeni, the Namnasa [Nansa] down through the territory of the Autrigones and Orgenomescos, and the < . . . >. One nation, the Vardulli, spreading from here to the promontory of the Pyrenees, terminates the Spains.

Gaul

16. Gaul's second coast follows. At first its shoreline does not go out to sea at all, but after a while, proceeding almost as far beyond Spain as Spain had receded, it comes to lie opposite the lands of the Cantabri.[11] The coast then bends in a great curve and turns its flank so that it faces west. Then turning to face north, the coastline unfolds a second time in

---

10. Again the location is uncertain, this time because the evidence is in conflict: see Parroni 1984, 386, and Silberman 1988, 256–57 n. 8. There were three altars dedicated to Augustus and the Sun (cp. Ptolem. 2.6.3). L. Sestius, Augustus' legate (22–19 B.C.E.?), erected these altars in the princeps' honor, and they are known also to the elder Pliny (*HN* 4.111) and to others. This is the L(ucius) Sestius P(ublii) f(ilius) Alb(inianus) Quirinalis who was suffect consul in 23 B.C.E.; for the date of his governorship, see G. Alföldy, *Fasti Hispanienses* (Wiesbaden: F. Steiner, 1969). Dio (53.32.3–4) explains that Augustus developed the system of suffect consulships to increase the number of experienced politicians available for subsequent provincial appointments.

11. Here M. describes the Bay of Biscay, for which he has no proper name.

a long and straight stretch up to the banks of the Rhenus [Rhein/ Rhine]. **17.** The land is rich, primarily in grain and fodder, and it is lovely with its vast woods. It is conducive to good health and rarely populated with animals of a harmful kind, but it supports—with difficulty, and not everywhere—those plants that are intolerant of the cold.

18. The peoples are crude, superstitious, and sometimes even so monstrous that they used to believe that to the gods the best and most pleasing sacrificial victim was a human being. Traces of their savagery remain, even though it has been banned now. Nevertheless, after they have led their consecrated human victims to the altars, they still graze them slightly, although they do hold back from the ultimate bloodshed. And yet, they have both their own eloquence and their own teachers of wisdom, the Druids.[12] **19.** These men claim to know the size and shape of the earth and of the universe, the movements of the sky and of the stars, and what the gods intend. In secret, and for a long time (twenty years), they teach many things to the noblest males among their people, and they do it in a cave or in a hidden mountain defile. One of the precepts they teach—obviously to make them better for war—has leaked into common knowledge, namely, that their souls are eternal and that there is a second life for the dead. Therefore they cremate and bury with the dead things that are suitable for the living. Long ago, traders' accounts and debt collection were deferred until they died, and some individuals happily threw themselves onto the pyres of their loved ones as if they were going to live with them!

20. The whole region they inhabit is Gallia Comata. Its peoples have three very distinguished names, and those peoples are separated by mighty rivers. In fact the Aquitani reach from the Pyrenees to the Garunna [Garonne] River, the Celts from there to the Sequana [Seine], and from there to the Rhenus, the Belgae. Of the Aquitani the most famous are the Ausci; of the Celts, the Haedui; of the Belgae, the Treveri. The wealthiest cites are Augusta [Trier] among the Treveri, Augustodunum [Autun] among the Haedui, and among the Aquitani, Eliumberrum [Auch].

21. The Garunna, which descends from the Pyrenees, flows shallow for a long time and is barely navigable except when swollen by winter rain or melted snow. But when it has been increased by the intrusions

---

12. See now P.B. Ellis, *The Druids* (London: Constable, 1994), passim, on M. (see his index); and in general see Françoise Le Roux and Christian-J. Guyonvarc'h, *Les Druides* (Rennes: Ouest-France, 1986).

of the seething Ocean, and while those same waters are receding, the Garunna drives on its own waters and those of Ocean. The river, being considerably fuller, becomes wider the farther it advances, and at the end it is like a strait. It not only carries bigger ships but rises like the raging sea and violently buffets those who sail it, at least if the wind pushes one way and the current another. 22. In the river is the island named Antros, which the locals think floats on the surface and is raised up by the rising waves. The reasons they think so are [a] that while the adjacent shore seems more elevated, the river covers it when its level rises, whereas prior to flooding only this island is surrounded by water, and [b] that what the banks and hills had stood opposite (so that it was not seen) is completely visible at that time as if because of being on higher ground.

23. From the Garunna's outlet begins the horizontal stretch of land that runs into the sea, as well as the shore that lies opposite the coast of the Cantabri[13] and that bends from the Santoni all the way to the Ossismi (with other peoples living in between). Indeed, after the Ossismi, the oceanfront again faces back to the north, and it reaches to the farthest people of Gaul, the Morini. And it does not have anything more noteworthy than the port they call Gesoriacum [Boulogne].

24. The Rhenus, cascading down from the Alps, makes—more or less at its source—two lakes, Lake Venetus [Upper Bodensee/Upper Lake Constance] and Lake Acronus [Lower Bodensee/Lower Lake Constance]. Then solid for a long time and descending in a defined bank, not far from the sea it spreads in two directions. To the left the Rhenus actually remains a river until it reaches its outlet. On the right, however, the river is at first narrow and unchanged, but later its banks recede over a vast expanse. At this point it is no longer called a river but a huge lake—Lake Flevo—where it has flooded the fields. It surrounds an island of the same name [Vlieland], becomes narrower again, and again makes its outlet as a river.

Germany

25. Germany extends on the near side from the banks of the Rhenus as far as the Alps; on the south from the very Alps; on the east from the

---

13. See 3.16. M. still is describing the shoreline of the (to him) anonymous Bay of Biscay.

frontier with the Sarmatian peoples; and where it faces north, from the oceanfront. **26.** The people who live there are extraordinary in courage, as in physique, and thanks to their natural ferocity they exercise both prodigiously—their minds by making war, their bodies by habitual hard work but above all by habitual exposure to the cold. They live naked before they reach puberty, and childhood is very long among them. The men dress in wool clothing or the bark of trees even during the harsh winter. **27.** They have not only a tolerance for swimming but a fancy for it. They wage war with their neighbors, and they provoke the causes of those wars for sheer pleasure, not for the pleasure of ruling or enlarging what they possess (since they do not cultivate in earnest even what is already in their possession), but simply so that what lies around them may be laid waste. **28.** They consider that right lies in might, so much so that not even brigandage shames them, provided that they are good to their guests and compliant for their suppliants. They are so crude and uncivilized in their way of life that they even eat raw or fresh-killed meat, or else they eat meat that has been frozen in the actual hides of cattle and wild animals after they have softened the meat by working it with their own hands and feet.

29. The land itself is not easily passable, because of its many rivers; it is rugged on account of its numerous mountains; and to a large extent it is impassable with its forests and swamps. Of the swamps, the Suesia, the Metia, and the Melsyagum are the biggest. Of the forests, the Hercynian and some others that have names do exist, but because it covers a distance of sixty days' march, the Hercynian Forest is as much better known as it is bigger than the others. **30.** Of the mountains, excepting those with names scarcely to be pronounced by a Roman mouth, the tallest are Mt. Taunus and Mt. Retico. Of the rivers that pass into the territories of other peoples, the most famous are the Danube and the Rhodanus [Rhône]; of those that go into the Rhenus, the Moenis [Main] and the Lupia [Lippe]; and of those that go into the Ocean, the Amissis [Ems], the Visurgis [Weser], and the Albis [Elbe]. **31.** On the other side of the Albis, the huge Codanus Bay [Baltic Sea] is filled with big and small islands. For this reason, where the sea is received within the fold of the bay, it never lies wide open and never really looks like a sea but is sprinkled around, rambling and scattered like rivers, with water flowing in every direction and crossing many times. Where the sea comes into contact with the mainland, the sea is contained by the banks of islands, banks that are not far offshore and that are virtually equidistant everywhere. There the sea runs a narrow course like a strait, then, curving, it promptly adapts to a long brow of land. **32.** On the bay are the Cimbri and the Teutoni; farther on, the farthest people of Germany, the Hermiones.

Sarmatia

33. Sarmatia, wider to the interior than toward the sea, is separated by the Vistula [Wisła/Vistula] River from the places that follow, and where the river reaches in, it goes all the way to the Ister River. Its people are very close to the Parthians in dress and in weaponry, but the rougher the climate, the cruder their disposition. **34.** They do not live in cities or even in fixed abodes. Insofar as pastures have lured them on, or insofar as an enemy's flight or pursuit has forced them out, they live in camps all the time and drag their possessions and their wealth with them. They are warlike, free, unconquered, and so savage and cruel that women also go to war side by side with men; and so that women may be suited for action, their right breast is cauterized as soon as they are born. As a result, that breast, now exposed and ready to withstand blows, develops like a man's chest. **35.** Archery, horseback riding, and hunting are a girl's pursuits; to kill the enemy is a woman's military duty, so much so that not to have struck one down is considered a scandal, and virginity is the punishment for those women.

Scythia

36. After that, the Scythian peoples—almost all designated under one name as the Belcae—inhabit the Asian frontier except where winter remains continuous and the cold remains unbearable. On the Asiatic littoral, first of all, the Hyperboreans are located beyond the north wind,[14] above the Riphaean Mountains, and under the very pole of the stars, where the sun rises, not every day as it does for us, but for the first time at the vernal equinox, and where it eventually sets at the autumnal equinox. Therefore, for six months daylight is completely uninterrupted, and for the next six months night is completely uninterrupted. **37.** The land is narrow, exposed to the sun, and spontaneously fruitful. Its inhabitants live in the most equitable way possible, and they live

---

14. This is the etymological meaning of their name. See also 1.13.

longer and more happily than any mortals.[15] To be sure, because they delight in their always festive leisure, they know no wars, no disputes, and they devote themselves primarily to the sacred rites of Apollo. According to tradition, they sent their firstfruits to Delos initially in the hands of their own virgins, and later they sent them through peoples who handed them on in succession to farther peoples.[16] They preserved that custom for a long time until it was profaned by the sacrilege of those peoples. The Hyperboreans inhabit groves and forests, and when a sense of having been satisfied by life (rather than boredom) has gripped them, they cheerfully wreathe themselves in flowers and actually throw themselves into the sea from a particular cliff. For them that is the finest death ritual.

38. The Caspian Sea first breaks into the land like a river, with a strait as small as it is long, and after it has entered by its straight channel, the sea is diffused into three bays.[17] Opposite its very mouth, it passes into

---

15. This fabled people lives in the extreme north, enjoys perfect peace and happiness, and has perpetual sunshine. Pindar (*Pythian* 10.29–44) says that the Muse never leaves their company. There is a good article on Hyperboreans, with bibliography, in *Der Kleine Pauly: Lexikon der Antike*, vol. 2 (Munich: Alfred Druckenmüller, 1967), 1274–75. Romm 1992, 45–81, has a good discussion of the Hyperboreans and similar peoples. See the following note.

16. Herodotus (4.32–35) tells the Delians' story about the Hyperboreans. According to him, the Delians knew more about this people than anyone else did. Their story as recounted by Herodotus generally is considered to preserve a cultural memory of the archaeologically attested trade routes between northern Europe and the Mediterranean. Herodotus names two sets of virgins, (1) Arge and Opis and (2) Hyperoche and Laodice, in chronological order. The two stories involving sets of virgins are simply cultural doublets.

17. The Caspian is the world's largest landlocked sea. Herodotus (1.202.4) knew that the Caspian was technically a lake; so did Aristotle (*Meteorol.* 2.1.10). Like Manilius (*Astronomica* 4.646–49) and Strabo (2.5.18) before him, M. shares the common mistake that the Caspian (Hyrcanian) Sea is an inlet of the ocean. Ca. 284/3 Patrocles was dispatched to explore the Caspian but did not do the job completely: he identified the Caspian as a gulf of Ocean. His voyage was limited to the Caspian's southern coast and can be reconstructed from Strabo 11.6., 11.7.1, and 11.8.8, with Pliny *HN* 6.36. Patrocles' work was open to criticism, and Eratosthenes (third century B.C.E.) was criticized for depending on Patrocles for other data too (see Strabo 2.1.4). Eratosthenes accepted Patrocles' report on the Caspian, and his view became canonical until well into the fourteenth century C.E. According to Pliny (*HN* 6.36), Agrippa's commentary treated the Caspian as a gulf of Ocean, but see Bunbury's remark on M.'s phrasing here (see my introduction, n. 53).

the Bay of Hyrcania; on the left, into Scythian Bay; and on the right, into the one they call by the name of the whole, Caspian Bay. The sea as a whole is violent, savage, without harbors, exposed to storms everywhere, as well as crowded[18] with sea-monsters more than any other sea is, and for all these reasons it is not fully navigable. To the right as you enter,[19] the Scythian Nomads occupy the shores of the strait.[20] **39.** To the interior, beside Caspian Bay, are the Caspians and Amazons (at least the ones they call the Sauromatidae); alongside the Bay of Hyrcania are the Albani, the Moschi, and the Hyrcani; and on Scythian Bay are the Amardi, the Pestici, and, at this point near the strait, the Derbices.

Many rivers, great and small, flow into that bay, but the famous one, the < . . . >, descends in a single bed from the Ceraunian Mountains and makes its outlet into the Caspian in two beds. **40.** The Araxes [Araks], which cascades down from the side of the Taurus Range, slips along peacefully and quietly as long as it slices through the plains of Armenia, and it is not clear which way it is moving even if you watch it closely. When the Araxes goes down into rougher terrain, is squeezed to either side by cliffs, and is that much swifter because it is that much narrower, the river becomes as a result rough and choppy alongside the crags that block its path. Because of that it rolls on with a mighty crashing and roaring, so rapid that where it is about to drop precipitously onto lower-lying terrain, the Araxes does not even change its water's direction but shoots the water straight out beyond its channel. The river propels itself in the air at a height of more than a *iugerum*, its waters suspended in midair without a riverbed.[21] Then, after it descends in a

---

18. *Differtus -a -um* (stuffed) is an expression from colloquial Latin, often used to pleasant effect in more formal contexts; cp. Hor. *Sat.* 1.5.4, where Forum Appii is descibed as *differtum nautis* [stuffed (crowded) with boatmen].

19. According to M., then, these Scythian Nomads live on the right bank of the strait that brings the imagined traveler into the Caspian Sea and Hyrcanian Bay.

20. In Roman imperial times *Scythia* generally refers to most of Asia's northern reaches. Some names of various Scythian peoples are preserved, but the stories about these peoples are generally fantastic. Strabo (11.6.2) says that the Caspian divides the Scyths into a western group (living between the Tanaïs River and the Caspian) and an eastern group (stretching to the Eastern Ocean and south to India). These Nomads, the easternmost of the western Scyths, are presumably to be distinguished from other western Scyths also called Nomads by M., at 2.4, 2.5, and 2.11 (see book 2, n. 5).

21. As a unit of height, *iugerum* is of uncertain meaning. It is likely to equal either 240 or 120 Roman feet (i.e., 233 feet or 116 feet 6 inches English); both Sil-

curve with its stream bent like a bow, the river becomes tranquil, and again silently and scarcely moving through the plains, it rolls out to the coastline there.

41. The Cyrus [Kura] and Cambyses [Yori] Rivers, produced from springs near the roots of Mt. Coraxicus, travel in different directions. Both flow down through the territories of the Hiberi and the Hyrcani for a long time with their beds very far apart. Later, after entering the same lake not far from the sea, they arrive at the Bay of Hyrcania in a single outlet. **42.** The rivers Iaxartes [Syrdarya] and Oxos [Amudarya] go from the regions of the Sogdiani, through Scythia's deserts, into Scythian Bay. The former is large at its source, but the latter becomes larger by the incursion of other rivers. The latter rushes for a considerable distance from east to west, bends for the first time beside the Dahae, and, with its course turned to the north, opens its mouth between the Amardi and the Pestici.

43. The forests also bear other fierce animals, but they even bear tigers—Hyrcanian ones, to be sure—a savage breed of wild animal so swift that they easily, and typically, track a mounted rider, even one passing at a distance; and they do it not once only but several times, even when the trail is retraced each time right from where it began. The explanation comes from the fact that when that proverbial horseman runs off with stolen tiger cubs, and once he has let one of the several cubs go to thwart the fury of the adult animals as they near the city, these tigers pick up the abandoned cub and bring it back to their den. They go back again rather a lot and do the same thing until the fleeing thief reaches a more populous locale than the tigers dare to approach.[22]

44. For quite some time it was unclear what lay beyond Caspian Bay, whether it was the same Ocean or a hostile, cold land that extended without a border and without end. **45.** But in addition to the natural

---

berman (1988, 78: "sur plus de cent pieds") and Brodersen (1994, 159: "100 Fuß, ca. 30m") apparently take the measurement here as approximating the shorter side of the notional farmer's field (see book 1, n. 47). Not only are such measurements precarious in ancient texts, but no one else in antiquity describes the Araxes in the same terms as M.

22. Hyrcania (Gurgan) was renowned for the harshness of its way of life. The point of this parable is the fierceness of the mother tiger in protecting her young, and Pliny (*HN* 8.66) indicates that this story has its origin in Hyrcanian and Indian folklore. Pliny elsewhere (*HN* 8.7–8) reports Indian folklore about the instinctual intelligence of elephants. Stories like Pliny's underlie the tradition of the medieval bestiary. Cp. C. White, *The Alnwick Bestiary* (Turnhout: Brepols, forthcoming).

philosophers and Homer, who all said that the entire known world was surrounded by sea,[23] there is Cornelius Nepos, who is more dependable as an authority because he is more modern. Nepos, however, adduces Quintus Metellus Celer as witness of the fact, and he records that Metellus reported it as follows. When Celer was proconsul of Gaul, certain Indians were presented to him as a gift by the king of the Boii. By asking what route they had followed to reach there, Celer learned that they had been snatched by storm from Indian waters, that they had traversed the intervening region, and that finally they had arrived on the shores of Germany. Ergo, the sea is continuous, but the rest of that same coast is frozen by the unremitting cold and is therefore deserted.[24]

Islands

46. Next to these shores, which we have traced from the angle of Baetica all the way here, also lie many obscure islands that have no names. Of those islands not happily passed by, though, Gades is on the Strait. That island is separated from the continent by a narrow space, as if by a river, and has an almost straight bank where it lies nearer to the mainland. Where the island faces Ocean it reaches into the sea with two promontories, and the shoreline in between recedes. On one prong it supports a temple of Aegyptian Hercules famous for its founders, its cult, its age, and its wealth. The Tyrians founded the temple, and Hercules' bones, buried there, show why the place is consecrated. The temple began its existence in the Trojan era, and time has fed its wealth.[25]

47. In Lusitania are the isle of Erythia, which we are told was the home of Geryon,[26] and other islands without fixed names. The fields

---

23. Hom. *Il.* 21.196–97.

24. Q. Metellus Celer was proconsul of Gaul in 62 B.C.E., but as Pompey's legate in Asia four years earlier, Celer may well have acquired the information, garbled here, while on duty in the East (cp. Pliny *HN* 6.52). Of course, despite M.'s confidence, Nepos was notoriously gullible (see Pliny *HN* 5.4). Silberman (1988, 277–78 nn. 1–3) gives a full discussion of the problems raised by this passage.

25. Velleius Paterculus (1.2.3) describes the founding of Cádiz in close proximity to the apotheosis of Hercules (Vell. Pat. 1.2.1), but the dating is troublesome.

26. Geryon is described as either a three-headed or a triple-bodied monster. He was a mythical king in Hesperia, the land of the evening sun. His home was

of Erythia are so fertile that as soon as grain is planted, as soon as the seed falls to the ground and renews the crop, they produce at least seven harvests, sometimes even more. On the Celtic coast[27] are a number of islands that, because they are all rich in lead, people call by one name, the Cassiterides [Grk., Tin Islands; Isles of Scilly].[28] **48.** In the Britannic Sea, opposite the coast of the Ossismi, the isle of Sena [Sein] belongs to a Gallic divinity and is famous for its oracle, whose priestesses, sanctified by their perpetual virginity, are reportedly nine in number. They call the priestesses Gallizenae and think that because they have been endowed with unique powers, they stir up the seas and the winds by their magic charms, that they turn into whatever animals they want, that they cure what is incurable among other peoples, that they know and predict the future, but that it is not revealed except to sea-voyagers and then only to those traveling to consult them.

49. Next, as to what kind of place Britain is and what kind of people it produces, information that is more certain and better established will be stated. The reason is that—lo and behold!—the greatest princeps is opening the long-closed island, and as conqueror of previously unsubdued and previously unknown peoples, the princeps brings with him the proof of his own accomplishments, since he will reveal in his triumph as much as he has laid claim to in war.[29]

50. Moreover, just as we have thought until now, Britain projects between the west and the north in a wide angle and looks toward the mouths of the Rhenus. It then draws its sides back obliquely, facing Gaul with one side, Germany with the other; then returning with a continuous line of straight shore on its rear side, Britain again wedges itself into two different angles—being triangular and very much like

---

Erythia (Grk., Red Land])—named for the color of the setting sun? Originally the Greeks identified Erythia with Ambracia, when Ambracia was still a remote place on Greece's western shore. Later, as the Greeks expanded their horizons, Geryon's home was located on an island in Ocean and off the coast of Spain. Geryon possessed miraculous red cattle but lost them to Hercules the civilizer (in the tenth of his canonical labors: see Apollod. 2.5.10).

27. See 3.10.

28. If this name actually means the Isles of Scilly, then the term *Cassiterides* probably also includes mainland Cornwall, a major tin-producing area. Silberman (1988, 281 n. 3) gives the evidence.

29. For the significance of this passage, see my introduction, the section titled "Pomponius Mela the Man" and n. 37 there.

Sicily. Britain is flat, huge, fertile, but more generously so for what feeds sheep than for what sustains humans. **51.** It supports groves and meadows and colossal rivers that sometimes flow to the sea, sometimes back again, with alternating currents, and certain other rivers that produce gems and pearls. It supports peoples and their kings, but all are uncivilized. The farther from the sea, the more ignorant they are of other kinds of wealth, being wealthy only in sheep and land, and—whether for beauty or for some other reason—they have their bodies dyed blue.[30] **52.** They produce, nevertheless, the causes of war and actual wars, and they take turns harassing one another constantly, mainly because they have a strong desire to rule and a strong drive to expand their holdings. They make war not only on horseback or on foot but also from two-horse chariots and cars armed in the Gallic fashion—they call them *covinni*—on which they use axles equipped with scythes.

53. On the far side of Britain, Iuverna [Ireland][31] is more or less equal in area, but it is oblong with equally extended lateral coastlines. Its climate is hideous for ripening seeds, but the island is so luxuriant with grass—not only abundant but sweet—that sheep stuff themselves in a fraction of the day, and unless they are kept from the pasture, they burst from feeding too long. Its inhabitants are undisciplined and ignorant of

---

30. Julius Caesar (*BG* 5.14) gives a reason: "All the Britons actually dye themselves with woad [*vitrum*], which effects a blue color, and for this reason they are more horrifying in appearance during battle. . . ." The Romans used woad (*Isatis tinctoria*) to dye wool, and it was not displaced as a dyeing agent until indigo was shipped to Europe from India in the seventeenth century, although indigo (Lat. *Indicum*) was known to the Romans (see Pliny *HN* 35.46).

31. Here called Iuverna, which echoes its Greek name, *Ierne*, instead of the more familiar *Hibernia* in Latin. Caesar knew of Ireland but did not visit it (*BG* 5.13). Nor did the Romans ever try to conquer the island. In general, what the Romans knew of Ireland was learned from merchants and especially from the British peoples in contact with it. In thinking Ireland "more or less equal" to Britain in area, M. apparently followed the measurements established by Agrippa in the Age of Augustus (see Pliny *HN* 4.102), although Caesar previously had reported that Ireland was reported to be half the size of Britain. Caesar's information was the better estimate, but the actual proportion is more like a third than a half. Tacitus (*Agric.* 24) knew that Ireland was small compared to Britain, but still his father-in-law, Agricola, who may have planned an invasion in 81 C.E., severely underestimated how big an army of occupation would be required.

all virtue, to a greater degree than any other nation, and they are very much inexperienced in piety.³²

54. The thirty Orcades [Orkney Islands] are separated by narrow spaces between them; the seven Haemodae [Denmark] extend opposite Germany in what we have called Codanus Bay;³³ of the islands there, Scadinavia,³⁴ which the Teutoni still hold, stands out as much for its size as for its fertility besides. **55.** Because of the sea's tidal ebb and flow, and because the distance between them is sometimes covered by waves and other times bare, what faces the Sarmatae sometimes seems to be islands and at other times seems to be one continuous land mass. **56.** In addition to what is handed down in legend, I discover—in authors whom I am not embarrassed to follow—that on these islands are the Oeonae [Grk., Birds of Prey], who feed only on oats and the eggs of marsh birds, and that the Hippodes [Grk., Horsefeet], with their equine hooves, are also there, and the Panotii [Grk., All-Ears] too, who for clothing have big ears broad enough to go around their whole body (they are otherwise naked).

57. Thule is located near the coast of the Belcae, who are celebrated in Greek poetry and in our own. On it—because there the sun rises far from where it will set—nights are necessarily brief, but all winter long they are as dark as anywhere, and in summer, bright. All summer the sun moves higher in the sky at this time, and although it is not actually seen at night, the sun nevertheless illuminates adjacent places when its radiance is close by; but during the solstice there is no night, because at that time the sun is now more visible and shows not only its brilliance but most of itself too. **58.** Talge [Cheleken], on the Caspian Sea, is fertile

---

32. M. shares the ancient prejudice about the savagery of the inhabitants (cp. Strabo 2.5.8 with details at 4.5.4, where Strabo is embarrassed by the lack of reliable sources), and M.'s view of the irreligious and barbaric inhabitants of Ireland thus gives a small insight into his ethnocentrism. The text here was revised by an Irish hand or by a scribe favorable to the Irish. Where M. wrote of the inhabitants of Ireland that they are "ignorant of all virtue, to a greater degree than any other nation" [omnium virtutium ignari <magis> aliae gentes], the scribe added the gloss "at least they know virtue to some degree" [aliquatenus tamen gnari]. M. regularly uses *virtutium* for *virtutum* in the genitive plural (cp. 2.45 and 3.86).

33. So named at 3.31.

34. On the name Scadinavia [*sic*], see Parroni 1984, 410, and Silberman 1988, 286–87 n. 10.

without being cultivated and is abundant in every root crop and fruit, but the local peoples consider it an abomination and a sacrilege to touch what grows there. They think that these things have been prepared for the gods and must be saved for the gods. Alongside those coasts that we have called[35] deserted lie a number of equally deserted islands, which, being without names of their own, are called the Scythian Islands.

India and the East

59. The route curves from here to the Eastern Sea and to the earth's eastern rim. This coast, which is first impassable because of the snows and then uncultivated because of the monstrous savagery of the inhabitants, reaches from Scythian Point to Point Colis [Cape Comorin]. The Androphagoe[36] and the Sacae are Scyths, and they are separated by a region that is uninhabitable because it is teeming with wild animals. **60.** Next, monstrous beasts again render vast tracts unsafe all the way to Mt. Tabis, which overhangs the sea. At a distance from there the Taurus Range rises. The Seres [Lat., Silk People] are in between, a people full of justice and best known for the trade they conduct in absentia, by leaving their goods behind in a remote location.[37]

61. India is situated not only on the Eastern Sea but also on the south-facing sea that we have called the Indian Ocean,[38] and it is bounded from this point by the Taurus Range and on the west by the Indus. India occupies a coastline that equals a sail of sixty days and nights. It is so

---

35. At 3.45.

36. Grk., literally Man-Eaters. The Greek stem *andro-* from *anêr* means "man" in the sense of Latin *vir* (see book 1, n. 29). Herodotus (4.18 and 106) knows by this name brutish nomads who live in the upper Borysthenes valley, but he distinguishes them from Scyths. M. uses *Androphagoi* as a term here to distinguish these Scyths from their European cousins, the *Anthropophagoi* mentioned at 2.14 (see n. 13 there). Pliny (*HN* 6.53) speaks only of Anthropophagoi but locates them on the other side of the Caspian Sea.

37. The Seres, or Silk People (Lat. *Seres* from *sericum*, "silken cloth"), also mentioned at 1.11, are the Chinese. It is not clear whether Alexander the Great intended to reach the Eastern Ocean and hence the Seres (see book 3, n. 50). Although it deals with a period later than *The Chorography*, John Thorley's "The Silk Trade between China and the Roman Empire at Its Height, *circa* A.D. 90–130" (*Greece and Rome* 18 [1971]:71–80) provides background as well as an overview of the silk trade as it related to Rome.

38. At 1.11.

remote from our regions that in a certain part of India neither north star is visible and—again different from elsewhere—shadows fall to the south.[39] **62.** Moreover, it is fertile and teems with a different type of human being and other animals. It sustains ants that are no smaller than the biggest dogs, ants that reportedly guard, like griffins,[40] gold that is mined from deep within the earth, and that pose the greatest threat to anyone who touches it. India also sustains monstrous snakes that with their bite and the winding constriction of their bodies can stop an elephant in its tracks. It is so rich in some places and has such productive soil that in this country honey drips from the leaves, trees bear wool,[41] and rafts of split bamboo even convey, like ships, two persons at a time, some even conveying three at a time.

63. The dress and customs of the inhabitants vary a good deal. Some dress in linen or what we have called wool,[42] others in the skins of birds or wild animals. One subculture goes naked; another covers only their private parts. Some are short and puny, others so tall and huge in body that routinely and with ease they even use elephants—the biggest ones there—in the same way we use horses. **64.** Certain individuals think it right to kill no animal at all and to eat no meat at all, and fish alone is used to sustain certain others. Some kill their parents (when they are on the verge of decline) like sacrificial animals before the parents decline from age and illness, and it is both morally right and absolutely pious to feast on the viscera of the slain parents. **65.** By contrast, when disease or old age have set in, the old and infirm withdraw far from the others and without any fear at all[43] await death in isolation. More prudent

---

39. The two polestars, of course, are Ursa Major and Ursa Minor. On this passage, see Silberman 1988, 292 n. 14.

40. The behavior of griffins is described at 2.1.

41. That is, cotton. Cp. German *Baumwolle* (etymologically, "tree-wool"), used to mean "cotton." Cotton *wool* is also the rolled form in which cotton is sold in pharmacies.

42. M. recognizes the unfamiliarity of the "tree-wool" he described in the preceding paragraph. Herodotus also refers to "garments made from trees" (7.65; cp. 3.106), and he means Indian cotton. M.'s whole account of India shows the (direct or indirect) influence of Herodotus (esp. Hdt. 3.97–102, 3.104, and 5.3). Parroni (1984, 415–16) and Silberman (1988, 293 n. 5) give further references.

43. This portrait reflects a romanticization of the noble primitive. The Roman Stoic ideal considered death as an *indifferent* (Grk. *adiaphoron*) thing; i.e., it made no difference and was neither to be feared nor desired for itself but was simply to be accepted when its time came.

individuals, those who are involved emotionally in the practice and pursuit of wisdom, do not wait for death but happily and gloriously bring it on by hurling themselves onto fires.[44]

66. Of the cities they inhabit—and there are quite a lot of them—Nysa [Nagarahara] is the most famous and the biggest. Of its mountains, Meros [Mar-Koh] is sacred to Jupiter. Those two places have special renown for the following reason: they think that Liber was born in that city and that he was suckled in a cave on this mountain. And for this reason either their traditional material or plain error has forced Greek writers to say that Liber was placed in Jupiter's thigh [Grk. *mêros*].[45]

67. The Palibothri hold the coastline from Point Tamus [Cape Negrais?][46] to the Ganges. From the Ganges to Point Colis, except where it is too hot to be inhabited, are found black peoples, Aethiopians so to speak. From Point Colis to the Indus the shores are straight, and peoples live there who are timorous and quite prosperous because of the sea's riches. 68. Tamus is a spur that the Taurus raises; Colis is the second angle on the eastern part and begins the side that faces south; the Ganges and the Indus are rivers. The Ganges originates from many sources in the Haemodes [Himalaya] Range, and as soon as it has formed a single bed, it becomes the greatest of all rivers and gets even wider in some places. It is ten miles wide where it flows in its narrowest bed, and it spreads into seven mouths. 69. The Indus[47] rises in the

---

44. "More prudent" because they do not await a death that is hemmed in by their own increasing debilitation. M. considers these individuals philosophically disposed since they practice and pursue *sapientia*. (See the preceding note and book 1, n. 37.) Indian "sophists" fascinated the Greeks and Romans. An ascetic cremated himself before Alexander, and in 20 B.C.E. at Athens, so did the ascetic Zarmanochegas (Sanskrit *Śramaṇācārya*) before Augustus while he was discharging a mission from King Pandion (Sanskrit *Pāṇḍya*), another Porus (Sanskrit *Paurava*), i.e., the king of the Pandyas and the latest Paurava dynastic ruler. (See Strabo 15.1.4 with 15.1.73; cp. also Dio 54.9.)

45. The Roman Liber and his female counterpart, Libera, were native Italic vegetation gods, and hence they were associated from early times with Ceres. Under Greek influence Liber had long since been identified with and assimilated to the Greek Dionysus, Libera to Persephone, and Ceres to Demeter.

46. If the identification of Point Tamus with Cape Negrais in Myanmar (formerly Burma) is correct, then Point Tamus is the easternmost geographic place about which M. has specific physical information.

47. This region was not well known to Greek and Roman writers, although over the following century that situation changed. John Thorley writes that "In Ptolemy's *Geography*, the information for which was mostly gathered c. A.D.

Propanisus Range [Hindu Kush][48] and in fact admits other rivers, the most famous being the Cophes, Acesinus, and Hydaspes [Jhelum].[49] It carries in its broad span a single river born of several streams. As a result of this circumstance the Indus roughly equals the Ganges[50] in size. Later, after it has circumvented a huge mountain chain by making several sweeping bends, the river descends a second time, straight and uninterrupted, until it divides left and right and makes its outlet to the sea through two widely separated mouths.

70. Alongside Point Tamus is the island of Chryse [Grk., Golden], beside the Ganges the island of Argyre [Grk., Silvery]. The first has

---

120–50, we find a quite startling advance in the geographical knowledge of north-west India over all previous western geographers": see Thorley, "The Roman Empire and the Kushans," *Greece and Rome* 26 (1979):187.

48. Alexander the Great crossed the Indus (located in modern Pakistan) in spring of 326 B.C.E. He had crossed the Hindu Kush and occupied the Kabul region as he descended the Kabul valley to the Indus. Omphis (Sanskrit *Āmbhi*) of Taxila (Sanskrit *Takṣaśilā*; Sirkap) allied with Alexander because Omphis feared another local ruler, King Porus (Sanskrit *Paurava*). Omphis' official title in the sources is Taxiles, ruler of Taxila, whose territory extended between the Indus and the Hydaspes (cp. Plut. *Alex.* 59; Arrian *Alex.* 4.22; Curt. 8.12.14; Strabo 15.1.28). Taxila is in Pakistan, northwest of modern Rawalpindi by about twenty miles. See the following note.

49. In 326 B.C.E. Alexander the Great crossed the Hydaspes to crush King Porus (Sanskrit *Paurava*), who resisted his advance. After his victory Alexander overran the Punjab (the easternmost reach of his conquests), until his troops refused to advance to the Ganges in September of that year. (The summer monsoons may have affected the troops' mood: see Strabo 15.1.27.) Near the Hydaspes, Alexander lost his favorite horse, Bucephalas, in whose honor he founded the city of Bucephalia (Ptolemy's Bucephala) on the river's banks (see Plut. *Alex.* 61). The Greek army then fought its way downriver to the Indus Delta. The Indians impressed the Greeks and left an indelible impression on Greek historiography and folklore, but no Indian source even names Alexander. However, according to Plutarch (*Alex.* 62), Sandrocottus (Sanskrit *Candragupta*) may have been inspired in part by Alexander when he founded the great Mauryan Empire ca. 320 B.C.E. See the following note.

50. The Ganges, roughly 250 miles east of the Hydaspes, was Alexander's immediate goal (see Plut. *Alex.* 61) when his troops mutinied on the Hydaspes and refused any further advance. There is some evidence (Arrian *Alex.* 5.26) that Alexander intended to reach the Eastern Ocean in order to sail home and prove that the three continents were entirely surrounded by Ocean. Historians still divide on the issue of Alexander's plans if he had crossed the Ganges. Strabo knows of writers who have gone as far as the Ganges and Palibothra (15.1.27), but only a small number of merchants engaged in private enterprise ever sailed as far as the Ganges in his day (15.1.4).

golden soil—so the old writers have handed down—the other has silver soil. Moreover, as seems to be the case really, either the name comes from the fact, or the legend comes from the designation. Taprobane [Sri Lanka] is said to be either a very large island or the first part of the second world, but because it is inhabited, and because no one reportedly has circumnavigated it, the latter interpretation is as good as true.[51] 71. Opposite the mouths of the Indus are the so-called Islands of the Sun, so unlivable that the pressure of the atmosphere instantly sucks the life out of anyone who enters, and between the rivers' very mouths is the district of Patalene, which is unbearable in some places because of the heat and lacks inhabitants. From there the district of Ariane, itself impassable and deserted, stretches to the beginning of the Red Sea [Arabian Gulf]. Its land is more like ashes than dust, and that is why the rivers that trickle through it are scarce and scant. We are told that its best-known rivers are the Tubero and the Arusaces.

The Persian Gulf, Red Sea [Arabian Gulf], and Arabian Gulf [Red Sea]

72. The Greeks call the Red Sea [Arabian Sea][52] the Erythra Thalassa [Grk., Red Sea] either because it is that color or because Erythras ruled there as king. It is a stormy, rough sea, and deep; it has monsters to a greater extent than all the other seas.[53] At first the Red Sea thrusts the

---

51. The origin of the name *Taprobane* (Sri Lanka; formerly Ceylon) appears to be disputed. It may be derived either from Sanskrit *tāmbrapaṇī*, "pond covered with red lotus," or Pali *tāmba vanna*, "copper-colored": see H. Williams, *Ceylon: Pearl of the East* (London: Robert Hale, 1950), 412–13. In any event, the island was named for its first capital city. Pliny (*HN* 6.81–91) indicated that he had much more information at his disposal than M. did. Pliny knew that Sri Lanka was recognized as an island in the time of Alexander the Great. The idea that this island belonged to the *antichthôn*, or counterworld, is pre-Alexandrian and had been outdated for almost four hundred years when M. was writing. Even so, Pliny makes the point that an embassy came from Sri Lanka to Rome in the principate of Claudius and that its visit freshened and refined the scientific and other data about the island that was available in the West.

52. It must be emphasized at the outset that (a) what the Greeks and Romans commonly called the Red Sea (Grk. *Erythra Thalassa*) we call the Arabian Sea, and (b) what they called the Arabian Sea (or Arabian Gulf) we call the Red Sea. In this instance modern terminology reverses ancient terminology.

53. M. made this claim also about the Caspian Sea. In a sense the Caspian and M.'s Red (Arabian) Sea are counterparts of one another, but see book 3, n. 17 on the Caspian.

receding shoreline in evenly, and there is a considerably wide gulf with the result that the sea does not go farther inland. But twice it breaks through those receding banks, and the second time it creates two gulfs. **73.** The one nearer to the lands under discussion is called the Persian Gulf; the farther one is the Arabian Gulf. Where the Persian Gulf receives the sea, it encloses its large mouth with two straight sides, like a neck, and then, encompassing the sea with a great ring of shoreline as the land pulls back over a vast expanse and in equal degree everywhere, the gulf makes the form of a human head appear. **74.** The mouth of the Arabian Gulf is narrower and its interior width smaller; its inner recess extends somewhat farther, and its sides are much longer. This gulf penetrates far inland until it virtually reaches Aegypt and Mt. Casius in Arabia, after becoming at a particular point less and less wide and narrower the more it penetrates.

75. From what we have described here to the Persian Gulf, except where the Chelonophagi [Grk., Turtle/Tortoise-Eaters] linger, are deserts. On the gulf itself are located the Carmanii on the right of those sailing in. They have no regular clothes or fruit, no flock or fixed abodes. They dress in fish skins, eat fish meat, and are hairy all over except for their heads. The Cedrosi inhabit the interior, and after them, the Persae. The Saetis [Rud-Gez] reaches the sea through the territory of the Carmanii, and beyond it are the Sandis [Minab] and the Coros [Kor].

76. Directly opposite the mouth to the sea are the territory of the Babylonians, that of the Chaldaeans, and two famous rivers, the Tigris nearer to Persia and, farther away, the Euphrates. **77.** The Tigris descends as it originated, and it goes right through to the coast. Not only does the Euphrates emerge from an immense open mouth where it rises, but it even falls over a broad expanse. It does not, as a consequence, cut through the fields immediately but spreads out in pools over a wide area. For a long time it is sluggish with standing water and extends without a bed. Later it really is a river when it breaks through the rim of these standing pools, and once it is taken by banks, it is swift and roaring and goes west through Armenia and Cappadocia, on its way to Our Seas if the Taurus did not stop it. **78.** From there the Euphrates turns south, and first it enters Syria, then Arabia. It does not last all the way to the sea and as a result dies off in an insignificant trickle even though in some places it is huge and navigable. The Euphrates never makes a distinct outlet as other rivers do but dwindles off.

79. A stretch of land that runs between both seas surrounds the other shore of the Persian Gulf. It is called Arabia Eudaemon,[54] and it is narrow but very productive of cinnamon, incense, and other scents. The Sabaeans occupy the greater part of it, the Macae the part nearest the mouth and across from the Carmanii. Forests and cliffs roughen the seafront between the mouths of the two gulfs. A number of islands are located in the middle region of this gulf, but Ogyris is more famous than all the others because the funerary monument of King Erythras is on it.[55] 80. The Arabs surround the second gulf on all sides. On the right, and in order for anyone who enters the gulf, are the cities of Charra, Arabia, and Adanus [Aden]; on the other side, from the reentrant angle, the first Berenice, between the Bay of Heroöpolis and the Bay of Strobilus; then, between Point Maenorenon and Point Coloba, Philoteris and Ptolemaïs; farther on, Arsinoë and the other Berenice; then a forest that produces the ebony tree and perfumes; and then a man-made river, which is worth reporting because it is drawn from the Nile in a canal.

81. Outside the gulf, but nevertheless on the Red Sea's main bay, one locale is infested with brute beasts and is therefore a wasteland; and the Panchaei, whom they call Ophiophages [Grk., Snake-Eaters] because they eat snakes, live in another. There were Pygmies to the interior, a diminutive species that became extinct from fighting the cranes for the crops they had planted.[56] 82. There are many kinds of flying creatures and many kinds of snakes. The snakes most worth remembering are very small and of ready poison. The tradition about these snakes is that they emerge at a fixed time of year from the muck of the congealed swamps, that they head for Aegypt by flying in a great swarm, and that on their very entry into its borders they are intercepted in a hostile formation and defeated in a fight by the birds they call ibises. 83. Of the birds, the Phoenix, always unique, is especially worth mentioning. It is not conceived by copulation or born through parturition, but after it

54. Greek *eudaimôn* ("happy, lucky, prosperous") is translated by Latin *felix*. This region is known in Latin as Arabia Felix, but the Latin form apparently had not established itself at the time M. was writing.

55. Pliny (*HN* 6.153) confirms the site of this burial, but according to Strabo (16.3.5), the information about the island, King Erythras, and the monument goes back to Alexander's admiral Nearchus and his voyage with Orthagoras from the mouth of the Indus to the mouth of the Euphrates in 325/4 B.C.E.

56. The story is as old as Homer (*Il.* 3.3–6), but the Homeric Pygmies lived on Africa's southern rim.

has lasted continuously for a lifetime of five hundred years, the Phoenix lies down on a funeral pile heaped up with different scents and decomposes. **84.** Next, after congealing from the moisture of its putrefying limbs, the bird conceives itself and is reborn from itself. When the Phoenix has reached maturity, it carries the bones of its former body, shut inside a ball of myrrh, to Aegypt, and in what they call the City of the Sun, it puts the ball on the burning pyre of an altar and consecrates it in a memorable funerary ritual.[57] That promontory by which the sea is enclosed there is impassable because of the Aceraunian Canyons.

Africa's Outer Coasts

85. The Aethiopians reside beyond there.[58] They occupy the land of Meroë, which the Nile makes into an island by embracing it in its first ambit. Because they have a lifetime longer than ours by almost half, certain Aethiopians are called Macrobii [Grk., Long-Lived]. Others are called Automoles [Grk., Deserters], because they came here from Aegypt; they are beautiful in physique and worship body and strength exactly as other peoples worship the best virtues. **86.** They have the custom of choosing by appearance and strength the chief they are to obey at all costs. Among these people there is more gold than copper, and for that reason they consider gold less valuable. They bedeck themselves with copper, but for criminals they make chains out of gold. **87.** It is a place always bursting with sumptuous banquets. Because, as pleases them, it is lawful for anyone who wants to eat to do so, they call the place Heliu Trapeza [Grk., Table of the Sun], and they claim that everything that has been served there is replenished by a miracle.

88. There is a lake from which bodies, once they have been immersed, continue to shine as brightly as if they had been oiled. The same water is used for drinking. The water is so clear and so incapable of supporting what falls or is thrown into it that the water does not allow even leaves that fall from the closest branches to float on its surface but takes them right to the very bottom. There are also very fierce

---

57. "City of the Sun" [urbs Solis] translates the Greek name Heliopolis. For the Phoenix, see Silberman 1988, 310 nn. 5–7, but add Tac. *Ann.* 6.28 to his list of Latin sources.

58. It helps to understand that M. may have conceived the African continent as basically trapezoidal (see book 1, n. 19).

animals, namely, variegated wolves[59] of every color and sphinxes of the sort we have heard about. There are amazing birds, horned *tragopanes*,[60] and pegasuses with equine ears.

89. Moreover, nothing noteworthy meets those who follow the shores eastward. Everything is a wasteland, defined by desolate mountains, and more a riverbank than an oceanfront. After that, there is a huge tract without inhabitants. For quite a long time it was uncertain whether there was sea beyond and whether the earth had a periphery, or whether, with the seawaters eliminated, Africa extended without end.

90. Hanno the Carthaginian,[61] however, was dispatched by his people to explore it. When he had exited Our Sea through the mouth of Ocean and circumnavigated a great part of it, he had reported back that Africa was deficient not in sea but in the hustle and bustle of human life.[62] In the time of our ancestors, while running away from King Lathyrus of Alexandria, a certain Eudoxus set out from the Arabian Gulf by this sea, as Nepos affirms, and he sailed all the way to Gades.[63] That is why its coasts are, to a certain extent, known.

---

59. M.'s word here for wolf, *lycaon*, is borrowed from Greek, where it means "werewolf," but its meaning seems to be somewhat different in Latin. M.'s description of these Aethiopian beasts does not fit the folklore motifs of the werewolf (see book 2, n. 14). Pliny describes the African lynx in a context similar to M.'s (*HN* 8.72) and uses *lycaon* of the Indian hyena (*HN* 8.123). It is not possible to press M. further on this point.

60. These birds are a product of legend, possibly arising from the strange impression given by local hornbills. Pliny devotes a whole section (*HN* 10.70) to nonexistent, fantastic birds, among which he counts *tragopanes* and pegasus birds. *Tragopan* means "Goat-Pan," the name of a bird here, but a related word, *Aegipanes* (Grk., Goat-Pans), is the name of a different kind of anthropoid or semianthropoid creature at 1.23, 1.48, and 3.95.

61. Part of Hanno's *Periplus* (Circumnavigation [of Africa]) has survived in a Greek translation of his Punic original. He is one of the rare geographic authorities cited by name in *The Chorography*. Hanno's date is uncertain, but the purpose of his trip beyond the Pillars of Hercules was to found trading towns. For Hanno's text and a translation, see Blomqvist 1979. On Hanno, see also Soren et al. (cited in book 1, n. 37), 65–72.

62. "Hustle and bustle" translates Latin *commeatus*, "traffic." The idea seems to be that Africa was not settled in cities or trading posts outside the Mediterranean region.

63. The king referred to is Ptolemy Lathyros (Ptolemy IX). On the adventures of the merchant and sailor Eudoxus of Cyzicus (second century B.C.E.), see Strabo 2.98–102, and see Silberman 1988, 316 n. 4, for discussion.

91. There are, then, on the other side of what we have just called wastelands, mute peoples for whom nodding their head is a substitute for speaking. Some make no sound with their tongue. Others have no tongues. Still others have lips that even stick together except for a hollow reed beneath their noses through which to drink by means of a straw, and when the desire for eating comes over them, they reportedly suck in, one by one, kernels of the grain that grows all over. 92. To some, fire was so unfamiliar before Eudoxus arrived, and seemed so amazing, and pleased them so much, that they really even felt like embracing the flames and hiding the burning sticks in their clothing until it did them harm. 93. Beyond them a bend of the great seacoast encloses a large island on which they tell that only women live. These women are hairy all over and essentially fertile without having sex with men; they have such a rough and brutish character that chains can barely prevent certain ones from resisting. Hanno reported this information, and because he had brought back leather skinned from the ones he slaughtered, credibility has been given to it.[64]

94. Beyond this bay a tall mountain, Theôn Ochêma [Grk., Chariot of the Gods; Mt. Kakulima?],[65] as the Greeks call it, burns with perpetual fire. 95. Beyond the mountain, there is a verdant hill, which extends over a long stretch on a long coastline; from this hill are to be seen the

---

64. Hanno (see book 3, n. 61), following his interpreters, called them gorillas (*Periplus* 17–18), but they may have been chimpanzees or baboons. Schoff (1913, 26–27) thought these hairy savages might be pygmies. His view has not been accepted, but his interpretation follows the Greek version and shows why *gorilla* was first used in English as if it meant "savage person." (*Gorilla* was first used in our familiar sense in 1847 by T.S. Savage, who in turn had adapted the word from a 1799 translation of Hanno's *Periplus* by Thomas Falconer.) That Hanno brought back skins virtually guarantees that these creatures were anthropoid apes and not people. Because of a shortage of supplies, this unnamed island is as far as Hanno's expedition got. Hanno also described the place as being an island in a lake that is contained within a larger island (now regarded widely as being in Sherbro Sound in Sierra Leone). Hanno's facts are different from M.'s: most of these "savage people" were females, and there were males whom he chased but did not catch. Pliny (*HN* 6.200) refers to the same incident and adds that Hanno brought back the skins of two females (Hanno said three), which he left in the temple of Juno/Tanit at Carthage, where they could be seen until the Roman destruction of Carthage in 146 B.C.E.

65. The Kakulima massif is located northeast of Conakry, Guinea. Greek *ochêma* can be used of any platform or support but commonly designates a chariot.

fields—more extensive than can be taken in completely—that belong to the Goat-Pans[66] and Satyrs. As a result, this explanation has received credence: although there is nothing civilized on this hill, no place of residence, no footprints, and although by day there is only a solitary wasteland and an even emptier silence, nevertheless by night fires flare up close together and are revealed like a sizable army camp, and they shake cymbals and beat drums, and horns are heard that sound louder than human ones.

96. Then the Aethiopians again. These people, the Hesperioe [Grk., Westerners] by name, are not at this point the rich ones we have mentioned,[67] and being smaller and uncouth, they are not very much like them in physique. In their territory there is a spring that is at least credible as the Nile's source. The spring is called Nunc by the locals and can apparently be called by no other name, but it has been mispronounced by the barbarian mouth. It also nurtures papyrus and animals that are rather small, in fact, but all of the same species. **97.** While other rivers turn toward Ocean, this one alone runs east into the midlands, and it is uncertain where it ends. From that fact it is inferred that the Nile originates at this spring, moves for quite a distance through inaccessible terrain, and is therefore undiscovered in that interval, but that it reappears where there is access. By inference again, the interval where the river is hidden from view creates the effect that on this side the river appears to give way to another river, while on the far side it appears to spring from a different place.

98. The *catoblepas*[68] is not a large wild animal, but it can scarcely hold up its own large and very heavy head, and it therefore moves around with its face very much to the ground. This animal is born among these Aethiopians and is even worthier of report because of its unique power, namely, that to look it in the eye is deadly even though the *catoblepas* never ever behaves violently by attacking and biting. **99.** Off their coast

---

66. Pliny has a similar description vis-à-vis the Goat-Pans and Satyrs (*HN* 5.6–7).

67. The rich Aethiopians (3.85–87) are the ones living in eastern Africa and spilling over into Asia, i.e., the ones living in Aethiopia proper. Pliny (*HN* 6.195) divides the Aethiopians into eastern and western groups, and the division goes back to Homer (*Od.* 1.22–25).

68. The *catoblepas* (Grk., down-looker) is an unknown, but small (as specified here and suggested by 3.96), wild animal found in this part of Africa. Because the *catoblepas* is small, it is not likely (as has been supposed) to be the gnu, which is a rather large member of the antelope family.

are the Gorgades Islands, once the home, they say, of the Gorgons. They are bounded by the projection of the mainland known as Hesperu Ceras [Grk., Horn of the West].

Africa's Atlantic Coast

100. From that point begins the oceanfront that faces west and is bathed by the Atlantic Ocean. The Aethiopians take up its first part, but no one takes up the middle, which is either parched, covered with sand, or infested with snakes. Islands that the Hesperides[69] reportedly lived in are located off the coast of the parched region. **101.** On the sandy part is Mt. Atlas, which rises abruptly.[70] It is, in fact, precipitous (with its deep-cut cliffs everywhere), inaccessible, and more impenetrable the higher it rises. Mt. Atlas rises right into the clouds since its peak is higher than can be seen, and it reportedly not only reaches the sky and the stars with its peak but even holds them up.[71] **102.** Opposite the sandy part, the Fortunate Isles [Canary Islands] abound in spontaneously generated plants; and with various ones always producing new fruit in rapid

---

69. The Hesperides are associated by their name with evening and the west. They helped the monstrous serpent Ladon to guard the golden apples that were the object of Hercules' eleventh labor (as recorded by Apollodorus [2.5.11], who also asserts arbitrarily that the Hesperides lived among the Hyperboreans, not in Africa). These apples grew on a magical golden tree, and they symbolize the immortal life that Hercules sought. In that way their symbolism overlaps with that of Hercules' visit to the underworld to retrieve Cerberus (his twelfth labor). M. refers to the retrieval of Cerberus through the Acherusian Cave at 1.103 (see n. 74 there).

70. Bunbury (1883, 2:368) notes that M. "describes Mt. Atlas in connection with this western coast [sc. of Africa], in a manner that clearly shows him to refer to the part of the mountain-chain that approaches the Atlantic, rather than that more familiar to the Romans in the north of Mauretania."

71. Thus M. connects the mountains to their legendary namesake. In antiquity, Atlas often was shown holding the celestial sphere, as in the so-called Farnese Atlas. Likewise, in the central frame of its upper register, the remarkable "Asiatic"-style sarcophagus of Junius Bassus, the prefect of the city who died in 359 C.E., shows a mixed theological conception but has the correct mythological representation of the Titan: Atlas holds stretched out above himself the protective mantle of the universe, above which sits the enthroned Jesus, portrayed as a young rabbi, with Peter and Paul standing beside him and wearing full beards in the style of mature Greek philosophers. The sarcophagus is discussed briefly by Nancy H. Ramage and Andrew Ramage, *Roman Art: Romulus to Constantine* (Englewood Cliffs, N.J.: Prentice Hall, 1991), 283–85 (illustration 12.27).

succession, the islands nourish people who want for nothing, and whose islands are more blissfully productive than others are.[72] One of the islands is primarily famous for the uniqueness of its two springs: those who have sipped the one laugh to death; the cure for those so affected is to drink from the other.

103. Next after the stretch that the wild beasts infest are the Himantopodes [Grk., Spindleshanks], hunched and rubber-legged, who reportedly slither rather than walk; then the Pharusii, who were well-off in the days when Hercules went to the Hesperides, but who are now squalid and, except for eating mutton, very poor. **104.** Hereafter richer fields and lovely meadows abound in citron, terebinth, and ivory. Not even the coasts of the Nigritae and the Gaetuli, who are quite nomadic, are infertile. Those coasts are very famous for purple and murex—the most effective dyeing materials. Anything they have dyed is instantly recognizable anywhere.

105. The remainder is the outer coast of Mauretania and Africa's extreme corner as it comes to its last point. The region is richly endowed, but less so, with those same sources of wealth.[73] As to the rest, it is even richer in soil and so fertile that it not only yields in extreme abundance the kinds of grain that are sown but also puts forth

---

72. Also called the Isles of the Blessed, but to be distinguished from the Macarôn Islands (described at 2.100), these islands are associated in Greek, Roman, and Celtic culture with the place where the souls of the good go after death. On the location of these isles, see Pliny *HN* 6.201–5; Pliny cites Juba II of Mauretania (see book 1, n. 33, in the present volume) as his authority. They are sometimes identified either with the Canary Islands, which compose two modern Spanish provinces and lie opposite the coast of Africa, near the former frontier between Morocco and Western Sahara, or with the Madeira group, a modern Portuguese administrative district far off the coast of today's Morocco. Pliny indicates ancient confusion but identifies the Fortunate Isles as the Canary Islands (Insulae Canariae), as in effect M. does too. *Canary* is now misleading in English, since the islands are associated with what used to be called "Canary birds" but are more commonly known now simply as "canaries." The birds take their name from the islands, to be sure, but the islands obtained their name because of the large number of big dogs (*canes*; cp. *canarius -a -um*, "connected with dogs") once available there. Juba himself acquired two dogs from what is now Grand Canary Island. There is no specific mention in antiquity of Canary birds per se (as opposed to finches in general). The Madeira group was better known to the Romans as the Insulae Purpurariae (the Purple Islands), where Juba had begun a dyeing operation using Gaetulian purple.

73. That is, purple and murex.

freely some kinds that are not sown. **106.** Here Antaeus reportedly ruled as king.[74] A sign—and quite a famous one—of this legend is also visible, namely, the modest hill that looks like a man reclining on his back, which the locals report is the funeral mound of Antaeus.[75] As a consequence, when any part of the hill has become eroded, the rains regularly sprinkle the ground, and they keep coming until the erose sections are restored.

107. Some humans[76] occupy the forests, but being less nomadic than those we have just mentioned,[77] others live in cities. The wealthiest cities, albeit the wealthiest among small ones, are considered to be Gilda, Volubilis, and Banasa, all far from Ocean, but nearer to it Sala and Lixos [Larache],[78] which is right on the Lixus [Lukkus] River. Farther on is the colony of Zilia, and the Zilia River, and the place we started from,[79] Point Ampelusia, which now turns into Our Strait, which is the terminus both of this work and of the Atlantic coastline.

ENDORSEMENT[80]

POMPONIUS MELA'S THREE BOOKS ON CHOROGRAPHY
HAVE BEEN COPIED OUT.

---

74. The mention of Antaeus here recalls 1.26, where Antaeus first appeared at the outset of M.'s *periplus*. M. has come full circle, as we are reminded in the next paragraph by M's concluding mot (for which cp. Hor. *Sat.* 1.5.104).

75. Hercules killed the giant Antaeus in a wrestling match after he retrieved the golden apples from the Hesperides (see book 3, n. 69). Hercules' civilized art triumphed over Antaeus' raw, brute force. Lucan (4.593–655) tells the story; see also Plut. *Ser.* 9.3–5 and Strabo 17.3.8 on the alleged size of the skeleton (60 cubits long).

76. M. uses the term *homines* here (see book 1, n. 29). He conceives a rough-and-tumble *multitudo*, not an orderly, identifiable *populus*.

77. The Nigritae and Gaetuli at 3.104.

78. Lixos, an early Phoenicio-Carthaginian foundation, was a Roman colony in the Claudian Age (see Pliny *HN* 5.2).

79. At 1.26.

80. Because it uses technical vocabulary from a later period, I print the Latin endorsement (*subscriptio*) here:

POMPONII MELAE DE CHOROGRAPHIA LIBRI TRES EXPLICITI.
FELICITER. FL. RUSTICIUS HELPIDIUS DOMNULUS V(IR)
C(LARISSIMUS) ET SP(E)C(TABILIS) COM(ES)
CONSISTOR(IANUS) EMENDAVI RABENNAE.

WITH GOOD RESULTS. I, FL. RUSTICIUS HELPIDIUS DOMNULUS, SENATOR AND ADVISOR IN THE IMPERIAL CONSISTORY, HAVE CORRECTED THEM AT RAVENNA.[81]

Parroni (1984) and Silberman (1988) take *Consistor* in the endorsement as the abbreviation of *Consistorii*, "in the Consistory," but the status designation seems more likely.

81. He is known also to have copied out the epitome of Valerius Maximus by Iulius Paris. J.R. Martindale's *The Prosopography of the Later Roman Empire*, vol. 2 (Cambridge: Cambridge University Press, 1980), hereafter cited as *PLRE*, is an indispensable tool here. Silberman (1988, xlvi) and J. Reynolds and N. Wilson (*Scribes and Scholars*, 2d ed. [1974], 93–94) follow Billanovich ([1956] 1958) and identify the Domnulus who signed here with the Christian poet Rusticius Helpidius (see *PLRE* 537, s.v. "Rusticius Helpidius" no. 7), who belongs to the late fifth and early sixth century. However, Gormley et al. (1984, 270–71), citing Cavallin (1955), say that this Domnulus is not this poet but a fifth-century personality. J. Harries (*Sidonius Apollinaris and the Fall of Rome, A.D. 407–485* [Oxford: Clarendon, 1994], 122–24), speculates that the signatory of this manuscript (see *PLRE* 374–75, s.v. "Fl. Rusticius Helpidius Domnulus" no. 2) is to be identified both with Sidonius' friend Domnulus (see *PLRE* 374, s.v. "Domnulus" no. 1) and also with the Christian poet Rusticius Helpidius.

Bibliography

This bibliography lists selected works that bear on Mela or *The Chorography*, including some that are not cited anywhere else in this volume. All works cited in this volume by author's last name and date of publication are listed here. Additional works, not related to Mela but bearing on individual topics, are cited in full in the notes to the translation when they first occur, and subsequent cross-references are supplied as needed.

Texts, Commentaries, Concordances

Brodersen, Kai. *Pomponius Mela: Kreuzfahrt durch die alte Welt.* Darmstadt: Wissenschaftliche Buchgesellschaft, 1994. Text and German translation, with nineteen regional maps reproduced from an early printed edition (1564) and other illustrations.

Frick, C. *Pomponii Melae De chorographia libri tres.* Bibliotheca Scriptorum Graecorum et Romanorum. Leipzig: Teubner, 1880, reprint, Stuttgart, 1968.

Guzmán, Carmen, and Miguel E. Perez, eds. *Concordantia in libros Pomponii Melae De Chorographia.* Hildesheim, Zurich, and New York: Olms, 1989.

Parroni, P. *Pomponio Mela: De chorographia libri tres.* Racolta di studi e testi 160. Rome: Editore di Storia e Letteratura, 1984. Text with index of proper names and extensive commentary.

Parthey, G. *Pomponii Melae De chorographia libri tres.* Berlin: F. Nicolai, 1867.

Ranstrand, G. *Pomponii Melae De chorographia libri tres.* Studia Graeca et Latina Gothoborgensia 28. Göteborg: Almqvist and Wiksell, 1971. Text with *index verborum cunctorum.*

Silberman, A. *Pomponius Mela: Chorographie.* Paris: Belles Lettres, 1988. Text, French translation, extensive commentary, and index of proper names.

Tzschucke, C.H. *Pomponii Melae De situ orbis libri tres.* 7 vols. Leipzig: Siegfried Lebrecht Crusius, 1806–7.

Specialized Studies

Barlow, C.W. "Codex Vaticanus Latinus 4929." *Memoirs of the American Academy in Rome* 15 (1938): 87–124.

Billanovich, G. "Dall'antica Ravenna alle biblioteche umanistiche." *Aevum* 30 (1956): 319–53. Reprinted, with corrections, in *Annuario dell'Univ. Catt. d. S. Cuore,* 1955–57 (1958): 71–107.

Bunbury, E.H. *A History of Ancient Geography.* 2 vols., 2d ed. London: J. Murray, 1883.
Bursian, Conrad. "Zur Kritik des Pomponius Mela." *Neue Jahrbücher für Philologie und Pädagogik* 39 (1869): 629–55.
Carvalho, Joaquim Barradas de. *La traduction espagnole du 'De situ orbis' de Pomponius Mela par Maître Joan Faras et les notes marginales de Duarte Pacheco Pereira.* Centro de estudos de cartografia antiga 15. Lisbon: Junta de Investigações Científicas do Ultramar, 1974.
Detlefsen, D. *Die Geographie Afrikas bei Plinius und Mela und ihre Quellen.* Quellen und Forschungen zur alten Geschichte 14. Berlin: Weidmann, 1908.
Folmer, H. *Stilistika Studier öfver Pomponius Mela.* Uppsala: Almqvist and Wicksell, 1920.
Gisinger, F. "Pomponius" no. 104. *Real-Enzyklopädie der klassischen Altertumswissenschaft* 21 (1952): 2360–411.
Gormley, C.M., M.A. Rouse, and R.H. Rouse. "The Medieval Circulation of the 'De Chorographia' of Pomponius Mela." *Mediaeval Studies* 46 (1984): 266–320.
Klotz, A. *Quaestiones Plinianae geographicae.* Quellen und Forschungen zur alten Geschichte und Geographie 11. Berlin: Weidmann, 1906.
Milham, Mary Ella. "A MS Inventory of Pomponius Mela." *Scriptorium* 35 (1981): 319–21.
Oertel, H. *Über den Sprachgebrauch des Pomponius Mela.* Erlangen: T. Jacob, 1898.
Parroni, P. "Il proemio della *Chorographia* di Pomponio Mela." *Rivista di Filologia e di Istruzione Classica* 96 (1968): 184–97.
Romer, F.E. "The 'Map' of Pomponius Mela: A Proposal." Paper presented at the annual meeting of the American Philological Association, New York, 30 December 1996.
Wissowa, Georg. "Die Abfassungszeit der Chorographia des Pomponius Mela." *Hermes* 51 (1916): 89–96.
Zimmermann, H. *De Pomponii Melae sermone.* Programm des Gymnasium zum Heiligen Kreuz. Dresden, 1895.

Other Ancient Geographic Writers

Blomqvist, Jerker. *The Date and Origin of the Greek Version of Hanno's Periplus.* Lund: CWK Glerup, 1979.
Casson, Lionel. *The Periplus Maris Erythraei.* Princeton: Princeton University Press, 1989.
Peretti, A. *Il periplo di Scilace.* Biblioteca di studi antichi 23. Pisa: Giardini, 1979.
Schoff, W. H. *The Periplus of the Erythraean Sea.* New York: Longman's Green and Co., 1912.
———. *The Periplus of Hanno.* Philadelphia: Commercial Museum, 1913.

General Studies

Barrett, Anthony A. *Caligula: The Corruption of Power.* New Haven: Yale University Press, 1989.
Bolgar, R.R. *The Classical Heritage and Its Beneficiaries.* Cambridge: Cambridge University Press, 1954.
Cary, M., and T.J. Haarhoff. *Life and Thought in the Greek and Roman World.* London: Methuen, 1940.
Cavallin, S. "Le poète Domnulus: Étude prosopographique." *Sacris Erudiri* 7 (1955): 49–66.
Conte, Gian Biagio. *Latin Literature: A History.* Baltimore: Johns Hopkins University Press, 1994. Originally published as *Letteratura latina: Manuale storico dalle origini alla fine dell'impero romano* (Florence: Casa Editrice Felice Le Monnier, 1987).
Cornell, T.J., and J.F. Matthews. *Atlas of the Roman World.* Oxford: Phaidon, 1982.
Dilke, O.A.W. *Greek and Roman Maps.* London: Thames and Hudson, 1985.
Doob, Penelope. *The Idea of the Labyrinth from Classical Antiquity through the Middle Ages.* Ithaca: Cornell University Press, 1990.
Ferrill, Arther. *Caligula: Emperor of Rome.* London: Thames and Hudson, 1991.
Fluss, M. "Manilius" no. 31. *Real-Enzyklopädie der klassischen Altertumswissenschaft* 14 (1928): 1143–44.
Jacoby, Felix. *Fragmente der griechischen Historiker.* Vol. 2c. Leiden: Brill, 1963.
Janson, T. *Latin Prose Prefaces.* Studia Latina Stockholm 13. Stockholm: Almqvist and Wiksell, 1964.
Kenney, E.J., and W.V. Clausen, eds. *The Cambridge History of Classical Literature.* Vol. 2, *Latin Literature.* Cambridge: Cambridge University Press, 1982.
Nicolet, Claude. "Les 'Quatre sages' de Jules César et la 'mesure du monde' selon Julius Honorius: Réalité antique et tradition médiévale." *Journal des Savants* (1986): 157–218.
———. *Space, Geography, and Politics in the Early Roman Empire.* Jerome Lectures 19. Ann Arbor: University of Michigan Press, 1991. Originally published as *L'Inventaire du monde: Géographie et politique aux origines de l'Empire romain* (Paris: Fayard, 1988).
Rawson, Elizabeth. *Intellectual Life in the Late Roman Republic.* Baltimore: Johns Hopkins University Press, 1985.
Romm, James S. *The Edges of the Earth in Ancient Thought: Geography, Exploration, and Fiction.* Princeton: Princeton University Press, 1992.
Stahl, W.H. *Roman Science.* Madison: University of Wisconsin Press, 1962.
Thomson, J.O. *A History of Ancient Geography.* Cambridge: Cambridge University Press, 1948.
Trüdinger, Karl. *Studien zur Geschichte der griechisch-römischen Ethnographie.* Leipzig: B.G. Teubner in Kommission, 1918.

Index

All references are specified by the book and section number of *The Chorography*.

Geographic Names

All places named by Mela are listed here. Modern place-names are given in parentheses after the main entry; they are also cross-referenced in the index. Where the Latin name differs significantly from the form used in this translation, it is preceded by the abbreviation Lat. and given in parentheses after the main entry. Where both the Latin name and a modern place-name are provided, they are separated by a semicolon, and the Latin name comes first. In keeping with the demands of the genre, islands and rivers are clearly marked.

Abdera, in Thrace, 2.29
Abdera (Adra), in Spain, 2.94
Abila (Jebel Musa), 1.27, 2.95
Absyrtis, 2.114
Abydos (Maltepe), 1.97, 2.26
Academia, 1.90
Acanthus (Hierissos), 2.30
Acarnania, 2.39, 2.43, 2.53
Aceraunian Canyons (Lat. Acerauni saltus), 3.84
Acesinus R., 3.69
Achaean Harbor. *See* Achaeôn Limen
Achaeôn Limen, 1.93
Achaia-and-Elis (Lat. Achaia Elis), 2.39, 2.42
Acheloüs R. (Aspropótamo), 2.53
Acherusian Cave (Lat. Acherusius specus), 1.103, 2.51
Achillea, is., 2.98
Achilles' Racecourse. *See* Dromos Achilleos

Acritas, Mt., 2.49, 2.50, 2.110
Acrocorinth (Lat. Acrocorinthos), 2.48
Acronus, Lake (Lower Bodensee/Lower Lake Constance), 3.24
Acrothoon, 2.32
Actium, 2.54
Adanus (Aden), 3.80
Aden. *See* Adanus
Adiabene, 1.62
Adra. *See* Abdera, in Spain
Adramytion, 1.91
Adria (Lat. Hadria), in Italy, 2.65
Adriatic Gulf (Lat. sinus Hadriae), 2.57
Adriatic Sea (Lat. Hadriaticum mare), 1.17, 1.18, 2.17, 2.39, 2.54, 2.58, 2.67, 2.110, 2.114
Adrobrica, 3.13
Aeaee, is., 2.120
Aeas (Vijosë) R., 2.57

137

Index

Aegatae, 2.105
Aegean Sea (Lat. Aegaeum mare), 1.17, 1.18, 2.25, 2.27, 2.37, 2.48, 2.106, 2.109
Aegina, is., 2.109
Aegina (error for Aegialia), is., 2.111
Aegion, 2.53
Aegira, 2.53
Aegos R., 2.26
Aegypt (Lat. Aegyptus), 1.40, 1.49, 1.51, 1.64, 3.74, 3.82, 3.84, 3.85
Aenaria, is., 2.121
Aenos (Enez), 2.28
Aeolis, 1.14, 1.90
Aesis R., 2.64
Aestria, is., 2.114
Aethiopia, 1.49, 1.50, 1.53
Aethiopians (Lat. Aethiopes), 1.12, 1.14, 1.22, 3.67, 3.85–87, 3.96, 3.100
Aethiopian Sea (Lat. Aethiopium mare), 1.21
Aetna, 2.119, 2.120
Aetolia, 2.39, 2.43
Africa, 1.8, 1.9, 1.12, 1.20–23, 1.25, 1.33, 1.40, 1.48, 1.50, 1.60, 2.95, 2.96, 2.105, 2.116, 2.120, 3.89, 3.105
African Sea (Lat. Africum pelagus), 2.123
Agatha (Agde), 2.80
Agde. *See* Agatha
Agragas, 2.118
Ak R. *See* Cestros
Al Ladhiqiyāh. *See* Laodicea
Albenga. *See* Albingaunum
Albingaunum (Albenga), 2.72
Albis (Elbe) R., 3.30, 3.71
Aleria, 2.122
Alexandria, 1.60, 2.104, 2.114, 3.90
Algiers. *See* Icosium
Alicante. *See* Lucentia
Alicudi. *See* Heraclea
Allone, 2.93
Alope, 2.45
Alopeconnesus, 2.27
Aloros, 2.35
Alpheus R., 2.51, 2.117

Alps (Lat. Alpes), 2.58, 2.59, 2.72, 2.73, 2.76, 3.24, 3.25
Altars of Sestius (Lat. Sestianae arae), 3.13
Altars of the Philaeni (Lat. arae Philaenorum), 1.33, 1.38
Altino. *See* Altinum R.
Altinum (Altino) R., 2.61
Amanus, Mt. (Elma Daği), 1.69
Amazonian Mountains (Lat. Amazonici montes), 1.109
Amazonius (Lat. Amazonius campus), 1.105
Ambracia (Árta), 2.54
Ambracian Gulf (Lat. Ambracius sinus), 2.54, 2.110
Amisos, 1.105
Amissis (Ems) R., 3.30
Ampelusia, Point (Cape Spartel), 1.25, 2.96, 3.107
Amphilochian Argives (Lat. Argi Amphilochii), 2.54
Amphipolis, 2.30
Ampsacus (Kabir) R., 1.30
Amudarya. *See* Oxos R.
Amyclae, 2.41
Anas (Guadiana) R., 2.87, 3.3, 3.6, 3.7
Anchialos (Pomoriye), 2.22
Anchorage. *See* Naustathmos
Ancon, 2.64
Ancona, 2.64
Andros, is., 1.92, 2.111
Anemurium (Anamur Burun), 1.77
Annaba. *See* Hippo Regius
Antandrus, 1.91–92
Anthedon, 2.45
Antibes. *See* Antipolis
Antichthones, 1.4, 1.54
Anticyra, 2.53
Antiochia, 1.63, 1.69
Antipolis (Antibes), 2.76
Antissa, 2.101
Antium (Anzio), 2.71
Antronia, 2.40
Antros, is., 3.22
Anzio. *See* Antium

Apennines (Lat. Apenninus mons), 2.58, 2.59
Aphrodisium, 2.71
Aphrodisium, Point, (Caria), 1.84
Apollo, Point (Lat. Apollinis promunturium; Ras Si Ali Mekki), 1.34
Apollonia, in Macedonia, 2.30
Apollonia (Polan), 2.57
Apollonia (Sozopol), 2.22
Apollonia (Sūsah), 1.40
Apsorus, is., 2.114
Apulum litus, 2.66
Aquileia, 2.61
Arabia, 1.14, 1.60, 1.61, 3.74, 3.79
Arabia (city), 3.80
Arabian Gulf (Lat. Arabicus sinus), 3.73, 3.74, 3.90
Arabian Sea (Lat. Arabicum mare; Red Sea), 1.9. *See also* Red Sea
Arados (Rûad), is., 2.103
Araks. *See* Araxes R.
Arauris (Hérault) R., 2.80
Arausio (Orange), 2.75
Araxes (Araks) R., 3.40
Araxos, 2.49, 2.52
Arcadia, 2.39, 3.43
Ardea, 2.71
Arelate (Arles), 2.75
Aremphaei. *See* Arimphaei
Argolid (Lat. Argolis), 2.39, 2.41
Argolis, Gulf of (Lat. Argolicus sinus), 2.50, 2.51
Argos, 2.41
Argyre, is., 3.70
Arles. *See* Arelate
Aria, 1.12
Aria, is., 2.98
Ariane, 1.12, 3.71
Arimaspoe, 2.2
Ariminum (Rimini), 2.64
Arimphaei/Aremphaei, 1.13, 1.117
Armene, 1.104
Armenia, 3.40
Armenian Gates (Lat. Armeniae pylae), 1.81
Arsinna, 1.31

Arsinoë, 1.40
Arsinoë (Tūkrah), 3.80
Árta. *See* Ambracia
Arusaces R., 3.71
Arzew, Gulf of. *See* Laturus Gulf
Ascalon (Ashqelon), 1.64
Ashdod. *See* Azotus, Port
Ashqelon. *See* Ascalon
Asi R. *See* Orontes
Asia, 1.8, 1.10, 1.11, 1.15, 1.19, 1.20, 1.22, 1.49, 1.68, 1.88, 1.101, 2.1, 2.3, 2.26, 2.34, 2.102, 3.36, 3.68; Asiatic littoral (Lat. Asiaticum litus), 3.36; Asiatic regions (Lat. Asiaticae regiones), 2.100
Asiaces (Tiligul) R., 2.7
Asine, Gulf of (Lat. Asinaeus sinus), 2.50, 2.51
Asine, in the Peloponnesos, 2.51
Asine, is., 2.114
Aspendos, 1.78
Aspropótamo. *See* Acheloüs R.
Assos, 1.93
Astabores R., 1.50
Astacos, 1.100
Astape R., 1.50
Asteria, is., 2.110
Astigi (Ecija), 2.88
Astura, 1.91
Astypalaea, is., 2.114
Aswân. *See* Syene
Atax (Aude) R., 2.81
Aternus (Pescara) R., 2.65
Athenopolis (Saint-Tropez), 2.77
Athens (Lat. Athenae), 2.41
Athos, Mt. (Lat. Atho mons), 2.30, 2.31, 2.45, 2.106
Atlantic Ocean (Lat. Atlanticus oceanus), 1.15, 1.21, 1.22, 1.25, 2.87, 3.3, 3.6, 3.100, 3.107
Atlas, Mt., 3.101
Atthis (Attica), 2.26, 2.39, 2.41, 2.49, 2.109
Aturia R., 3.15
Atyras (Karasu) R., 2.24
Auch. *See* Eliumberrum

Aucus (Harrach) R., 1.31
Aude. *See* Atax R.
Aufidus (Ufente) R., 2.66
Augusta (Trier), 3.20
Augustodunum (Autun), 3.20
Aulis, 2.45
Autun. *See* Augustodunum
Ave. *See* Avo R.
Avennio (Avignon), 2.75
Avernus, Lake, 2.70
Avignon. *See* Avennio
Avo (Ave) R., 3.10
Axene Sea (Lat. Pontus Axenus), 1.102. *See also* Pontus
Axios. *See* Axius R.
Axius (Vardar/Axios) R., 2.35
Ay Todor. *See* Criu Metopon
Azotus (Ashdod), Port, 1.61
Azov, Sea of. *See* Maeotis, Lake

Babylon, 1.63
Babylonia, 1.62
Baesippo (Barbate), 2.96
Baetica, 2.87, 2.88, 2.94, 3.6, 3.46
Baetis (Guadalquivir) R., 3.5
Baetulo (Besos) R., 2.90
Baetulo (Madalona), 2.90
Bagrada (Mejerda) R., 1.34
Baiae, 2.70
Balchik. *See* Dionysopolis
Balearic (Lat. Baliares) Isles, 2.124
Balsa (Torre de Tavira), 3.7
Baltic Sea. *See* Codanus Bay
Banasa, 3.107
Barbate. *See* Baesippo
Barbesula, 2.94
Barcelona. *See* Barcino
Barcino (Barcelona), 2.90
Bargylos, 1.85
Bari. *See* Barium
Barium (Bari), 2.66
Basilic Gulf (Lat. Basilicus sinus), 1.85, 1.86
Basilid nation. *See* Basilidae (in Peoples and Groups index)
Batroûn. *See* Botrys

Beautiful Harbor. *See* Calos Limen
Beirut. *See* Berytos
Belasitza. *See* Orbelos, Mt.
Belgae, 3.20
Bello, 2.96
Bellunte, 3.15
Berenice (I), 3.80
Berenice (II), 3.80
Berytos (Beyrouth/Beirut), 1.69
Besos. *See* Baetulo R.
Beterrae (Béziers), 2.75, 2.80
Beyrouth. *See* Berytos
Biferno. *See* Tifernus R.
Birket Qârûn. *See* Moeris
Bisanthe (Tekirdağ), 2.24
Bithynis, 2.98
Bizerte. *See* Hippo Diarrhytos
Bizone (Kavarna), 2.22
Black Corcyra (Lat. Corcyra nigra; Korchula), 2.114
Black Gulf. *See* Melas Gulf
Black R. *See* Melas (Karak) R., in Thrace
Black Sea. *See* Axene Sea; Euxine Sea; Pontus
Blanc, Cap. *See* White Point
Blanda, 2.69
Blande, 2.90
Boar's Harbor. *See* Capru Limen
Bodensee, Lower. *See* Acronus, Lake
Bodensee, Upper. *See* Venetus, Lake
Bodrun. *See* Halicarnassos
Boeo, Capo. *See* Lilybaeum, pr.
Boeotia, 2.39, 2.40, 2.107
Bolbitic mouth (of the Nile), 1.60
Bologna. *See* Bononia
Bon, Cap. *See* Mercury Point
Bononia (Bologna), 2.60
Borion (Lat. Borion promunturium; Ras Taiùnes), 1.37
Borysthenes (Dnepr) R., 2.6, 2.98
Borysthenida, 2.6
Bosphorus, Cimmerian (Kerchenskiy Proliv, Strait of Kerch), 1.7, 1.112, 1.114, 1.115, 2.2, 2.3
Bosphorus, Thracian (Karadeniz

Boğazi), 1.7, 1.10, 1.14, 1.101, 1.108, 2.24, 2.99
Botrys (Batroûn), 1.67
Bougaroun, Cape. See Metagonium, Point
Brauronia, 2.46
Brindisi. See Brundisium
Britain (Lat. Britannia), 3.49, 3.53
Britannic Ocean (Lat. Britannicus oceanus), 1.15, 2.85; Britannic Sea (Lat. Britannicum mare), 3.48
Brundisium (Brindisi), 2.66, 2.114
Bruttium, 2.68; (Lat. Bruttius ager), 2.115
Bubassius Gulf, 1.84
Bubastis, 1.60
Buca (Termoli), 2.65
Bucephalos, 2.49
Buces (Nogaïka) R., 2.2
Bug. See Hypanis R.
Butroton, 2.54
Buxentum, 2.69
Buxeri, 1.107
Byblos (Jbail), 1.67
Bytinis (Vize), 2.24
Byzantion (Istanbul), 2.24

Cabo da Roca. See Great Point
Cabo de la Nao. See Ferraria, promontory
Cabo de Santa Maria. See Wedge Field
Cabo de Sâo Vicente. See Sacred Point
Caecina (Cecina) R., 2.72
Caepio. See Monument of Caepio
Caesaraugusta (Saragossa), 2.88
Caesarea, 1.30
Cagliari. See Caralis
Caïcus R., 1.90
Calabria, 2.66
Calarnaea. See Tower of Calarnaea
Calauria, is., 2.109
Calbis R., 1.83
Calchedon, 1.101
Callatis (Mangalia), 2.22

Calliaros, 2.40
Callipolis, in Greece, 2.52
Callipolis (Gallipoli), 2.66
Calos Limen, 2.3
Calpe (Gibraltar), 1.27; (Lat. Calpes), 2.95
Calpes. See Calpe
Calydon, 2.53
Calymnia, is., 2.111
Cambyses (Yori) R., 3.41
Camiros, 2.101
Campanella, Punta della. See Minerva, Point
Campania, 2.59, 2.70
Campomarino. See Cliternia
Canary Islands. See Fortunate Isles
Canastraeum, Point, 2.34, 2.35
Candidum promunturium. See White Point
Canopic mouth (of the Nile), 2.103
Canopos, is., 2.103
Canosa di Puglia. See Canusium
Canusium (Canosa di Puglia), 2.66
Caphereus, Point, 2.107
Capo Passero. See Pachynum, Point
Capraia. See Capraria
Capraria (Capraia), is., 2.122
Capreae (Capri), is., 2.121
Capri. See Capreae
Capru Limen, 2.30
Capua, 2.60
Caralis (Cagliari), 2.123
Carambis, Point (Kerempe Burun): (Lat. Carambis), 1.104; (Lat. Carambicum promunturium), 2.3
Carbania, is., 2.122
Carcine (Skadovsk), 2.4
Carcinites (Karkinitskiy), 2.4
Carcinus, 2.68
Cardia (Karaköy), 2.27
Caria, 1.14, 1.83, 2.101
Carian Port (Lat. Caria; Shabla), 2.22
Carpathian Sea (Lat. Carpathium mare), 2.114
Carpathos, is., 2.114
Carteia, 2.96

Carthage, Gulf of (Lat. Carthaginis sinus), 2.105
Carthage (Lat. Carthago), 1.34, 1.38
Carthage (Lat. Carthago Nova; Cartagena), 2.94
Cartinna (Ténès), 1.31
Caruanda, 1.85
Carystos, 2.108
Casius, Mt. (El Kas), 1.61, 3.74
Caspian Gates (Lat. Caspiae pylae), 1.81
Caspian Gulf (Lat. Caspianus sinus), 1.11, 1.12, 1.13, 3.38, 3.39
Caspian Mountains (Lat. Caspii montes), 1.109
Caspian Sea (Lat. Caspium mare), 1.9, 3.38, 3.58
Cassandria, 2.35
Cassiterides (Isles of Scilly), is., 3.47
Castanaea, 2.35
Castel Rousillon. See Ruscino
Castra Cornelia, 1.34
Castra Delia, 1.34
Castrum Novum (Torre Chiaruccia), 2.72
Catabathmos (Senke on the Gulf of Salûm), 1.39, 1.40, 1.49
Cataptystic mouth (of the Nile), 1.60
Catarhactes (Düden) R., 1.79
Catina, 2.117
Caucasus (Lat. Caucasus), 1.81; (Lat. Caucasii montes), 1.109
Caudos, is., 2.114
Caulonia, 2.68
Caunus, 1.83
Cavado. See Celadus R.
Cave of Hercules (Lat. specus Herculi), 1.26
Caÿster (Lat. Caÿstros) R., 1.88
Cebennae. See Cebennici Mountains
Cebennici (Cévennes) Mountains, 2.74; (Lat. Cebennae), 2.80
Cecina. See Caecina R.
Cedrosis, 1.12
Celadus (Cavado) R., 3.10
Celendris, 1.77

Celtic Point (Lat. Celticum promunturium; Punta de Narija), 3.9, 3.12
Cenaeum, Point, , 2.107
Cenchreae, 2.48
Çenet Deresi. See Corycian Cave
Centuripe. See Centuripinum
Centuripinum (Centuripe), 2.118
Ceos, is., 2.111
Cephallania, is., 2.110
Cepoe, 1.112
Ceramicus Gulf, 1.84
Cerasunta, 1.107
Ceraunian Mountains (Lat. Ceraunii montes; Mali i Çikë with Kara Burun), 1.109, 2.54, 3.39
Cerbère. See Cervaria
Cercasorum (El Arkas), 1.51
Cercina (Kerkenah), is., 2.105
Cervaria (Cerbère), 2.84, 2.89
Cestros (Ak) R., 1.79
Ceuta. See Seven Brothers
Ceyhan. See Pyramus R.
Ceyreste. See Citharistes
Chalcis, is., 2.111
Chalcis, on Euboea, 2.108
Chariot of the Gods. See Theôn Ochema
Charra, 3.80
Charybdis, 2.115
Cheleken. See Talge
Chelidonian (Lat. Chelidoniae) Islands, 2.102
Chelonates R., 2.49, 2.52
Chemmis, is., 1.55
Chercell. See Iol
Cherronesus (Sevastopol), 2.3
Chersonessus (Méthana), 2.49
Chersonessus, Thracian (Gelibolu/Gallipoli), 2.25, 2.27
Chios, is., 2.101
Chomarae, 1.3
Chott Jerid. See Triton, Lake
Chrysa, in Aeolis, 1.91
Chryse, is. off Crete, 2.114
Chryse, is. off India (Golden Is.), 3.70
Chyarae, is., 2.105

Cicynethos, is., 2.106
Cilicia, 1.14, 1.63, 1.77, 2.102
Cimo, 1.78
Cinolis, 1.104
Cinyps (Khāne) R., 1.37
Cios, 1.100
Circeia, 2.71
Cirrha (Itéa), 2.53
Cirta (Constantine), 1.30
Cisthena, 1.91
Cithaeron, Mt., 2.40
Citharistes (Ceyreste), 2.77
City of the Sun (Lat. Solis urbs), 3.84
Ciudadela. *See* Iamno
Clampetia (San Lucido), 2.69
Clazomenae, 1.89
Cleonae, 2.30
Cliternia (Campomarino), 2.65
Clodianum R., 2.89
Cluana, 2.65
Clupea (Kelibia), 1.34
Cnemides, 2.45
Cnidus, 1.84
Codanus Bay (Baltic Sea), 3.31, 3.54
Coele, 1.62
Coelos (Kilya), Port, 2.26
Colchis, 2.44
Colis, Point (Cape Comorin), 3.59, 3.67, 3.68
Collyris, 1.104
Coloba, Point, 3.80
Colonna, Capo. *See* Lacinium, Point
Colophon, 1.88
Colubraria (Formentera), is., 2.126
Columna Rhegia, 2.68
Comorin, Cape. *See* Colis, Point
Commagene, 1.62
Concordia, 2.61
Consentia (Cosenza), 2.68
Constance, Lower Lake. *See* Acronus, Lake
Constance, Upper Lake. *See* Venetus, Lake
Constanta. *See* Tomoe
Constantine. *See* Cirta
Coös (Kos/Cos), is., 2.101

Cophes R., 3.69
Cophos, 2.34
Coracanda R., 1.112
Coraxic Mountains (Lat. Coraxici montes), 1.109
Coraxicus, Mt., 3.41
Corcyra, Black. *See* Black Corcyra
Corcyra (Kérkira/Corfu), is., 2.110
Cordova. *See* Corduba
Corduba (Cordova), 2.88
Corfu. *See* Corcyra
Corinth, Gulf of. *See* Rhion
Corinth (Lat. Corinthos), 2.48
Coros (Kor) R., 3.75
Corsica, is., 2.122, 2.123
Corycian Cave (Lat. Corycius specus; Çenet Deresi), 1.72
Corycos (Korghoz), 1.71
Coryna, 1.89
Cos. *See* Coös
Cosa, 2.72
Cosenza. *See* Consentia
Cossura (Pantelleria), is., 2.120
Cothonius, is., 2.111
Cragus, Mt. (San Dagh), 1.82
Crau. *See* Litus Lapideum
Crete (Lat. Creta), is., 2.112
Creusis, 2.53
Crimea. *See* Peninsula
Criu Metopon, in Crete, 2.112
Criu Metopon (Ay Todor), 2.3
Cromnos, 1.104
Croto (Crotone), 2.68
Crotone. *See* Croto
Crunos, 2.22
Crya, 1.83
Cumae, 2.70
Cupra (Cupramarittima), 2.65
Cupramarittima. *See* Cupra
Cyaneae, is., 2.99
Cyanos, 2.111
Cyclades, is., 2.111
Cycnus, 1.110
Cydna, 2.35
Cydnus (Tarsus) R., 1.70
Cydonea, 2.113

Cyllene, 2.52
Cyllene, Mt. (Lat. Cyllenius mons), 2.43
Cyme, 1.90
Cyna, 1.91
Cynos, 2.40
Cynos Sema, 2.26
Cyparissos, 2.51
Cyparissos, Gulf of (Lat. Cyparissius sinus), 2.50, 2.51
Cypros, is., 2.102, 2.112
Cypsela (Ipsala), 2.24
Cyrenaïca, 1.39
Cyrene (Shahhāt), 1.40; province, 1.22
Cyrnos, 1.84
Cyrus (Kura) R., 3.41
Cythera, is., 2.110
Cytoros, 1.104
Cyzicum, 1.98

Damascene, 1.62
Danube (Lat. Danuvius) R., 2.8, 2.57, 3.30. *See also* Ister R.
Dardanelles. *See* Hellespont
Dardania, 1.96
Dascylos, 1.99
Decium, 3.15
Delos, is., 2.111, 3.37
Delphi, 1.82, 2.40
Delta, 1.51
Demetrias, 2.44
Denmark. *See* Haemodae Is.
Deris, 2.34
Dertosa (Tortosa), 2.90
Despoto Dagh. *See* Haemos, Mt.
Devales R., 3.15
Dianium (Giannutri), is., 2.122
Dictynna, 2.113
Didyma (Salina), is., 2.120
Diomedia, is., 2.114
Dionysia, is., 2.111
Dionysopolis (Balchik), 2.22
Dioscorias, 1.111
Dnepr. *See* Borysthenes R.
Dnestr. *See* Tyra R.
Dodonaei Iovis templum, 2.43

Don. *See* Tanaïs R.
Doris, 2.39
Doriscos, 2.28
Dromos Achilleos (Tendrovskaya Kosa), 2.15
Düden. *See* Catarhactes R.
Duero. *See* Durius R.
Dulichium, is., 2.110
Durazzo. *See* Dyrrachium
Durius (Duero) R., 3.8, 3.10
Durrës. *See* Dyrrachium
Dyrrachium (Durazzo/Durrës), 2.56
Dyscelados, is., 2.114

Eastern Ocean (Lat. Eous oceanus), 1.9
Eastern Sea: (Lat. Eoum mare), 3.59; (Lat. Eoum pelagus), 3.61
Ebora, Port. *See* Port Ebora
Ebora, in Baetica, 3.4
Ebora (Evora), in Lusitania, 3.7
Ebro. *See* Hiberus R.
Ebusos (Ibiza), is., 2.125, 2.126
Eceabat. *See* Madytos
Echidna, 2.11
Echinades, is., 2.110
Echinia, 2.30
Echinos, 2.44
Ecija. *See* Astigi
Egypt. *See* Aegypt
El Arkas. *See* Cercasorum
Elaea, 1.90
Elba. *See* Ilva
Elbe. *See* Albis R.
Elche. *See* Ilice
Electrides, is., 2.114
Elephantine (Gesiret Aswân), 1.51, 1.60
Eleus (Eski Hissarlik), 2.26
Eleusin, 2.41
Eliberrae (Elne), 2.84
Elis. *See* Achaia-and-Elis
Elis (territory), 2.42
Eliumberrum (Auch), 3.20
Emerita (Mérida), 2.88
Emporiae, 2.89

Ems. *See* Amissis R.
Encheleae, 2.55
Enez. *See* Aenos
Enna. *See* Henna
Ephesus, 1.88
Epidamnos, 2.36
Epidaurus, 2.50, 2.109
Epiros, 2.39, 2.43, 2.54, 2.110
Erasinus R., 2.51
Ereğli. *See* Heraclea; Perinthos
Eresos, 2.101
Eretria, 2.108
Ergene. *See* Ergine
Erginos (Ergene) R., 2.24
Erice. *See* Eryx
Erymanthus R., 2.43
Erythia, is., 3.47
Erythra Thalassa, 3.72. *See also* Red Sea
Eryx (Erice), 2.119
Eski Hissarlik. *See* Eleus
Etesian Winds (Lat. Etesiae), 1.53
Etruria, 2.59; Etruscan localities and rivers (Lat. Etrusca loca et flumina), 2.72
Euboea, is., 2.107
Eudaemon Arabia, 3.79
Euphrates R., 1.63, 3.76, 3.77
Euripos, 2.108
Europe (Lat. Europa), 1.8, 1.9, 1.15, 1.20, 1.25, 1.101, 2.1, 2.95, 2.96, 2.106
Eurotas R., 2.51
Eurymedon R., 1.78
Eurymenae, 2.35
Euteletos, is., 2.105
Euthana, 1.84
Euxine Sea (Lat. pontus Euxinus), 1.102, 1.109, 2.3, 2.17. *See also* Pontus
Evenos R., 2.53
Evora. *See* Ebora
Ex, 2.94
Exampaeus, 2.7

Face of God. *See* Theuprosopon
Fano. *See* Fanum

Fanum (Lat. Fanestris colonia; Fano), 2.64
Faro. *See* Ossonoba
Feodosiya. *See* Theodosia
Fermo. *See* Firmum
Ferraria (Cabo de la Nao), promontory, 2.91, 2.125
Fethiye. *See* Telmesos
Filicudi. *See* Phoenicusa
Firmum (Fermo), 2.65
Flevo, Lake, 3.24
Flevo (Vlieland), 3.24
Fondi. *See* Fundi
Fontaine de Salses. *See* Salsulae
Formentera. *See* Colubraria
Formiae (Formia), 2.71
Fortunate Isles (Lat. Fortunatae insulae; Canary Is.), 3.102
Forum Iulii (Frejús), 2.77
Fountain of the Sun (Lat. fons Solis), 1.39
Francoli. *See* Tulcis R.
Frejús. *See* Forum Iulii
Friendly Sea. *See* Euxine Sea
Fundi (Fondi), 2.71

Gades (Cádiz), is., 2.97, 3.46, 3.90; Port of (Lat. Gaditanus portus), 3.4
Gaesus R., 1.87
Galata, is., 2.120
Gallia. *See* Gaul
Gallice, 3.52
Gallipoli. *See* Callipolis
Gallipoli/Gelibolu. *See* Chersonessus, Thracian
Ganges R., 3.67, 3.68, 3.69, 3.70
Garganus (Gargano), Mt., 2.65
Gargara, 1.93
Garonne. *See* Garunna
Garunna (Garonne) R., 3.20, 3.21, 3.23
Gaul (Lat. Gallia), 1.18–19, 2.79, 2.84, 2.86, 2.87, 2.124, 3.14, 3.16, 3.20, 3.45, 3.50; Gallia Bracata, 2.74; Gallia Narbonensis, 2.74; Gallia Togata, 2.59
Gaulos (Gozo), is., 2.120

Gaza, 1.64
Gelibolu/Gallipoli. *See* Chersonessus, Thracian
Gelonos, 1.116
Gelos, 1.84
Genoa/Genova. *See* Genua
Genua (Genova/Genua), 2.72
Geraestos, Point, 2.107
Germany (Lat. Germania), 2.8, 2.73, 3.25, 3.32, 3.45, 3.50, 3.54
Gerrhos (Malochnaya) R., 2.4
Gesiret Aswân. *See* Elephantine
Gesoriacum, 3.23
Giannutri. *See* Dianium
Gibraltar. *See* Calpe
Giglio. *See* Igilium
Gilda, 3.107
Gnatia (Torre d'Egnazia), 2.66
Gnossos, 2.113
Goat R. *See* Aegos R.
Golden Is. *See* Chryse, is. off India
Gorgades, is., 3.99
Gortyna, 2.113
Gozo. *See* Gaulos
Granicus R., 1.98
Graviscae (Porto Clementino), 2.72
Great Point (Lat. Magnum promunturium; Cabo da Roca), 3.7
Great Port. *See* Portus Magnus
Greater Balearic Isles (Mallorca). *See* Balearic Isles
Greece (Lat. Graecia), 1.18, 1.90, 2.26, 2.34, 2.37, 2.116
Guadalquivir. *See* Baetis R.
Guadiana. *See* Anas R.
Gusty Mountains. *See* Riphaean Range
Gyaros, is., 2.111
Gythium, 2.51

Habromacte, 1.34
Hadria. *See* Adria
Hadriatic Sea. *See* Adriatic Sea
Hadrumetum (Sousse), 1.34
Haemodae Islands (Denmark), 3.54

Haemodes (Himalaya) Range, 1.81, 3.68
Haemos, Mt. (Rodopi Planina/Despoto Dagh), 2.17
Halicarnassos (Bodrun), 1.84, 1.85
Halmydessos (Midye), 2.23
Halonessos, is., 2.106
Halos, 2.44
Halys R. (Kizil Irmak), 1.105
Hamiz R. *See* Nabar
Hammo, 1.39
Hammodes, Point, 1.70
Harrach R. *See* Aucus
Hasta (Mesa de Asta), 3.4
Hebrus (Merica) R., 2.17, 2.28
Helene, is., 2.109
Heliu Trapeza, 3.87
Hellas, 2.37, 2.46, 2.48. *See also* Greece
Hellespont (Lat. Hellespontus; Dardanelles), 1.7, 1.14, 1.15, 1.90, 1.96, 2.25, 2.26, 2.100; (Lat. Hellesponticum fretum), 1.7
Henna (Enna), 2.118
Heraclea, in Italy, 2.68
Heraclea, in Sicily, 2.118
Heraclea (Alicudi), is., 2.120
Heraclea (Ereğli), 1.103
Hérault. *See* Arauris R.
Herculaneum, 2.70
Hercules. *See* Cave of Hercules; Pillars of Hercules
Hercynian Forest (Lat. Hercynia silva), 3.29
Hermiona, 2.50
Hermisium, 2.3
Hermonassa, 1.112
Hermus R., 1.89
Heroöpolis, Bay of (Lat. Heroöpoliticus sinus), 3.8
Hesperia, 1.40
Hesperides, is., 3.100, 3.103
Hesperu Ceras, 3.99
Hiberus (Ebro) R., 2.90
Hiera (Vulcano), is., 2.120
Hierissos. *See* Acanthus
Hill of Pandion, 1.84

Index

Himera (city), 2.118
Himera R., 2.119
Hindu Kush. *See* Propanisus
Hippis, 1.86
Hippo Diarrhytos (Bizerte), 1.34
Hippo, Gulf of (Lat. Hipponensis sinus), 1.34
Hipponium, 2.69
Hippo Regius (Annaba), 1.33
Hippuris, is., 2.111
Hispal (Seville), 2.88
Hispania. *See* Spain
Hister. *See* Ister R.
Histonium (Vasto), 2.65
Histria. *See* Istria
Histropolis. *See* Istropolis
Horn of the West. *See* Hesperu Ceras
Huelva. *See* Onoba
Hybla, 2.118
Hydaspes (Jhelum) R., 3.69
Hydria, is., 2.114
Hydrus, Mt., 2.66
Hyla, 1.84
Hypacaris (Kuban) R., 2.4
Hypanis (Bug) R., 2.7
Hypatos, 1.69
Hyrcania, 3.43; Bay of (Lat. Hyrcanius sinus), 3.38, 3.39, 3.41

Iader (Zadar), 2.57
Ialysos, 2.101
Iamno (Ciudadela), 2.124
Iasian Gulf (Lat. Iasius sinus), 1.85
Iaxartes (Syrdarya) R., 3.42
Ibiza. *See* Ebusos
Icaria, is., 2.111
Ichthys, 2.49, 2.50
Icosium (Algiers), 1.31
Ida, Mt., in Aeolis (Lat. Idaeus mons; Kaz), 1.91, 1.93, 1.94
Ida, Mt., on Crete (Lat. Idaeus mons), 2.113
Igilium (Giglio), is., 2.122
Igneada Burun. *See* Thynias
Îles d'Hyères. *See* Stoechades
Ilice (Elche), 2.93

Ilice, Bay of (Lat. Ilicitanus sinus), 2.93
Ilium. *See* Troy
Illyricum, 2.57
Illyris, 1.18
Iluro (Mataró), 2.90
Ilva (Elba), is., 1.122
Imbros, is., 2.106
Inachus R., 2.51
India, 3.61
Indian Ocean: (Lat. Indicus oceanus), 1.9; (Lat. Indicum mare), 1.11; (Lat. Indicum pelagus), 3.61. *See also* 3.45
Indus R., 3.61, 3.67, 3.68, 3.69, 3.71
Ingulets. *See* Panticapes R.
Iol (Chercell), 1.30
Iolcos, 2.40
Ionia, 1.14, 1.86, 1.89, 2.101
Ionian Sea (Lat. Ionium mare), 1.17, 1.18, 2.37, 2.38, 2.48, 2.58, 2.110, 2.115, 2.117
Iope (Tel Aviv-Yafo), 1.64
Ipsala. *See* Cypsela
Ireland. *See* Iuverna
Ischia. *See* Pithecusa
Iskenderun Körfezi, 1.68
Islands of the Blessed. *See* Macarôn Islands
Islands of the Sun (Lat. Solis insulae), 3.71
Isles of Aeolus (Lipari Is.), 2.120
Isles of Scilly. *See* Cassiterides
Issa, is., 2.114
Issos, Gulf of (Lat. Issicus sinus), 1.70
Issos, 1.70
Istanbul. *See* Byzantion
Ister (Lat. Hister) R., 2.8, 2.16, 2.22, 2.57, 2.63, 2.79, 2.98, 3.33. *See also* Danube R.
Isthmian Games (Lat. Isthmici ludi), 2.48
Isthmos, on Thracian Chersonessus, 2.25, 2.27
Isthmos, of Corinth, 2.48, 2.49, 2.52
Istria (Lat. Histria), 2.56, 2.63

Istriya. *See* Istropolis
Istropolis (Lat. Histropolis; Istriya), 2.22
Italy (Lat. Italia), 1.18, 2.58, 2.67, 2.72, 2.116, 2.120
Itéa. *See* Cirrha
Ithaca, is., 2.110
Itharis, 2.35
Iubia R., 3.13
Iuverna (Ireland), is., 3.53

Jbail. *See* Byblos
Jebel Musa. *See* Abila
Jerba. *See* Menis
Jhelum. *See* Hydaspes R.
Júcar. *See* Sucro R.
Judaea, 1.62
Juno, Point (Lat. Iunonis promunturium), 2.96
Jupiter, Mt. (Lat. Iovis mons), 2.89, 2.90

Kabir R. *See* Ampsacus
Kabousi. *See* Seleucia
Kakulima, Mt.. *See* Theôn Ochema
Kaliakra Burun. *See* Tiristis, Point
Kara Burun. *See* Ceraunian Mountains
Karadeniz Boğazi. *See* Bosphorus, Thracian
Karaköy. *See* Cardia
Karasu. *See* Atyras R.
Karkinitskiy. *See* Carcinites
Kassándra. *See* Pallene
Kavarna. *See* Bizone
Kefken Adsasi. *See* Thynias
Kelb R. *See* Lycos
Kelibia. *See* Clupea
Kerch. *See* Panticapaeon
Kerch, Strait of. *See* Bosphorus, Cimmerian
Kerchenskiy Proliv. *See* Bosphorus, Cimmerian
Kerempe Burun. *See* Carambis, Point
Kerkenah. *See* Cercina
Kérkira. *See* Corcyra

Kilya. *See* Coelos, Port
Kizil Irmak. *See* Halys R.
Koca Çayi. *See* Xanthus
Kor. *See* Coros R.
Korchula. *See* Black Corcyra
Kos. *See* Coös
Krym. *See* Peninsula
Kuban. *See* Hypacaris R.
Kura. *See* Cyrus R.

Labyrinth (Lat. Labyrinthos), 1.56
Laccobriga (Lagos), 3.7
Lacedaemon, 2.41
Lacinium, Point (Capo Colonna), 2.68
Lacippo, 2.94
Laconice, 2.39, 2.41
Laconian Gulf (Lat. Laconicus sinus), 2.50, 2.51
Lacydon, 2.77
Ladon R., 2.43
Laepa (Lepe), 3.5
Laeros (Lérez) R., 3.10
Lagos. *See* Laccobriga
Lake Geneva. *See* Lake Lemannus
Lake Lemannus (Lake Leman/Lake Geneva), 2.74, 2.79
Lambre. *See* Lambriaca
Lambriaca (Lambre), 3.10
Lampsacum, 1.97
Laodicea (Al Ladhiqiyāh/Latakia), 1.69
Larache. *See* Lixos
Larino. *See* Larinum
Larinum (Larino), 2.65
Larissa, 2.40
Larumna (Caria), 1.84
Larumna (Greece), 2.45
Latakia. *See* Laodicea
Latara, 2.80
Latium, 2.59
Latmus, Mount (Lat. Latmius mons), 1.86
Laturus Gulf (Lat. Laturus sinus; Gulf of Arzew), 1.31
Laurentum, 2.71
Lebedos, 1.88

Lebinthos, is., 2.111
Le Brusc. *See* Tauroïs
Lecce. *See* Lupiae
Ledum (Les) R., 2.80
Lemnos, is., 2.106
Lemta. *See* Leptis
Lentini. *See* Leontini
Leontini (Lentini), 2.118
Lepe. *See* Laepa
Leptis (Lemta), 1.34
Leptis, 1.37
Lérez. *See* Laeros R.
Lerne, 2.51
Les. *See* Ledum R.
Lesbos, is., 2.101
Lesser Balearic Isles (Minorca). *See* Balearic Isles
Leuca, in Caria, 1.85
Leuca, in Ionia, 1.89
Leucadia (Leucas), is., 2.110
Leucas, in Acarnania (town), 2.53
Leucas, is. *See* Leucadia
Leucata, 2.86
Leuce/Leuce Achillea, is., 2.98
Leucothea, is., 2.121
Libethra (Litókhoron), 2.36
Libyan Sea (Lat. Libycum mare), 1.21, 1.22, 1.23, 2.119
Lilybaeum, pr., (Capo Boeo/Capo Lilybeo), 2.116, 2.118
Lilybeo, Capo. *See* Lilybaeum, pr.
Limia R., 3.10
Limyra R., 1.82
Lindos, 2.101
Linguarum, is., 2.114
Lipara (Lipari), is., 2.120
Lipari. *See* Lipara
Lipari Islands. *See* Isles of Aeolus
Liri. *See* Liris
Liris (Liri) R., 2.71
Lisboa. *See* Ulisippo
Lisbon. *See* Ulisippo
Liternum, 2.70
Litus Lapideum (the Crau), 2.78
Lixos (Larache), 3.107
Lixus (Lukkus) R., 3.107

Llobregat. *See* Rubricatum R.
Locris, 2.39, 2.40
Long Wall. *See* Macron Tichos
Lower Sea. *See* Tuscan Sea
Lucania, 2.59, 2.69
Lucentia (Alicante), 2.93
Lucrine Lake (Lat. Lacus Lucrinus), 2.70
Lukkus. *See* Lixus R.
Luna (Luni), 2.72
Luni. *See* Luna
Lupia R., 3.30
Lupiae (Lecce), 2.66
Lusitania (Portugal), 2.87, 2.88, 3.6, 3.47
Lycastos, on Crete, 2.13
Lycastos, on the Pontus, 1.105
Lycia, 1.14, 1.80, 1.82, 2.101
Lycos (Kelb) R., 1.69
Lyctos, 2.113
Lysimachia, 2.24

Macarôn Islands (Lat. Macarôn Insulae), 2.100
Macedonia, 1.18, 2.39
Macron Tichos, 2.24
Madalona. *See* Baetulo
Madonna, Cape. *See* Theuprosopon
Madytos (Maydos/Eceabat), 2.26
Maeander R., 1.86
Maenalus, Mt., 2.43
Maenoba, 2.94
Maenorenon, Point, 3.80
Maeotic Lake. *See* Maeotis, Lake
Maeotis, Lake (Sea of Azov), 1.7, 1.8, 1.10, 1.15, 1.109, 1.110, 1.115, 2.1, 2.2, 2.4, 2.97. *See also* Swamp
Magnesia, 2.39, 2.40
Mago (Mahón), 2.124
Magrada, 3.15
Mahón. *See* Mago
Maidenshead. *See* Parthenion, Point
Main. *See* Moenis R.
Maius R. 90
Malaca (Malaga), 2.94
Malaga. *See* Malaca

Malea, 2.49, 2.50, 2.110
Mali i Çikë. *See* Ceraunian Mountains
Malia, Gulf of (Lat. Maliacus sinus), 2.45
Mallorca. *See* Balearic Isles
Mallos, 1.70
Malochnaya. *See* Gerrhos R.
Malta. *See* Melita
Maltepe. *See* Abydos
Mangalia. *See* Callatis
Marathon, 2.45
Marathos, 1.67
Mare Nostrum. *See* Our Sea
Maria Nostra. *See* Our Seas
Marian Canal (Lat. fossa Mariana), 2.78
Mariana, 2.122
Maritima Avaticorum, 2.78
Mar-Koh. *See* Meros, Mt.
Marmara, Sea of. *See* Propontis
Marmaraereğlisi. *See* Perinthos
Maronia, 2.28
Marsa Matrûh. *See* Port Paraetonius
Martil R. *See* Tumuada
Martius Narbo (Narbonne), 2.75, 2.81
Massilia (Marseilles), 2.77, 2.124
Massilia (Marseilles), Port of, (Lat. Massiliensium portus), 2.77
Mastusia, 2.25, 2.27
Matapán. *See* Taenaros, Cape
Mataró. *See* Iluro
Matrinus R., 2.65
Mauretania, 1.25, 1.30, 3.105
Mausoleum, 1.85
Maydos. *See* Madytos
Mearus R., 3.13
Mediterranean Sea. *See* Our Sea
Medma, 2.69
Megara, 2.41, 2.47, 2.48
Megarid, in Greece (Lat. Megaris), 2.39, 2.41
Megaris, in Sicily, 2.117
Megyberna (Molivópyrgos), 2.34
Megyberna Bay: (Lat. Megybernaeus flexus), 2.34, (Lat. Megybernaeus sinus), 2.35

Mekyberna. *See* Megyberna
Mejerda. *See* Bagrada R.
Melaria, 2.96
Melas R., in Pamphylia, 1.78
Melas (Kavak) R., in Thrace, 2.27
Melas Gulf (Lat. Melas sinus), 2.27
Meliboea, 2.35
Melilla. *See* Rusigada
Melita (Malta), is., 2.120
Melos, is., 2.111
Melsyagum, swamp, 3.29
Melys, 1.51
Memphis (Mit Rahina and Saqqâra), 1.60
Mende, 2.33
Mendesian mouth (of the Nile), 1.60
Menis (Jerba), is., 2.105
Mercury Point (Lat. Mercurii promunturium; Cap Bon), 1.34
Merica. *See* Hebrus R.
Mérida. *See* Emerita
Meroë, is., 1.50, 3.85
Meros (Mar-Koh), Mt., 3.66
Mértola. *See* Myrtili
Mesa de Asta. *See* Hasta
Mesopotamia, 1.62
Messana, 2.117
Messembria (Nesebŭr), 2.22
Messene, 2.41
Messenia, 2.39, 2.41
Mesta. *See* Nestos R.
Mesua Hill, 2.80
Metagonium, Point (Cape Bougaroun), 1.33
Metaponto. *See* Metapontum
Metapontum (Metaponto), 2.68
Metaurum, 2.68
Metaurus R., 2.64
Méthana. *See* Chersonessus
Methone, 2.41
Methymna, 2.101
Metia, swamp, 3.29
Midye. *See* Halmydessos
Mignone. *See* Minio R.
Miletus, 1.86
Minab. *See* Sandis R.

Index

Minerva, Point (Lat. Minervae Promunturium; Punta della Campanella), 2.69
Minio (Mignone) R., 2.72
Minius (Miño) R., 3.10
Miño. *See* Minius
Minorca. *See* Balearic Isles
Minotaur (Lat. Minotaurus), 2.112
Minturnae, 2.71
Minyans (Lat. Minyae), 1.98, 2.44
Miseno. *See* Misenum
Misenum (Miseno), 2.70
Mit Rahina. *See* Memphis
Mitylene, 2.101
Modena. *See* Mutina
Moenis (Main) R., 3.30
Moeris (Birket Qârûn), 1.55
Molivópyrgos. *See* Megyberna
Mondego. *See* Munda R.
Monument of Caepio, 3.4
Moratusa, 2.113
Moschic Mountains (Lat. Moschici montes), 1.109
Mother, spring (Lat. Mater), 2.7
Moulouya. *See* Mulucha R.
Mulucha (Moulouya) R., 1.25, 1.29
Munda (Mondego) R., 3.8
Murmecion, 2.3
Musagorus, is., 2.114
Mutina (Modena), 2.60
Mycenae, 2.41
Myconos, is., 2.111
Myndos, 1.85
Myriandros, 1.69
Myrina, 1.90
Myrlea, 1.99
Myrtili (Mértola), 3.7
Myrtoän Sea. *See* Myrtos, Sea of
Myrtos, Sea of (Lat. Myrtoum pelagus), 2.37, 2.110
Myscella, 2.34
Mysia, 1.90
Mysius, Mount. *See* Olympus, Mt., in Mysia
Mystiae, 2.68

Nabar (Hamiz) R., 1.31
Nabeul. *See* Neapolis
Nagarahara. *See* Nysa
Nagidos, 1.77
Nansa. *See* Namnasa
Namnasa (Nansa) R., 3.5
Naples. *See* Neapolis
Nar (Neretva) R., 2.57
Nara. *See* Sestos
Narbo. *See* Martius Narbo
Narbonne. *See* Martius Narbo
Narona, 2.57
Natiso (Natisone) R., 2.61
Natisone. *See* Natiso
Naumachos, is., 2.114
Naupactos, 2.43
Naustathmos (Ra's el Hilāl), 1.40
Naxos, is., 2.111
Neapolis (Nabeul), 1.34
Neapolis (Naples), 2.70
Neapolis (uncertain, near Myndos), 1.85
Nebis (Neyva) R., 3.10
Negrais, Cape. *See* Tamus, Point
Nemausus (Nîmes), 2.75
Neretva. *See* Nar R.
Neritos, is., 2.110
Nesebŭr. *See* Messembria
Nesos, 2.108
Nestos (Mesta) R., 2.17, 2.30
Neyva. *See* Nebis R.
Nicaea (Nice), 2.76
Nice. *See* Nicaea
Nile (Lat. Nilus) R., 1.8, 1.9, 1.10, 1.14, 1.20, 1.22, 1.49, 1.50, 1.60, 2.8, 2.103, 2.104, 3.80, 3.85, 3.96, 3.97
Nilus. *See* Nile
Nîmes. *See* Nemausus
Niphates, 1.81
Noega, 3.13
Nogaïka. *See* Buces R.
North Point. *See* Borion
Numana (Umana), 2.65
Numantia, 2.88
Numidia, 1.30
Nunc, 3.96

Nysa (Nagarahara), 3.66
Nyspiros, 2.111

Oblivion (Lat. Oblivio) R., 3.10
Ocean (Lat. Oceanus), 1.5, 1.24, 1.27, 1.117, 2.74, 2.86, 2.87, 2.96, 2.97, 3.1, 3.21, 3.46, 3.90, 3.97, 3.107
Odessos (Varna), 2.22
Oea (Tarābulus/Tripoli), 1.37
Oeanthia, 2.53
Oechalia, 2.108
Oenussae, is., 2.110
Oeta, Mt., 2.36
Ogyris, is., 3.79
Olbia, Gulf of (Lat. Olbianos sinus), 1.100
Olbia, in France, 2.77
Olbia, in the Ukraine, 2.6
Old Paphos (Lat. Palaepaphos), 2.102
Olearos, is., 2.111
Oleastrum, 3.4
Olintigi, 3.5
Olopyxos, 2.113
Olympus, Mt., in Mysia, 1.98
Olympus, Mt., on the Greek peninsula, 2.36
Olynthos, 2.30
Olyros, 2.53
Onoba (Huelva), 3.5
Opuntian Gulf (Lat. Opuntius sinus), 2.45
Orange. *See* Arausio
Orb. *See* Orbis R.
Orbelos, Mt. (Vihren/Belasitza), 2.17
Orbis (Orb) R., 2.80
Orcades (Orkney Is.), 3.54
Orchomenos, 2.43
Oricum (Eriko), 2.56
Orkney Is. *See* Orcades
Orontes (Asi) R., 1.69
Ossa, Mt., 2.36
Ossonoba (Faro), 3.7
Osteodes (Ustica), is., 2.120
Ostia, 2.71
Our Sea (Mediterranean Sea), 1.6, 1.14, 1.24, 1.25, 1.49, 2.8, 2.16, 2.86, 2.87, 3.1, 3.90; Our Seas, 1.13, 1.81, 2.1, 2.96, 3.77
Our Strait (Lat. Noster fretum), 3.107. *See also* Strait
Oxos (Amudarya) R., 3.42

Pachynum, Point (Capo Passero), 2.116, 2.117, 2.118
Padova/Padua. *See* Patavium
Padus (Po) R., 2.62, 2.64
Paestum, 2.69
Paestum, Gulf of (Lat. Paestanus sinus; Gulf of Salerno), 2.69
Pagae, 2.53
Pagasa, 2.44
Pagasa, Gulf of (Lat. Pagaseus sinus), 2.44, 2.106
Paglione. *See* Paulo R.
Palermo. *See* Panhormus
Palestine (Lat. Palaestine/Palaestina), 1.63, 1.64
Palantia (Palencia), 88
Palencia. *See* Palantia
Palinuro, Capo. *See* Palinurus
Palinurus (Capo Palinuro), 2.69
Pallene (Kassándra), 2.30, 2.33
Palma, 2.124
Palmaria (Palmarola), is., 2.121
Palmarola. *See* Palmaria
Pamisum R., 2.51
Pamphylia, 1.14, 1.77, 1.78–79
Panchai, 3.81
Pandateria, is., 2.121
Pandion. *See* Hill of Pandion
Panhormus. *See* Palermo
Pan-Ionian Sanctuary (Lat. Panionium), 1.87
Pantelleria. *See* Cossura
Panticapaeon (Kerch), 2.3
Panticapes (Ingulets) R., 2.5
Paphlagonia, 1.104
Paphos, 2.102
Paraetonius, 1.40
Parion, 1.97
Parnassos, 2.40
Paropamisus. *See* Propanisus

Paros, is., 2.111
Parthenion, Point, 2.3
Parthenius R., 1.104
Parthenius, Mt., 2.43
Patalene, 3.71
Patara, 1.82
Patavium (Padova/Padua), 2.60
Pathmetic mouth (of the Nile), 1.60
Patrae (Pátrai/Pátras), 2.52
Pátrai. See Patrae
Pátras. See Patrae
Paulo (Paglione) R., 2.72
Pedalion, 1.83
Pelion, Mt., 2.36
Pelle, 2.34
Peloponnesos, 2.38, 2.39, 2.48, 2.49, 2.117
Pelorias, pr., 2.116; (Lat. Peloris), 2.118
Pelusiac mouth (of the Nile), 1.60
Pelusium, 1.60
Peneus R., 2.35
Peninsula (Crimea/Krym), 2.4
Perekop. See Taphrae
Perga (Perge), 1.79
Perinthos (Marmaraereğlisi/Ereğli), 2.34
Persian Gulf (Lat. Persicus sinus), 1.12, 1.14, 3.73
Persian Sea (Lat. Persicum mare), 1.9. See also Persian Gulf
Persis, 1.12, 3.76
Pesaro. See Pisaurum
Pescara. See Aternus R.
Petelia (Strongoli), 2.68
Petrae, 2.69
Peuce (Picizina), is., 2.98
Phanagorea, 1.112
Pharos, is. off Aegypt, 2.104
Pharos, is. off Italy, 2.114
Phaselis, 1.79
Phasis (Rioni) R., 1.108, 2.22
Philaeni. See Altars of the Philaeni
Philiae, 2.23
Philippi, 2.30

Philoteris, 3.80
Phinopolis, 2.23
Phocaea, 1.89
Phocis, 2.39, 2.40
Phoenicia (Lat. Phoenice), 1.63, 1.85, 2.103
Phoenicusa (Filicudi), is., 2.120
Pholoe, Mt., 2.43
Phoristae, 1.13
Phrygia, 1.100
Phthia, 2.40
Phthiotis, 2.39, 2.40
Phycon (Ras Sem), 1.37
Phygela, 1.88
Phyre, 1.34
Picentia (Vicenza), 2.69
Picenum, 2.65
Picizina. See Peuce
Pieria, 2.36
Pillars of Hercules (Lat. columnae Herculis), 1.27, 2.95
Pinara, is., 2.111
Piraeus, 2.47
Pisa, in Greece, 2.42
Pisa, in Italy. See Pisae
Pisae (Pisa), 2.72
Pisaurum (Pesaro), 2.64
Pitane, 1.90
Pithecusa (Ischia), is., 2.121
Pityussa, is., 2.109
Placia, 1.98
Plotae, is., 2.110
Po. See Padus R.
Pogon, Gulf of (Lat. Pogonos portus), 2.50
Pola, 2.57
Pola, Gulf of (Lat. Polaticus sinus), 2.57
Polan. See Apollonia
Pollenca. See Pollentia
Pollentia (Pollenca), 2.124
Polyaegos, is., 2.106
Pomoriye. See Anchialos
Pompeii (Lat. Pompei), 2.70
Pompeiopolis, 1.71
Pontiae (Ponza), is., 2.121

Pontus (Black Sea), 1.7, 1.14, 1.15, 1.101, 1.102, 1.108, 1.111, 1.112, 1.113, 1.115, 2.2, 2.3, 2.17, 2.22, 2.23, 2.51, 2.98; Pontic shore (Lat. Ponticus latus), 1.10, 1.18, 2.16
Ponza. *See* Pontiae
Populonia (Porto Baratti), 2.72
Port Ebora, 3.11
Port Hannibal (Lat. portus Hannibalis; Portimâo), 3.7
Port Paraetonius (Marsa Matrûh), 1.40
Port Venus (Lat. portus Veneris), 2.84
Portimâo. *See* Port Hannibal
Porto Baratti. *See* Populonia
Porto Clementino. *See* Graviscae
Portugal. *See* Lusitania
Portus Magnus (Bettioua), 1.29
Poseidon, Point, 1.86
Potentia (Santa Maria di Potenza), 2.65
Potidaea, 2.33
Pozzuoli. *See* Puteoli
Priapos, 1.97
Priene, 1.87
Prochyta (Procida), is., 2.121
Procida. *See* Prochyta
Proconnesos, is., 2.99
Propanisus (Hindu Kush), 3.69
Propanisus (Paropamisus), 1.81
Propontis (Sea of Marmara), 1.7, 1.15, 1.98, 2.24, 2.99
Prote, is., 2.110
Psophis, 2.43
Pteleon, 2.44
Ptolemaïs (Tulmaythah), 1.40
Ptolemaïs, on the Red Sea, 3.80
Punta de Narija. *See* Celtic Point
Puteoli, Bay of (Lat. Puteolanus sinus; Bay of Naples), 2.70
Puteoli (Pozzuoli), 2.70
Pylos, 2.52
Pyramus (Ceyhan) R., 1.70
Pyrenees (Lat. Pyrenaeus mons), 2.74, 2.81, 2.84, 2.85, 2.89, 3.15, 3.20, 3.21

Pyrgi, 2.72
Pyrrha (Lesbos), 2.101
Pyrrha (Euboea), 2.108

Quiza, 1.31

Ram's Brow. *See* Criu Metopon
Ras Si Ali Mekki. *See* Apollo, Point
Ra's el Hilāl. *See* Naustathmos
Ras es Saq'a. *See* Theuprosopon
Ras Sem. *See* Phycon
Ras Taiùnes. *See* Borion
Ravenna, 2.64
Red Sea. *See* Arabian Sea
Red Sea (Lat. Rubrum mare; Arabian Sea), 3.72, 3.81
Reggio. *See* Rhegium
Retico, Mt., 3.30
Rhamnus, 2.46
Rhegium (Reggio), 2.68
Rhein. *See* Rhenus R.
Rhenea, is., 2.111
Rhenus (Rhein/Rhine) R., 2.74, 2.79, 3.16, 3.20, 3.24, 3.30, 3.50
Rhessos, 2.24
Rhine. *See* Rhenus R.
Rhion (Grk. rhion Akhaïkon, the Gulf of Corinth), 2.52, 2.53
Rhoda, 2.89
Rhodanus (Rhône) R., 2.78, 2.79, 3.30
Rhodes (Lat. Rhodos), is., 2.101
Rhodope, 2.17
Rhoeteum, 1.96
Rhône. *See* Rhodanus R.
Rhosos, 1.69
Rhyndacos R., 1.99
Rimini. *See* Ariminum
Rioni. *See* Phasis R.
Riphaean Mountains. *See* Riphaean Range
Riphaean Range, or Mountains: (Lat. Riphaeus mons), 1.115, 1.117; (Lat. Riphaei montes), 1.109, 2.1, 3.36
Rocky Beach. *See* Litus Lapideum
Rodopi Planina. *See* Haemos, Mt.
Rome (Lat. Roma), 2.60

Rubraesus, Lake, 2.81
Rubricatum (Llobregat) R., 2.90
Rud-Gez. *See* Saetis R.
Rudiae (Rugge), 2.66
Rugge. *See* Rudiae
Ruscino (Castel Rousillon), 2.84
Rusiccade (Skikda), 1.33
Rusigada (Russadir/Melilla), 1.29
Russadir. *See* Rusigada
Ruthisia, 1.31

Sa el-Hagar. *See* Saïs
Sabatia, 2.72
Sacred Point (Lat. Sacrum promunturium; Cabo de Sâo Vicente), 3.7
Saetis (Rud-Gez) R., 3.75
Saguntum, 2.92
Saint-Tropez. *See* Athenopolis
Saïs (Sa el-Hagar), 1.60
Saja. *See* Saunium R.
Sala, 3.107
Salacia Bay, 3.8
Salaeni, 3.15
Salamis, on Cyprus, 2.102
Salamis, is. off Attica, 2.109
Salduba, 2.94
Salerno, Gulf of. *See* Paestum, Gulf of
Salia R., 3.14
Salina. *See* Didyma
Sallentine Fields (Lat. Sallentini campi), 2.66
Sallentum, 2.66
Sallentum, Point (Lat. Sallentinum promunturium), 2.68
Salona (Solin), 2.57
Salonica. *See* Thessalonice
Salsulae (Fontaine de Salses), 2.82
Salûm, Gulf of. *See* Catabathmos
Same, is., 2.110
Samonium, Point, 2.112
Samos, is.,2.101
Samothrace, is., 2.106
San Antioco. *See* Sulci
San Dagh. *See* Cragus, Mt.
San Lucido. *See* Clampetia
Sandis (Minab) R., 3.75

Sane, 2.35
Santa Maria di Potenza. *See* Potentia
Santa Maria di Siponto. *See* Sipontum
Saqqâra. *See* Memphis
Sar. *See* Sars R.
Saragossa. *See* Caesaraugusta
Sardabale R., 1.31
Sardemisos, 1.79
Sardinia, is., 2.123
Sarmatia, 3.33
Saronic Gulf (Lat. Saronicus portus), 2.50
Sarpedon, Point, 1.77
Sars (Sar) R., 3.11
Saunium (Saja) R., 3.15
Sauso R., 3.15
Scadinavia, is., 3.54
Scamander R., 1.93
Scandile, is., 2.106
Scarphia, 2.45
Schoenitas, 2.50
Schoenus, 1.84
Schoenus, Gulf of (Lat. Schoenitas portus), 1.84
Sciathos, is., 2.106
Scione, 2.33
Scironian Rocks (Lat. Scironia saxa), 2.47
Scylace, 1.98
Scylla, in Italy, 2.68
Scylla, in Sicily, 2.115, 2.116
Scyllaceum (Squillace), 2.68
Scyllaceum, Bay of (Lat. Scyllaceus sinus; Gulf of Squillace), 2.68
Scyllaeon, 2.49, 2.50
Scyros, is., 2.106
Scythia, 1.18, 2.6, 2.8, 3.42
Scythian Bay (Lat. Scythicus sinus), 3.38, 3.39, 3.42
Scythian Islands (Lat. Scythicae insulae), 3.58
Scythian Ocean, 1.9, 1.11
Scythian Point (Lat. Scythicum promunturium), 3.12, 3.59
Sebennytic mouth (of the Nile), 1.60
Sein. *See* Sena

Seine. *See* Sequana R.
Sele. *See* Silerus R.
Seleucia (Kabousi), 1.69
Selimiye. *See* Sida
Selymbria (Silivri), 2.24
Sena (Sein), is., 3.48
Senke. *See* Catabathmos
Sepias, Point, 2.35, 2.44
Seven Brothers (Lat. Septem Fratres; Ceuta), 1.29
Sequana (Seine) R., 3.20
Seriphos, is., 2.111
Serpis. *See* Sorobis R.
Serrhion (Mákri), Cape, 2.28
Sesamus, 1.104
Sestos (Nara), 2.26
Sevastopol. *See* Cherronesus
Seville. *See* Hispal
Shabla. *See* Carian Port
Sicilian Sea: (Lat. Siculum pelagus), 2.58; (Lat. Siculum mare), 2.115; Strait (Lat. Siculum fretum), 2.120
Sicily (Lat. Sicilia), is., 2.115, 2.120, 3.50
Sicinos, is., 2.111
Sicyon, 2.53
Sida (Selimiye/Side), 1.78, 1.80
Sidon (Saïda), 1.66
Sidonia, is., 2.121
Siga (Takembrit), 1.29
Sigeum, 1.93, 2.100
Silerus (Sele) R., 2.69
Silivri. *See* Selymbria
Silvery Island. *See* Argyre
Simoïs R., 1.93
Simyra, 1.67
Sindos, 1.111
Sinoessa, 2.71
Sinonia, is., 2.121
Sinop. *See* Sinope
Sinope (Sinop), 1.105
Siphnos, is., 2.111
Sipiuntum, 2.66
Sipontum (Santa Maria di Siponto), 2.66
Skadovsk. *See* Carcine

Skikda. *See* Rusiccade
Smyrna (Izmir), Gulf of (Lat. Smyrnaeus sinus), 1.89
Sun. *See* Fountain of the Sun; Islands of the Sun
Solin. *See* Salona
Sonans, 3.15
Sophene, 1.62
Sorobis (Serpis) R., 2.92
Sorrento. *See* Syrrentum
Soûr. *See* Tyre
Sousse. *See* Hadrumetum
Sozopol. *See* Apollonia
Spain (Lat. Hispania), 1.18, 1.19, 1.25, 1.27, 2.85, 2.86, 2.93, 2.124, 3.14, 3.15, 3.16
Spartel, Cape. *See* Ampelusia
Sperchios R., 2.44
Sporades, is., 2.111
Squillace. *See* Scyllaceum
Squillace, Gulf of. *See* Scyllaceum, Gulf of
Sri Lanka. *See* Taprobane
Stairs of Hannibal (Lat. scalae Hannibalis), 2.89
Sthenos R., 2.28
Stoechades (Îles d'Hyères), is., 2.124
Strait (Strait of Gibraltar), 1.7, 1.16, 1.27, 2.96, 2.97
Stratos, 2.43
Strobilus, Bay of (Lat. Strobilus sinus), 3.80
Stromboli. *See* Strongyle
Strongoli. *See* Petelia
Strongyle (Stromboli), is., 2.120
Strophades, is., 2.110
Struma. *See* Strymon
Strymon (Struma) R., 2.17, 2.30
Styra, 2.108
Subur, 2.90
Sucro (Júcar) R., 2.92
Sucro, Bay of (Lat. Sucronensis sinus), 2.92, 2.125
Suel, 2.94
Suesia, swamp, 3.29
Sulci (San Antioco), 2.123

Sunium, 2.27, 2.45, 2.46
Sūsah. *See* Apollonia
Swamp (Lat. Palus), 1.15, 1.112, 2.3, 2.4. *See also* Maeotis, Lake
Syene (Aswân), 1.60
Symplegades, is., 2.99
Syracusae, 2.117
Syrdarya. *See* Iaxartes R.
Syria, 1.14, 1.62, 1.69, 2.102, 2.116
Syros, is., 2.111
Syrrentum (Sorrento), 2.70
Syrtis, greater Bay of (Lat. Syrtis sinus maior), 1.37, 2.105
Syrtis, lesser Bay of (Lat. Syrtis sinus minor), 1.34, 1.35, 2.105

Tabarka. *See* Thabraca
Tabis, Mt., 3.60
Table of the Sun. *See* Heliu Trapeza
Tachempso, is., 1.51
Taenaros (Matapán), Cape, 2.49, 2.50, 2.51
Tagus (Tejo/Tajo) R., 3.8
Tajo. *See* Tagus R.
Takembrit. *See* Siga
Talge (Cheleken), is., 3.58
Tamaris (Tambre) R., 3.11
Tambre. *See* Tamaris R.
Tamus, Point, (Cape Negrais?), 3.67, 3.68, 3.70
Tanaïs (Don) R., 1.8, 1.9, 1.10, 1.14, 1.15, 1.18, 1.109, 1.114, 1.115, 2.1
Tangiers. *See* Tinge
Taphrae (Perekop), 2.4
Taprobane (Sri Lanka), is., 3.70
Tarābulus. *See* Oea
Taranto. *See* Tarentus
Tarentum, Gulf of (Lat. Tarentinus sinus), 2.68
Tarentus (Taranto), 2.68
Tarracina (Terracina), 2.71
Tarraco (Tarragona), 2.90
Tarraconensis, 2.124, 2.87, 2.88, 3.5
Tarragona. *See* Tarraco
Tarsus, 1.70
Tarsus R. *See* Cydnus R.

Tartessos, 2.96
Taunus, Mt., 3.30
Taurianum, 2.68
Tauric mountains. *See* Taurus Range
Tauroïs (Le Brusc?), 2.77
Tauromenium, 2.117
Taurus Range, 1.80, 1.81, 2.100, 2.102, 3.40, 3.60, 3.61, 3.68, 3.77; (Lat. Taurici montes), 1.109
Taÿgetus, Mt., 2.41
Teanum, 2.65
Tegea, 2.43
Tejo. *See* Tagus R.
Tekirdağ. *See* Bisanthe
Tel Aviv-Yafo. *See* Iope
Telis R., 2.84
Telmesos (Fethiye), 1.82
Temessa, 2.69
Tempe, 2.36
Tendrovskaya Kosa. *See* Dromos Achilleos
Tenedos, is., 2.100
Ténès. *See* Cartinna
Tenos, is., 2.111
Teos, 1.89
Tergeste (Trieste), 2.57, 2.61; (Lat. Tergestum), 2.55
Terme. *See* Thermodon R.
Termoli. *See* Buca
Terracina. *See* Tarracina
Thabraca (Tabarka), 1.33
Thasos, is., 2.106
Thatae, 1.114
Thebae, in Aegypt, 1.60
Thebae, in Boeotia, 2.40
Thebe, 1.91
Theganusa, is., 2.110
Themiscurum, 1.105
Theodosia (Feodosiya), 2.3
Theôn Ochema (Mt. Kakulima?), 3.94
Therapnae, in Laconice, 2.41
Therapnae, on Crete, 2.113
Thermae, 2.118
Thermaïc Gulf (Lat. Thermaïcus sinus), 2.35
Thermodon (Terme) R., 1.105

Thermopylae, 2.45
Thessaly (Lat. Thessalia), 2.39, 2.40
Thessalonice (Thessaloníki/Salonica), 2.35
Thessaloníki. *See* Thessalonice
Theuprosopon (Cape Madonna/Ras es Saq'a), 1.67
Thoricos, 2.46
Thrace (Lat. Thracia), 1.18, 2.16, 2.24, 2.73, 2.106
Three-Cities. *See* Tripolis
Thurium, 2.68
Thyatira, is., 2.111
Thylae, is., 2.105
Thyle, is., 3.57
Thymnias, Gulf, 1.84
Thynias (Igneada Burun), 2.23
Thynias (Kefken Adsasi), 2.98
Thyssanusa, 1.84
Tiber (Lat. Tiberis) R., 2.71, 2.121
Ticis R., in Gaul, 2.84
Ticis R., in Spain, 2.89
Tifernus (Biferno) R., 2.65
Tigris R., 1.63, 3.76, 3.77
Tigulia, 2.72
Tiligul. *See* Asiaces R.
Timavo. *See* Timavus R.
Timavus (Timavo) R., 2.61
Tin Islands. *See* Cassiterides
Tinge (Tangiers), 1.26
Tingentera, 2.96
Tios, 1.104
Tiristis, Point, (Kaliakra Burun), 2.22
Titana, is., 2.114
Tolosa (Toulouse), 2.75
Tomb of the Dog. *See* Cynos Sema
Tomoe (Constanta), 2.22
Torone, 2.34
Torre Chiaruccia. *See* Castrum Novum
Torre d'Egnazia. *See* Gnatia
Torre de Tavira. *See* Balsa
Tortosa. *See* Dertosa
Toulouse. *See* Tolosa
Tower of Augustus (Lat. turris Augusti), 3.11

Tower of Calarnaea (Lat. turris Calarnaea), 2.30
Tower of Diomedes (Lat. turris Diomedis), 2.29
Trâblous. *See* Tripolis
Trabzon. *See* Trapezos
Tragurium (Trogir), 2.57
Trapezos (Trabzon), 1.107
Trier. *See* Augusta
Trieste. *See* Tergeste
Tripoli. *See* Oea
Tripolis (Trâblous), 1.67
Tritino, 3.15
Triton, Lake (Chott Jerid), 1.36
Triton R., 1.36
Troad (Lat. Troas), 1.14, 1.90, 2.101
Troezene, 2.50, 2.109
Trogir. *See* Tragurium
Troy: (Lat. Troia), 2.45; (Lat. Ilium), 1.93, 2.33
Tronto. *See* Truentinum R.
Truentinum, 2.65
Truentinum (Tronto) R., 2.65
Tshoban. *See* Zone
Tubero R., 3.71
Tūkrah. *See* Arsinoë
Tulcis (Francoli) R., 2.90
Tulmaythah. *See* Ptolemaïs
Tumuada (Martil) R., 1.29
Turia R., 2.92
Tuscan Sea: (Lat. Tuscum mare), 1.17, 1.18, 2.58, 2.69, 2.115, 2.119; (Lat. Tuscum pelagus), 2.74
Typhon, Cave of (Lat. Typhoneus specus), 1.76
Tyra (Dnestr) R., 2.7
Tyre (Lat. Tyra; Soûr), 1.66
Tyrrhenian Sea (Lat. Tyrrhenicum mare), 1.17. *See also* Tuscan Sea

Ufente. *See* Aufidus R.
Ulisippo (Lisboa/Lisbon), Bay of, 3.8
Ulla R., 3.10
Umana. *See* Numana
Unfriendly Sea. *See* Axene Sea
Upper Sea. *See* Adriatic Sea

Urci, 2.94
Urci, Bay of (Lat. Urcitanus sinus), 2.94
Urgo, 2.122
Urias Bay (Lat. Urias sinus; Lago di Varano), 2.66
Ustica. *See* Osteodes
Utica, 1.34

Vaison la Romaine. *See* Vasio
Valencia. *See* Valentia
Valentia (Valencia), 2.92
Valeso. *See* Valetium
Valetium (Valeso), 2.66
Vardar. *See* Axius R.
Varna. *See* Odessos
Var. *See* Varum
Varum (Var) R., 2.72, 2.74
Vasio (Vaison la Romaine), 2.75
Vasto. *See* Histonium
Velia, 2.69
Venetus, Lake, (Upper Bodensee/Upper Lake Constance), 3.24
Vesulus, Mt., (Monte Viso), 2.62
Vesuvius, Mt., 2.70
Vibo, 2.69
Vicenza. *See* Picentia
Vienna, 2.75
Vihren. *See* Orbelos, Mt.
Vijosë. *See* Aeas R.
Viso, Monte. *See* Vesulus, Mt.

Vistula (Wisła) R., 3.33
Visurgis (Weser) R., 3.30
Vize. *See* Bytinis
Vlieland. *See* Flevo
Vulcano. *See* Hiera
Volturno. *See* Volturnum
Volturnum (Volturno), 2.70
Volturnus R., 2.70
Volubilis, 3.107

Wedge Field (Lat. Cuneus ager; Cabo de Santa Maria), 3.7
Weser. *See* Visurgis R.
White Point (Lat. Candidum promunturium; Cap Blanc), 1.34
Wisła. *See* Vistula R.

Xanthos, 1.82
Xanthus R. (Koca Çayi), 1.82

Yori. *See* Cambyses R.

Zacynthos, is., 2.110
Zadar. *See* Iader
Zephyre, is., 2.114
Zephyr Point, in Cyrenaïca (Lat. Zephyrion promunturium), 1.40
Zephyr Point, in Italy (Lat. Zephyrium promunturium), 2.68
Zilia, colony, 3.107
Zilia R., 3.107
Zone (Tshoban), 2.28

Peoples and Groups

Divine, historical, and legendary peoples and groups named by Mela are listed here. Where the English form is not identical to the ancient form, the Latin name is given in parentheses after the main entry and marked by the abbreviation Lat.

Achaeans (Lat. Achaei), 1.13, 1.110
Achaeans (Lat. Achivi), 1.93, 2.33
Aeacids (Lat. Aeacides), 2.54
Aegipanes. *See* Goat-Pans

Aegyptians (Lat. Aegyptii), 1.14, 1.23, 1.59
Aeolians (Lat. Aeoli), 1.90, 1.93
Aetolians (Lat. Aetoli), 2.52

Index

Africans (Lat. Afri), 1.25
Albani, 3.39
All-Ears. *See* Panotii
Allobroges, 2.75
Amardi, 3.39, 3.42
Amazons (Lat. Amazones), 1.12, 1.13, 1.88, 1.90, 1.105, 1.116, 3.39
Androphagoe, 3.59
Anthropophagi, 2.14
Apulians (Lat. Apuli), 2.59
Aquitani, 3.20
Arabs (Lat. Arabes), 1.12, 1.49, 1.63, 3.78, 3.80
Arecomici, 2.75
Arimphaei, 1.13; (Lat. Aremphaei), 1.117
Argives (Lat. Argivi), 1.71, 1.78, 1.85
Armenians (Lat. Armenii), 1.13, 3.77
Artabri, 3.13
Asiacae, 2.7, 2.11
Assyrians (Lat. Assyrii), 1.14
Astyres, 3.13
Atacini, 2.75
Athenienses, 1.78, 2.26, 2.47
Atlantes, 1.23, 1.43
Augilae, 1.23, 1.46
Ausci, 3.20
Automoles, 3.85
Autrigones, 3.15

Babylonians (Lat. Babylonii), 1.14, 3.76
Bactri, 1.13
Basilidae, 2.4, 2.11
Bastuli, 3.3
Bechiri, 1.107
Belcae, 3.36, 3.57
Black-Robes. *See* Melanchlaeni
Birds of Prey. *See* Oeonae
Bithynians (Lat. Bithyni), 1.14, 1.97, 2.98
Blemyes, 1.23, 1.48
Boi, 3.45
Bruttii, 2.59
Budini, 1.116

Cadusi, 1.13
Calabri, 2.59
Callipidae, 2.7
Cantabri, 3.12, 3.15, 3.16, 3.23
Cappadocians (Lat. Cappadoces), 1.13, 3.77
Carmanii, 3.75, 3.79
Carni, 2.59
Carthaginians (Lat. Poeni), 2.94
Caspiani, 1.12
Caspians (Lat. Caspii), 3.39
Cavaran peoples. *See* Cavares
Cavares, 2.75, 2.79
Cave Dwellers. *See* Trogodytae
Cedrosi, 3.75
Celtic ancestry (Lat. Celtica gens), 3.13
Celts: (Lat. Celtae), 3.20; (Lat. Celtici), 3.10, 3.47
Cercetae, 1.13
Cercetici, 1.110
Chaldaeans (Lat. Chaldaei), 3.76
Chalybae. *See* Chalybes
Chalybes; (Lat. Chalybes), 1.105; (Lat. Chalybae), 1.106
Chelonophagi, 3.75
Choamani, 1.13
Chomarae, 1.13
Cilices, 1.69
Cimbri, 3.32
Cimmerii, 1.13
Cissianti, 1.13
Colchians (Lat. Colchi), 1.98, 1.108, 2.57, 2.98
Colician peoples (Lat. Colicae), 1.110
Colophonians (Lat. Colophonii), 1.99
Comari, 1.13
Commagenes (Lat. Commageni), 1.13
Coraxici, 1.110
Cretans (Lat. Cretes), 1.83
Cyclopes, 2.119
Cyrenaeans (Lat. Cyrenaïci), 1.38

Dahae, 1.13, 3.42
Dasaretae, 2.55
Daunians (Lat. Dauni), 2.59, 2.65

Index

Deciates, 2.76
Derbices, 3.39
Druids (Lat. Druidae), 3.18

Encheleae, 2.55
Eneti, 1.13
Epidaurians (Lat. Epidaurii), 2.49
Epigoni, 1.88
Eretrians (Lat. Eretrii), 2.33
Essedones, 2.2, 2.9, 2.13

Frentani, 2.59, 2.65

Gaetuli, 1.23, 3.104
Gallic peoples (Lat. Gallicae gentes), 2.55, 2.64, 3.23
Gallo-Greeks (Lat. Gallograeci), 1.13
Gamphasantes, 1.23, 1.47
Gandari, 1.13
Garamantes, 1.23, 1.45
Geloni, 2.14
Georgians (Lat. Georgi), 1.13, 2.5, 2.11
Germans (Lat. Germani), 1.19
Geryones, 3.47
Getae, 2.18
Gigantes, 2.36
Goat-Pans (Lat. Aegipanes), 1.23, 1.48, 3.95
Gorgones, 3.99
Greeks: (Lat. Graeci), 1.7, 1.25, 3.72, 3.94; (Lat. Grai), 1.17, 2.24, 2.32, 2.45, 2.64, 2.66, 2.83, 2.110; merchants, 1.110; writers, 3.66
Grovi, 3.110
Gynaecocratumenoe, 1.116

Haedui, 3.20
Hamaxobioe, 2.2
Heniochi, 1.110, 1.111
Hermiones, 3.32
Hesperides, 3.100, 3.103
Hesperioe, 3.96
Hiberi, 1.13, 3.41
Himantopodes, 3.103
Hippopodes, 3.56
Histri, Histrians, Histrici. *See* Istrians

Horsefoot. *See* Hippopodes
Hyperboreans (Lat. Hyperborei), 1.12, 1.13, 3.36
Hyrcani, 1.13, 3.39, 3.41

Ilienses, 2.123
Illyric peoples (Lat. Illyricae gentes), 2.55
Illyrii, 2.16, 2.56
Indians (Lat. Indi), 1.11, 1.12, 3.45
Ionians (Lat. Iones), 1.87
Iphigenia, 2.11
Isaurians (Lat. Isauri), 1.13
Istrians: (Lat. Histri), 2.57; (Lat. Histrici), 2.7
Italic peoples: (Lat. Italicae gentes), 2.55, 2.64; (Lat. Italici populi), 2.59
Ixamatae, 1.114

Lacedaemonians (Lat. Lacedaemonii), 2.26
Laconians (Lat. Lacones), 2.45
Legion II, 2.75
Legion VI, 2.75
Legion VII, 2.75
Legion VIII, 2.77
Legion X, 2.75
Leucoaethiopes. *See* White Aethiopians
Leucothea, 2.121
Liburnians (Lat. Liburni), 2.56, 2.57
Ligurians (Lat. Ligures), 2.59, 2.72, 2.124
Locri, 2.68
Long-Heads. *See* Macrocephali
Long-Lived. *See* Macrobii
Lotus-Eaters (Lat. Lotophagi), 1.37
Libyan Aegyptians (Lat. Libyes Aegyptii), 1.23
Lycaones, 1.13
Lydians (Lat. Lydi), 1.13

Macae, 3.79
Macedones, 2.34, 2.35
Macrobii, 3.85
Macrocephali (Long-Heads), 1.107

162 Index

Maeotici, 1.14, 1.114
Maeotidae, 1.116
Manes, 1.46
Mariandyni, 1.97, 1.103, 2.98
Massagetae, 1.13
Matiani, 1.13
Medes (Lat. Medi), 1.13
Megarians (Lat. Megarenses), 1.100, 1.101
Melanchlaeni, 2.14; (Lat. Melanchlaena gens), 1.110
Messenians (Lat. Messenii), 2.52
Milesians (Lat. Milesii), 1.104, 2.22
Minyans (Lat. Minyae), 1.98, 2.44
Moors (Lat. Mauri), 1.22
Morini, 3.23
Moschi, 1.13, 3.39
Mossyni, 1.106
Murimeni, 1.13
Musae, 2.36

Neri, 3.11
Neuri, 2.7, 2.14
Nigritae, 1.22, 3.104
Nomads (Lat. Nomades; western Scyths), 2.4, 2.5, 2.11
Nomads (Lat. Nomades; eastern Scyths), 3.38
Numidians (Lat. Numidae), 1.22

Octavanorum colonia, 2.77
Oeonae, 3.56
Ophiophagi, 3.81
Opoes, 2.45
Orgenomesci, 3.15
Ossismi, 3.23, 3.48

Palibothri, 3.67
Panotii, 3.56
Paphlagones, 1.104
Pariani, 1.13
Partheni, 2.55
Parthians: (Lat. Parthi), 1.14; (Parthica gens), 3.33
Pelasgians (Lat. Pelasgi), 1.83, 1.92, 1.98, 2.32

Peloponnesians: (Lat. Peloponnesiaci), 2.52; (Lat. Peloponnesiacae gentes), 2.43
Persians (Lat. Persae), 1.12, 1.64, 1.66, 1.70, 1.78, 1.98, 2.26, 2.45, 3.75
Pestici, 3.39, 3.42
Phaeaces, 2.55
Pharmacotrophi, 1.13
Pharusii, 1.22, 3.103
Phicores, 1.114
Philaeni, 1.33, 1.38
Phocaeans (Lat. Phocaei), 1.97, 2.77
Phoenicians (Lat. Phoenices), 1.34, 1.65, 1.78, 2.96
Phrygians (Lat. Phryges), 1.13
Phthirophagi, 1.110
Picentes, 2.59
Piraeans (Lat. Piraei), 2.56, 2.57
Pisidae, 1.13
Praetermarici, 3.11
Propanisadae, 1.13
Protesilaüs, 2.26
Psammetichus, 1.56
Pygmies (Lat. Pygmaei), 3.81
Pylians (Lat. Pylii), 2.52

Rhodians (Lat. Rhodii), 1.71, 1.84
Romans (Lat. Romani), 2.34, 2.56, 2.57, 2.60, 2.105
Ruled By Women. *See* Gynaecocratumenoe

Sabaeans (Lat. Sabaei), 3.79
Sacae, 3.59
Sallentines (Lat. Sallentini), 2.59
Samians (Lat. Samii), 1.77, 2.24
Santoni, 3.23
Sarmatae, 1.19, 3.55; (Lat. Sarmaticae gentes), 3.25
Satarchae, 2.3, 2.4, 2.10
Satyrs (Lat. Satyri), 1.23, 1.48, 3.95
Sauromatae, 1.14, 1.116, 2.2
Sauromatidae, 3.39
Scyths: (Lat. Scythae), 1.11, 1.12, 1.13, 2.2, 3.38, 3.59; (Lat. Scythici populi), 3.36

Seres (Silk People), 1.11, 3.60
Silk People. *See* Seres
Sindones, 1.110, 1.111
Sirachi, 1.114
Sirens (Lat. Sirenes), 2.68
Sittiani, 1.30
Snake-Eaters. *See* Ophiophages
Sordones, 2.84
Spindleshanks. *See* Himantopodes
Sugdiani, 1.13, 3.42
Supertamarici, 3.11
Syri, 3.78
Syro-Cilicians (Lat. Syrocilices), 1.13

Taulantii, 2.55
Taurians (Lat. Tauri), 2.11
Taurici, 2.3, 2.4
Tectosages, 2.75
Teutoni, 3.32, 3.54
Thatae, 1.114
Thebani, 1.88
Thessali, 2.35
Thracians (Lat. Thraces), 2.18, 2.110
Thyssagetae, 1.116
Tibarani: (Lat. Tibarani), 1.13; (Lat. Tibareni), 1.106
Tibareni. *See* Tibarani

Tolobi, 2.90
Toretici (Lat. Toretica gens), 1.110
Tortoise-Eaters. *See* Chelonophagi
Treveri, 3.20
Troezenians (Lat. Troezenii), 2.49
Trogodytae (Cave Dwellers), 1.23, 1.44
Trojans (Lat. Troiani), 1.90
Turcae, 1.116
Turduli, 3.3
Turduli, Old, (Lat. Turduli Veteres), 3.8
Turtle-Eaters. *See* Chelonophagi
Tuscans (Lat. Tusci), 2.60
Tyrians (Lat. Tyrii), 3.46

Vardulli, 3.15
Veneti, 2.59
Vocontii, 2.75
Volcan peoples (Lat. Volcae), 2.79, 2.80
Volsci, 2.59

Wagon-Dwellers. *See* Hamaxobioe
Westerners. *See* Hesperioe
White Aethiopians (Lat. Leucoaethiopes), 1.23

Individuals

Divine, historical, and legendary individuals named by Mela are listed here. Where the English name is not identical to the ancient form, the Latin name is given in parentheses after the main entry and marked by the abbreviation Lat.

Abdera, eponym, 2.29
Achilles, 2.5, 2.15, 2.98
Aeacids (Lat. Aeacides), 2.54
Aeneas, 1.92, 2.28, 2.119
Aesculapius, 2.49
Agamemnon, 2.45
Agathyrsis, 2.2, 2.10
Ajax (Lat. Aiax), 1.96
Alebion, 2.78

Alexander (the Great), 1.66, 1.70, 1.98, 2.34
Amasis, 1.59, 1.60
Ammon (Lat. Hammo), 1.39
Amphiaraüs, 2.46
Anaximander, 1.86
Andromeda, 1.64
Antaeus, 1.26, 3.106
Antenor, 2.60

Index

Apis, 1.58
Apollo, 1.55, 1.82, 1.86, 1.88, 2.40, 3.37
Aratus, 1.71
Arcesilas, 1.90
Archias, 1.101
Arethusa, 2.117
Apis, 1.58
Ariadne, 2.112
Artemisia, 1.85
Ascanius, 1.92
Augustus, 2.13, 3.11
Auster, 1.39

Bocchus, 1.29

Caepio, 3.4
Calypso, 2.120
Cambyses, 1.64
Canopus, 2.103
Castor, 1.111
Cato, 1.34
Cepheus, 1.64
Cerberus, 1.103
Ceres, 2.41, 2.118
Chimaera, 1.80
Circe, 2.71
Cornelius Nepos, 3.45, 3.90
Cyme, 1.90
Cynicus Diogenes, 1.105
Cytisorus, 1.104
Cyzicus, 1.98

Daedalus, 2.112
Darius, 1.70
Democritus, 2.29
Demosthenes, 2.109
Dercynos, 2.78
Diana, 1.79, 1.88, 2.3
Diogenes Cynicus, 1.105
Diomedes, 2.29

Endymion, 1.86
Ennius, 2.66
Erythras, 3.72, 3.79
Eudoxus, 3.90, 3.92
Europa, 2.112

Hannibal, 2.89, 2.116
Hanno, 3.90, 3.93
Hasdrubal, 2.94
Hecuba, 2.26
Helena, 2.109
Hercules, 1.26, 1.27, 1.103, 2.11, 2.29, 2.36, 2.78, 2.95, 3.46, 3.103
Homer, 1.60, 3.45; Homeric, 2.104

Iphigenia, 2.11

Jason (Lat. Iaso), 1.101, 1.111
Juba (Lat. Iuba), 1.30
Jugurtha (Lat. Iugurtha), 1.29
Juno, 2.41, 2.96, 3.4
Jupiter, 1.101, 2.42, 2.43, 2.78, 2.89, 2.90, 2.112, 2.113, 3.66

Lathyrus, king, 3.90
Leander, 2.26
Leucothea, 2.121
Liber, 2.17, 3.66

Macar, 2.100
Manto, 1.88
Mars, 2.15, 2.98
Mausolus, 1.85
Menelaüs, 2.103
Mercury (Lat. Mercurius), 1.34, 2.52
Metellus Celer, Q., 3.45
Minerva, 1.36, 2.69
Minotaur (Lat. Minotaurus), 2.112
Misenus, 2.70
Mopsus, 1.79, 1.88
Myrinus, 1.90

Nemesis, 2.46
Nepos. *See* Cornelius Nepos
Neptune (Lat. Neptunus), 1.100, 2.48, 2.51, 2.78

Oenomaüs, 1.90, 2.42
Orestes, 2.11
Orpheus, 2.17, 2.28

Palinurus, 2.69
Pandion, 1.80, 1.84
Paris, 1.94
Pasiphaë, 2.112
Pelops, 1.90
Pelorus, 2.116
Perseus, 1.64
Phidias, 2.42, 2.46
Philaeni, 1.33, 1.38
Philip, 2.34
Philoctetes, 2.35
Phineus, 1.64
Phoenix, 3.83
Phrixus, 1.104, 1.108
Pollux, eponym, 1.111
Pompey (Lat. Pompeius), 1.71
Poseidon, Point, 1.86
Protesilaüs, 2.26
Psammetichus, 1.56
Pyrrhus, 2.54

Rhessos, 2.24

Sarpedon, 1.77
Sciron, 2.47
Semiramis, 1.63
Sun (Lat. Sol), 1.39, 3.71
Syphax, 1.30

Talus, 2.112
Telamon, 2.72
Thales, 1.86
Themistagoras, 1.108
Theseus, 2.45
Timotheus, 1.86
Tiresias, 1.88
Turduli, Old, (Lat. Turduli Veteres), 3.8
Typhon, 1.76

Ulixes, 2.110

Venus, 2.102, 2.119

Xerxes (Lat. Xerses), 2.28, 2.32